WOMEN WRITERS OF THE BEAT ERA

Cultural Frames, Framing Culture

Robert Newman, Editor

WOMEN WRITERS OF THE BEAT ERA

Autobiography and Intertextuality

MARY PANICCIA CARDEN

University of Virginia Press

CHARLOTTESVILLE AND LONDON

University of Virginia Press
© 2018 by the Rector and Visitors of the University of Virginia
All rights reserved
Printed in the United States of America on acid-free paper

First published 2018

9 8 7 6 5 4 3 2 1

LIBRARY OF CONGRESS CATALOGING-IN-PUBLICATION DATA

Names: Carden, Mary Paniccia, author.
Title: Women writers of the Beat era : autobiography and intertextuality / Mary Paniccia
  Carden.
Description: Charlottesville : University of Virginia Press, 2018. | Series: Cultural frames,
  framing culture | Includes bibliographical references and index.
Identifiers: LCCN 2017054495 | ISBN 9780813941219 (cloth : alk. paper) |
  ISBN 9780813941226 (pbk. : alk. paper) | ISBN 9780813941233 (e-book)
Subjects: LCSH: Beat generation. | American literature—20th century—History
  and criticism. | American literature—Women authors—History and criticism. |
  Autobiography—Women authors. | Autobiography in literature.
Classification: LCC PS228.B6 C365 2018 | DDC 810.9/35082—dc23
LC record available at https://lccn.loc.gov/2017054495

Cover art: Washington Square Park, New York City, 1960, by Dave Heath.
(© Howard Greenberg Gallery, New York, and Stephen Bulger Gallery, Toronto)

For Julia and Patrick

CONTENTS

ABBREVIATIONS

Works by Bonnie Bremser

"A"   "Artista: Brenda (Bonnie) Frazer" (interview)
"B"   "Breaking out of D.C."
"P"   "Poets and Oddfellows"
T   *Troia: Mexican Memoirs*
"TV" "The Village Scene"

Works by Diane di Prima

M   *Memoirs of a Beatnik*
R   *Recollections of My Life as a Woman*

Works by Joyce Johnson

"AC" "A Conversation with Joyce Johnson" (interview)
"BQ" "Beat Queens"
DW *Door Wide Open*
MC *Minor Characters*

Works by Hettie Jones

"BB" "Babes in Boyland"
D   *Drive*
"D"   "Drive: Hettie Jones" (interview)

H	*How I Became Hettie Jones*
LH	*Love, H: The Letters of Helene Dorn and Hettie Jones*

Works by Joanne Kyger

JIJ	*The Japan and India Journals*
"PG"	"Places to Go: Joanne Kyger" (interview)
T	*The Tapestry and the Web*

Works by ruth weiss

C	*CAN'T STOP THE BEAT*
DJ	*DESERT JOURNAL*
F	*FOR THESE WOMEN OF THE BEAT*
"S"	"Single Out: ruth weiss" (interview)

PREFACE

There was . . . the first [poetry] conference to involve any of our writing community. . . . I had of course not been asked. I didn't find this strange then, I was often not asked to literary events, though I published with everyone in the usual places, worked side-by-side with the men putting out the magazines and books, read here and there with them on the East Side or in the Village.
As a woman, I was invisible. I took that as a matter of course.
— DIANE DI PRIMA, RECOLLECTIONS OF MY LIFE AS A WOMAN

The Beat movement is notable for the considerable number of women writers who were part of the community yet obscured or ignored, for the degree to which women went unrecognized for their literary and cultural contributions, and for Beat's indifference to [their] kindred spirit of rebellion.
— RONNA C. JOHNSON AND NANCY M. GRACE, "VISIONS AND REVISIONS OF THE BEAT GENERATION"

Not long ago, a colleague asked what I was working on. "Beat women writers," I said. She replied, "I didn't know there were any." Her comment, variants of which I hear with some frequency, echoes general assumptions about women (or the lack of women) within Beat literary cultures. As Amy Friedman observes, "for decades the women writers associated with the Beat Generation have been an ignored presence, only glancingly acknowledged" ("Being" 229). Glancing, perfunctory acknowledgment marginalizes even as it purports to recognize, freezes out as it putatively includes. Both there and not there, women writers have been essentially invisible in popular and scholarly accounts of the Beat movement, its impact on U.S. culture, and its contributions to the American literary tradition.

When not ignored completely, women affiliated with Beat circles have been dismissed as noncontributing hangers-on, as Beat groupies rather than "real" Beats. For the most part, readers know them as nonessential, extraneous characters (or caricatures) found at the margins of men's stories. *Women Writers of the Beat Era* has its origins in the (fairly obvious) premise that this scant recognition constitutes a fundamental *mis*-recognition, as it has come filtered through the dominant Beat mythos—that familiar compendium of already-known Beat legend and lore that defines the Beat Generation as a specifically male cohort. These already-heard narratives have engendered a social and literary nowhere for women who lived and wrote within Beat communities. In this context, as the poet Diane di Prima observes, the assumed absence of women seems less "strange" than the fact of their presence.

Di Prima is far from the only woman writer to recount experiences of invisibility and dislocation within Beat literary scenes. Joyce Johnson recalls that even though she was deeply invested in the energetic Beat community in New York, she knew that "as a female," she was "not quite part" of its transformative counterculture (*MC* 262). During the period she was living with Beat icon Jack Kerouac and writing *Come and Join the Dance* (1962), which Ronna Johnson has identified as the first Beat novel by a woman, she "thought of only the male writers as the Beat writers" ("AC" 114).[1] Joanne Kyger has contended that Allen Ginsberg essentially created "the Beat Generation" through active promotion of his "brotherhood of poets," a group in which she did not feel particularly welcome ("PG" 140). ruth weiss,[2] who wrote haiku with Kerouac and continues to perform her jazz poetry in North Beach (and around the world), counted Beat men among her "good friends." She remembers, however, that they did not welcome women "into the center of things," but relegated them to "the periphery." Many, she remarks, refused to even consider publishing women's texts ("S" 71, 73). In 1996, Hettie Jones—who lived and worked at the center of the New York Beat community as cofounder of the Beat literary magazine *Yugen*—asserted "I don't think women are *ever* going to be identified as the Beats" (qtd. in Charters, "Panel" 622).[3]

Narratives documenting, describing, and analyzing the Beat Generation have long divided Beat communities along gender lines, with female writers relegated to a set of "minor characters" labeled "Beat *women*."[4] The "Beat woman" classification has been applied to numerous and diverse writers affiliated (closely and loosely) with Beat literary circles, including Carol Bergé, Bonnie Bremser (Brenda Frazer), Elise Cowen, Diane di Prima, Mary Fabilli, Barbara Guest, Bobbie Louise Hawkins, Joyce (Glassman) Johnson, Kay Johnson, Hettie Jones, Lenore Kandel, Mary Norbert Körte, Joanne Kyger, Denise Levertov, Sheri Martinelli, Joanna McClure, Barbara Moraff, Rochelle Owens, Janine Pommy Vega, Margaret Randall, Diane Wakoski, Anne Waldman, and ruth weiss. On its surface, the "Beat woman" designation may appear to recognize and include women as Beats. But for the most part, its deployment of "woman" as a qualifier of "Beat" has had the opposite effect, positioning women as trespassers on male ground and discounting their contributions to the Beat movement and to the substantial social changes it put in motion.

However, in the years following revival of interest in the Beats that accompanied the twenty-fifth anniversary of Kerouac's publication of *On the Road* (1957) in 1982, women writers linked to the Beat movement began to garner wider and more serious acknowledgment. This reassessment has been spurred in large part by the appearance of anthologies dedicated to women's writing—Brenda Knight's *Women of the Beat Generation: The Writers, Artists and Muses at the Heart of a Revolution* (1996) and Richard Peabody's *A Different Beat: Writings by Women of the Beat Generation* (1997)—and by incisive and compelling scholarship produced by Nancy Grace, Ronna Johnson, Amy Friedman, Jennie Skerl, Linda Russo, Maria Damon, Tony Trigilio, Jane Falk, Kurt Hemmer, and others. Their critical work has shed light on women's "obscured or ignored" texts and reconsidered the gendered contexts in which the Beat "spirit of rebellion" manifested itself.

Women Writers of the Beat Era: Autobiography and Intertextuality builds on this critical foundation to explore intersections of Beat-associated women's life-writing and the dominant Beat Generation mythos, intersections where presence meets absence, voice contends with silence, and the categories "Beat" and "Beat woman" undergo supplementation and transformation. My intention is to extend critical reevaluations of the Beat movement currently under way, as evidenced by scholarly collections such as Johnson and Grace's *Girls Who Wore Black: Women Writing the Beat Generation* (2002), Skerl's *Reconstructing the Beats* (2004), and Grace and Skerl's *The Transnational Beat Generation* (2012). *Women Writers of the Beat Era* injects women's self-representation into evolving definitions of "Beat," investigating the strategies women develop to improvise identities within pre-scripted cultural boundaries that restrict female agency and deny female creativity.

My study has its roots in a series of questions about the repercussions of writing from Beat nowheres. For example: If one has been excluded from canonical and cultural accounts of the Beat movement, what sort of "Beat" life can one represent? And for what purposes? In what ways are women's Beat stories prompted, pervaded, and otherwise regulated by the already-known Beat Generation narrative? To what extent might writers enmeshed in the already-known write a different kind of Beat story? In what ways might women's stories exert reinterpretive, possibly transformative, pressure on the already-known?

Women Writers of the Beat Era: Autobiography and Intertextuality examines Beat-associated women writers' strategies of self-definition by focusing on their encounters with representations of themselves—both as individuals and in group classifications—produced and disseminated by others. In my investigation of these issues, I find that in conversation with each other and with the Beat canon, Beat-associated women autobiographers craft alternative models of identity which expand and complicate the dominant Beat Generation mythos. Seeking to convey female experience in excess of the masculinist Beat paradigm as somehow Beat nevertheless, the women writers included in this study devise intertextual strategies to supplement, revise, and transform the "Beat woman" label. In the process, they reconstitute the positions signified by the terms "woman," "writer," and "Beat" as sites of negotiation, difference, and creativity.

The era designated as the Beat period may have passed, but Beat's questing, experimental zeitgeist in many ways endures, as do cultural conditions in which women who live and work as ignored innovators in male-dominant arenas nevertheless find ways to create something new. Beat-associated women's life-writing, as Hettie Jones points out, offers other women something valuable they themselves lacked—"frontline stories of success and failure at trying to be an artist in a woman's life" (*LH* 5). I hope *Women Writers of the Beat Era* facilitates a more nuanced recognition of the complex ways in which women writers affiliated with the Beat movement—and other invisible women—negotiate intertextual matrices of identity and improvise on the often-fraught discursive materials near at hand to craft previously unforeseen possibilities.

The autobiographical texts explored in *Women Writers of the Beat Era* identify various and varied formations of community as central to Beat-associated women's lives and work. Some women directly credit friends, colleagues, and others with whom they formed literary relationships with empowering them to imagine and create themselves as writers. While I have certainly not encountered anywhere near the level of resistance faced by many of the writers included in this study, my ability to find time to write and to summon ways of rethinking established narratives and histories has been similarly enabled by my own supportive communities.

Colleagues and friends at Edinboro University of Pennsylvania and other institutions took an encouraging interest in this project, and a sabbatical leave granted by Edinboro University gave me time and space to complete a first draft. Robert Bernard Hass and Catherine Whitley read and commented on sections of this book as they evolved. As always, Sidonie Smith's incisive critiques pushed me in more interesting directions than those I had in mind when I set out. I am also indebted to Tatum Petrich and Kurt Hemmer for suggestions that improved the focus and coherence of this study.

I am grateful to the Beat Studies Association for cultivating an active and convivial climate for study of the Beats. Ronna Johnson and Nancy Grace have been inspiring examples of scholarly rigor and innovation in the field; with other members of the Beat Studies Association community, they laid the groundwork that made possible the publication of a scholarly book focused on Beat women's life-writing. The University of Virginia Press's Cultural Frames/Framing Cultures series, edited by Robert Newman, provided a welcoming home for a study that straddles categories that all too often partition and restrict academic endeavor. I am extremely grateful to Eric Brandt, Assistant Director and Editor in Chief, for his sharp eye and thoughtful guidance. My heartfelt thanks to Morgan Myers, Susan Murray, Nicholas Rich, Bonnie Gill, and the design and marketing staff of the University of Virginia Press for their high standards and for the care they took in bringing *Women Writers of the Beat Era* to print.

I have been beyond fortunate in the support and patience of my family—my husband, Kevin Carden; my children, Patrick and Julia Carden; my mother, Sally Dwyer Paniccia, and my father- and mother-in-law, William and Lela Carden. Together with my sisters and brothers and sisters- and brothers-in-law, their interest and encouragement, to borrow from Hettie Jones (who borrowed from another woman writer), keep me afloat. And never far from my thoughts is my first and primary model of hard work and persistence—my late father, Albert Paniccia.

I have also been fortunate in the generosity of authors (and their representatives) included in this study. I thank them for their gracious permission to use their words and images in *Women Writers of the Beat Era* and also for their informative conversation and advice. Poetry by Hettie Jones is reprinted from *All Told* ©2003 by Hettie Jones and from *Drive* © 1998 by Hettie Jones, by permission of Hanging Loose Press; poetry by Joanne Kyger is reprinted by permission of the Estate of Joanne Kyger; poetry by ruth weiss is reprinted by permission of the author.

My thanks to the following individuals, publishers, and corporations for allowing me to use cover images discussed in this study: Last Gasp 1988 *Memoirs of a Beatnik* front cover reprinted by permission of Last Gasp and Bobby Neel Adams; Penguin 1998 *Memoirs of a Beatnik* front cover reprinted by permission of Penguin Random House; Penguin 2001 *Recollections of My Life as a Woman* front cover reprinted by permission of Penguin Random House and Getty Images; Croton 1969 *Troia: Mexican Memoirs* and London Magazine Editions 1971 *For Love of Ray* front covers reprinted by permission of Michael Perkins; Divine Arts 2011 *CAN'T STOP THE BEAT* front cover reprinted by permission of Ingeborg Gerdes/Dennis Hearne and ruth weiss; Tombouctou Books 1981 *The Japan and Indian Journals* front cover reprinted by permission of Michael Wolfe and the Kenneth J. Botto Photography Trust; North Atlantic Books 2000 *Strange Big Moon: The Japan and India Journals* front cover reprinted by permission of North Atlantic Books; Nightboat Books 2016 *The Japan and India Journals* front cover reprinted by permission of Nightboat Books and Allen Ginsberg LLC; Houghton Mifflin 1983 *Minor Characters* front cover reprinted by permission of Houghton Mifflin Harcourt and Globe Photos; Penguin 1999 *Minor Characters* front cover reprinted by permission of Penguin Random House and Globe Photos; Penguin 2000 *Door Wide Open* front cover reprinted by permission of Penguin Random House and Bob Heriques/Magnum Photos; Dutton 1990 *How I Became Hettie Jones* front cover reprinted by permission of Getty Images. Every attempt has been made to obtain permission to reproduce copyrighted materials; if any proper acknowledgment has not been made, I invite copyright holders to inform me of the oversight. Photographs of book covers by Julie Scott.

Sections of chapter 2, "Truthiness: Diane di Prima's *Memoirs of a Beatnik* and *Recollections of My Life as a Woman*," originally appeared as "'What You Would Like to Hear': Sex, Lies, and Life Writing in Diane di Prima's *Memoirs of a Beatnik*," *a/b: Auto/Biography Studies* 22.1 (2007): 26–45.

WOMEN WRITERS OF THE BEAT ERA

INTRODUCTION
Writing from Nowhere

*It is necessary to bring the female persona, the feminine principle, fem-
inist concerns, the sense of women's struggle as wives, lovers, mothers,
artists, breadwinners—as well as taking into account the literal presence
of living breathing thinking creative women—into the whole macrocosm
that is the Beat literary movement. It thickens the plot.*
　　　　　　　　　　—ANNE WALDMAN, "FAST SPEAKING WOMAN"

The Beat movement—which emerged after World War II, flourished in
the 1950s, and continued through the 1960s—is characterized by disen-
gagement from the bourgeois mainstream and by rebellion against the
conventionality, conformity, and consumerism of the postwar United
States. Beat cultures began as underground communities, bohemian subcultures that coalesced in New York City and San Francisco, havens from
the repressive authoritarianism of the U.S. majority. These subcultures
were composed of outsiders—drifters and drug users, artists, musicians,
writers, and intellectuals, disaffected children of the middle and working
classes, and assorted other rebels—people who would not or could not fit
into post–World War II America.

In the United States of the 1950s, the historian Ruth Rosen observes,
national discourses urged homogeneity, and dissent "became linked in
the popular mind with Communist sympathizers." A national climate of
anticommunism "cast a shadow of self-censorship across the intellectual
landscape," muffling opposition and "forcing . . . political consensus" (12).
Beats rejected Cold War politics and conformist social values in a "bohemian retreat from the dominant culture" that constituted "a force for social change" and a "crucible for art" (Skerl 2). Like Diane di Prima, many
Beats viewed themselves as "artists first" and "held to their work as to their
very souls" (R 223). For them, "self-censorship" meant self-denial and self-
betrayal, capitulation to a stifling status quo.

Members of Beat communities valued spontaneity and pursuit of individual truth and creative vision; they were drawn to the improvisational

art of jazz, viewing it as emblematic of an authentic self-expression that forces life past the boundaries that would circumscribe, contain, and control it. They sought out the limits of human perception in their use of drugs and embraced the present moment in free and open sexuality. Beat lifestyles constituted a deliberate flouting of dominant national values, a disaffiliation from lives defined through nuclear family and organized in pursuit of upward mobility. John Tytell describes the Beat movement as "a crystallization of a sweeping discontent with American 'virtues' of progress and power" (4). Beats, he notes, "saw themselves as outcasts, exiles within a hostile culture, freaky progenitors of new attitudes toward sanity and ethics, rejected artists writing anonymously for themselves" (5). They often adopted characteristics of other marginalized populations, including African Americans, homosexuals, hustlers, and hoboes, outsider groups that provided Beat communities with "aspects of language, style, and culture" that enabled them to "fashion a heterogeneous space distanced from the center" (Holton 24–25). For Americans dissatisfied with the national norm, Beat bohemia offered dynamic new centers where difference and dissent produced creative possibilities, where being "beat" seemed more authentic and more desirable than comfortable normalcy.[1]

But even as Beat literary communities drew much of their creative energy from refusal of status quo lifestyles, they tended to reproduce the gender role expectations of the conservative American mainstream. As a result, social and familial arrangements within the New Bohemia were often rooted in assumptions that Beat women would by default perform essentially the same service and caretaking functions as their more respectable sisters. "Because they were women," Chelsea Schlievert points out, they were made to "[symbolize] parts of society to rebel against" and so "fell out of the range of Beat's hipness and instead constructed its borders" (1095). Texts produced by Beat men represent Beat women as both conventional (adherents to domestic values) and transgressive (promiscuous flouters of bourgeois morality), as sexualized "chicks" and as would-be hausfraus plotting marriage traps. More often than not, Beat men portray women as "spoilsports" (J. Johnson, *MC* 260) intent on interfering with their fun and camaraderie, against whose passive and unimaginative existences they measure the new, the exciting, the productive.

As lesser, suspect figures operating within male-dominated environments, women seeking to establish themselves as writers in Beat communities encountered a relatively narrow field for artistic self-determination. In *Recollections of My Life as a Woman: The New York Years* (2001), di Prima almost seems to shrug as she recalls that not only did LeRoi Jones, her coeditor on the Beat periodical the *Floating Bear*, often receive "the credit for the whole thing," but "most of the actual physical work devolved upon [her]." She concludes "in this he was not any different from any other male artist of his day. It was just the natural division of labor and credit" (253). This seemingly self-evident "division of labor and credit" and "natural" equation of Beatness with maleness demanded female invisibility and encouraged dismissal of women's creative endeavors as at best dilatory hobbies, at worst sycophantic imitation of male artistry.

Thickening the Plot

Despite the limitations of a period in which, as Joyce Johnson argues, American culture as a whole had "no respect for creative women" ("BQ" 44), Beat-associated women found ways to improvise on both traditional gender roles and the male-focused Beat ethos, participating in and pioneering elements of the social experimentation and literary innovation characteristic of Beat cultures. Critical commentary and scholarly research published in recent years has debunked common perceptions of Beat-associated women writers as lesser, copycat authors, irrelevant to the emergence and development of Beat literature. As Amy Friedman has demonstrated, their "commitment . . . to their work generally contests the view that they were accidental artists, or that they only gained access to writing through a connection with the men" ("Being" 233).[2] Women writers were frequent and prolific contributors to (and founders of) the literary magazines, newsletters, and journals that widened Beat literary circles and played a major role in establishing Beat literary principles and priorities.

Poetry by ruth weiss, a decades-long member of San Francisco jazz and literary communities, appeared in most of the early issues of *Beatitude* (Peabody 232). Barbara Guest and Denise Levertov contributed to *Yugen*, *Floating Bear*, and *Kulchur* ("Bibliographic Bunker"), important Beat literary publications based in New York. Barbara Moraff published in *Yugen*, *Evergreen Review*, *Origin*, *Beat Scene*, *Trobar*, and *Fuck You* (Egles 392; Peabody 230). Moraff, Carol Bergé, Lenore Kandel, and Rochelle Owens were among the regular contributors to *Fuck You* ("Bibliographic Bunker"). Bonnie Bremser (Brenda Frazer) published work in *Blue Beat*, *Fuck You*, *Intrepid*, and *Down Here* (Hemmer, "Frazer" 105). Joanne Kyger's poetry appeared in journals including *Poetry*, *Paris Review*, *World*, *Rocky Ledge*, and *Coyote's Journal* (Knight 348). In addition to contributing to others' publications, Anne Waldman founded and edited *Angel Hair* magazine and press; she directed the Poetry Project at St. Mark's Church in the Bowery from 1968 to 1977 ("Fast" 256). Hettie Jones cofounded and produced *Yugen*. Di Prima, probably the best-known Beat woman writer, contributed to more than seventy anthologies and more than three hundred periodicals (Quinn 175–76). As cofounder and coeditor of the *Floating Bear*, cofounder of the New York Poet's Theatre, and cofounder of the Poet's Press, di Prima was instrumental in the evolution of Beat literary practice.

In addition to contributing to Beat journals and anthologies, Beat-associated women published their own books of poetry and prose. Three poetry texts authored by Kandel came out in 1959: *An Exquisite Navel, A Passing Dragon,* and *A Passing Dragon Seen Again*. Her *Love Book* triggered an obscenity scandal and trial in 1966. In addition to originating an influential jazz poetics, weiss published poetry collections including *STEPS* (1958), *GALLERY OF WOMEN* (1959), *SOUTH PACIFIC* (1959), and *BLUE IN GREEN* (1960); her magnum opus, *DESERT JOURNAL,* written between 1961 and 1968, was finally published in 1977. *THE BRINK* (1961), a film based on one of weiss's poems, records "impressions from [her] wanderings around San Francisco and the Bay area" ("S" 63).

After leaving college in the late 1950s to immerse herself in San Francisco's burgeoning literary scene, Kyger authored multiple collections of poetry, including *The Tapestry and the Web* (1965), *The Fool in April: A Poem* (1966), *Joanne* (1970), *Places to Go* (1970), and *All This Every Day* (1975). Joyce (Glassman) Johnson began work on her novel *Come and Join the Dance* in 1955; it came out in 1962. Kay Johnson, a denizen of the Beat Hotel in Paris, published *Human Songs* with City Lights in 1964 (Peabody 227). Janine Pommy Vega's *Poems to Fernando* was published by City Lights in 1968. Among other collections of poetry, Waldman published *Giant Night* in 1968, *Baby Breakdown* in 1970, and *Fast Speaking Woman* in 1975. Di Prima has authored more than thirty books of poetry, including *This Kind of Bird Flies Backward* (1958), *Dinners and Nightmares* (1961), *The New Handbook of Heaven* (1962), *Haiku* (1966), *New Mexico Poem* (1967), *War Poems* (1968), *Earth Song* (1968), *LA Odyssey* (1969), *Revolutionary Letters* (1971), and *Loba: Parts 1–16* (1978, 1998), to name a few.[3] Like di Prima, many of these writers have continued to publish well into the twenty-first century.

Critical excavation of Beat-associated women's work has illustrated its significance as innovative literature, illuminating and provocative texts characterized by both "transcendent poetic achievement" and "lucid literary anarchy" (Friedman, "Being" 237, 235). Beat Studies scholars have also examined the roles Beat women writers played as harbingers of and contributors to the U.S. social revolutions that now enable, if not demand, their recognition as "protofeminist" explorers and innovators (Johnson and Grace, "Visions" 5). Interest in Beat women's texts continues to grow as previously unpublished writing comes to light and long out-of-print work is reissued, including Kandel's *Love Book* and weiss's *DESERT JOURNAL*. *Love, H: The Letters of Helene Dorn and Hettie Jones* was published in 2016, as was a third edition of Joanne Kyger's *Japan and India Journals*. Kyger passed away in March 2017, six months before the publication of *There You Are: Interviews, Journals, and Ephemera*, a compilation covering forty years of her life and work.[4] Joyce Johnson's *Come and Join the Dance* was reissued in 2014 with a cover blurb characterizing the novel as "a Beat ur-text." An edited collection of the surviving poetry of Elise Cowen—friend and intimate of so many Beat men and women, and poignant reminder of Beat women's marginality—reached print in 2014, fifty-two years after her death.[5]

Beat Consociates

Anne Waldman's foreword to Brenda Knight's *Women of the Beat Generation*, the anthology that introduced Beat-associated women writers and artists to a largely unaware reading public, describes the book as "a kind of resurrection" and "a necessary reckoning" with an "extraordinary unsung legacy" (xi, xii). She observes that while "men . . . have gotten most of the credit as the movers and shakers of the 'Beat' literary movement," *Women of the Beat Generation* allows readers to become "privy to what else—what 'other'—was going on at the same time, in parallel time, and how the various lives—of both men and women—interwove and dovetailed with one another" (xi). Waldman describes these "Beat" lives using Clifford Geertz's concept of consociation, which she defines as "interconnectedness of shared and experienced realities" that "takes into consideration the influences of time, place, mutually informed circumstance on individuals existing in proximity—yet not necessarily intimates—to create a larger cultural context for action and art" (xi). In a 2010 poem entitled "Keep the Beat," di Prima concurs, declaring: "It's not a 'Generation' / dig— / *it's a state of mind*" (81). I will argue that consociative exchange characterizes a good deal of the work by Beat-associated women considered in this study. As we will see in the chapters that follow, their texts propose widened and deepened definitions of Beat that construct "larger cultural context[s]" to accommodate female subjectivity and creativity.

Consociative principles also inform recent critical reconsiderations of Beat cultures. In *Reconstructing the Beats,* Skerl asserts that "the Beats" should be understood as "a movement, rather than a coterie" (5), "a loosely affiliated arts community . . . encompass[ing] two or three generations of writers, artists, activists, and nonconformists" (2). Characterizations of "the Beats" as a "generation," in contrast, erect rigid and exclusive boundaries around Beat identification. Pushed to its narrowest "generational" limits, "Beat" would likely encompass only the Kerouac–Ginsberg–Burroughs New York group; it would leave out many important male writers and most of the female writers, including women like weiss, who was performing her jazz poetry in North Beach before Kerouac and Ginsberg came to town, as well as women like Janine Pommy Vega, who sought out Beat communities after reading *On the Road* and feeling that "all the characters seemed to move with an intensity that was missing in [her] life" (2). Understanding Beat as a "movement" allows for recognition of its diffusion into multiple contexts and for acknowledgment of its fluid intersections with other modes of modernist and postmodernist expression. Additionally, the looser "movement" characterization of Beat literary cultures makes visible alternatives to popular and academic perceptions of Beat writing as gendered male, a function of Kerouac-style spontaneous prose.[6]

Conceptualizing Beat as a movement underscores the idea that being "Beat," as Waldman remarks, often comes down to a matter of "guilt by association" ("Fast" 277). Johnson and Grace argue persuasively that "Beat writers are united fundamentally by their . . . formative mutual associations; commonwealth and personal relations are integral to writers' identification as Beat. . . . [S]ocial, artistic, personal, geographical links— literary camaraderies and life relations—underlie most writers' identification with Beat" ("Visions" 3). Writers aligned with a number of interrelated experimental and antiestablishment literary circles of the 1940s, 1950s, and 1960s tend to be grouped under the Beat aegis. As the early Beat cohort in New York expanded, it incorporated writers such as di Prima, Gregory Corso, and LeRoi Jones, many of whom had close ties to Frank O'Hara and the New York School poets. These writers also formed common cause and creative community with Black Mountain poets including Charles Olson, Ed Dorn, and Denise Levertov. In 1955, Ginsberg performed "Howl" in San Francisco as part of the legendary 6 Gallery reading, an event that galvanized exchange with San Francisco Renaissance writers—Gary Snyder, Michael McClure, Philip Lamantia, Lawrence Ferlinghetti, and Philip Whalen, as well as Kyger, weiss, and others.

Most of the writers mentioned above published their work in the influential Beat literary magazine *Yugen;* LeRoi Jones, its editor, lists authors affiliated with Beat, New York School, Black Mountain, and San Francisco circles among the contributors to its early issues (Baraka 222–25). Charles Olson's paradigm-shifting "Projective Verse" was published by LeRoi Jones's Totem Press; Kerouac's "Essentials of Spontaneous Prose" appeared in *Black Mountain Review.* In Beat-allied communities, Tim Hunt observes, literary "labels were less the names of discrete schools or systems than tags for groups of people drawn together by both personal and aesthetic tendencies." He notes that "the practices of the writers in these overlapping communities were evolving and shifting throughout the period, and . . . writers could move from one group to another or even be functioning in several communities at once" (254).

With this flexibility of community and association in mind, I will conclude this introduction by returning to Waldman's characterization of male and female Beats as "consociates." Her suggestion that Beat sensibilities formed within and between individuals and groups sharing aesthetic and ethical stances and worldviews posits a kind of cultural and literary intertextuality as a primary principle of Beat identification. Approaching the Beat movement as an intertextual matrix demands attention to ways in which individual writers and their texts interact with and influence each other, testing parameters and reconstituting networks of signification in which "Beat" functions as a principle of identity and community.

Understood broadly, intertextuality refers to processes by which texts and subjectivities assemble out of encounter and exchange with others. As human beings constituted in and through language, we construct our relationships, interactions, and means of self-definition and self-representation within already-established vocabularies and prearranged systems of communication. Expressing one's sense of self in written or spoken language necessarily involves incorporating, synthesizing, and re-formulating available lexicons and discourses of identity. In this context, it is important to acknowledge that women composing narratives about their Beat experiences necessarily enter into self-conscious exchange with densely permeated narrative networks and already-known literary, cultural, and historical intertexts in which they appear primarily as minor characters in men's stories. It is even more important to investigate how and what they make out of these discursive positions.

Chapter 1, "Intertextual Lives: Reading the Autobiographical Texts of Women Writers of the Beat Era," attempts to lay the groundwork for this investigation. It explores the intertextual strategies Beat-associated women devise to account for their thickly plotted lives, focusing on their attempts to articulate defiant forms of femininity and alternative models of Beatness in and around and through already-established discourses and already-told stories. Subsequent chapters address autobiographical texts written by Diane di Prima, Bonnie Bremser (Brenda Frazer), ruth weiss, Joanne Kyger, Joyce Johnson, and Hettie Jones; they are arranged in roughly chronological order based on the publication date of the first text under consideration. While the choice of chronology as an organizing principle might seem arbitrary (or at least unimaginative), this configuration highlights shared autobiographical practices and sheds light on shifts occurring within still-evolving Beat narratives.

The juxtaposition of Diane di Prima (chapter 2) and Bonnie Bremser (chapter 3) brings into view subversive and ambivalent responses to the hypersexualized "Beat chick" caricature. Chapter 2, "Truthiness," begins with an examination of di Prima's *Memoirs of a Beatnik*—published in 1969 and set in New York in the early- to mid-1950s—through questions of sexual truth-telling. Di Prima recounts the story of "beatnik" hedonism she believes her reader wants to hear, telling lies that convey an odd sort of truth; in its parodic reproduction of Beat life, *Memoirs* forces reconsideration of Beat stereotypes and offers subtle alternatives for understanding Beat and female experience. Di Prima's later autobiography, *Recollections of My Life as a Woman: The New York Years* (2001), takes the opposite approach, promising to tell the truth and foregrounding artistic elements of Beat life obscured by the earlier text's focus on sex. Although *Recollections* uses different strategies of description and interpretation to (re)tell di Prima's Beat story, this text also reconstructs the "Beat woman" as a site of alternative femininities. However, in its rendering of di Prima's essential difference from other women, Beat and straight, *Recollections* ultimately denies the reader access to her reformulated paradigm of Beat.

In lies and in truth, di Prima writes a bold, confident, powerful identity—a self in no way worn down by poverty, threatened by sexual excess, endangered by disregard of social norms, or undone by the demands of art and motherhood. In short, her life-writing asserts an impossibly defiant female individualism. Bonnie Bremser's *Troia: Mexican Memoirs* (1969), in contrast, reveals a porous and unstable female identity under constant challenge by external forces. In *Troia*, originally composed as letters to her husband, Bremser attempts to account for her life in Mexico in the early 1960s, a period during which she was forced into prostitution to support her family. Chapter 3, "Diversification," analyzes her strategies for locating and expressing the truth of her experience as Beat, woman, wife, mother, prostitute, and author—categories shot through with inter-textual expectation.

In, perhaps, an attempt to impose control over the "diversified" (*T* 21) self formed and re-formed in Mexico, Bremser draws on discourses and metaphors of exchange to organize the incompatible models of identity encoded in/as her Beat experience. Instead, the exchange economies she constructs in her narrative generate an overdetermined, at points chaotic self, as "Bonnie Bremser" is repeatedly overwritten by changeable and contradictory identifications. Some Beat-associated women portray exchange as a source of creativity and satisfaction, but Bremser finds that it endangers her sense of self and makes autobiographical representation difficult, even dangerous. Nevertheless, as she sifts through the risks and rewards inherent in sexual and textual exchange with others, she reframes the male-centered Beat ethos, answers others' definitions of her, and discovers the "free[dom] to think . . . for [her]self" (*T* 188).

While all of the Beat-associated women writers addressed in this study represent themselves as liminal figures who reject dominant scripts of femininity in favor of alternative social arrangements, they do so in much different ways. Where Bremser tends to convey her Beat experience through tropes of separation and exclusion, jazz poet ruth weiss constructs inclusive modes of exchange to represent her sense of self and her relation to the Beat movement. Her autobiographical prose poetry breaks down dualistic boundaries and "trapped pattern[s]" ("TURNABOUT" 142) to present consociation as a generative and transformative ground for Beat identity.

Chapter 4, "Consociation," interprets the principles articulated in weiss's poetic manifesto *DESERT JOURNAL* (1977) as the foundation for the revisionary aesthetic she expresses in her Beat manifestos *FOR THESE WOMEN OF THE BEAT* (1997) and *CAN'T STOP THE BEAT: THE LIFE AND WORDS OF A BEAT POET* (2011). Having cultivated a worldview that seeks out communality rather than assenting to division, weiss's later work intervenes in exclusive and exclusionary definitions of "the Beat." Her Beat-claiming texts propose consociative formulations of identity that significantly widen and extend the already-known Beat story. Like many of the other authors examined in *Women Writers of the Beat Era*, weiss self-consciously alters Beat in order to reconstruct her place within its narrative parameters. In so doing, she situates her readers in a position akin to her own—negotiating overlapping but often opposed representations of Beat lives and Beat art.

Chapter 5, "Displacements," which explores Joanne Kyger's experimentation with self-representation in her life-writing and her poetry, considers dislocations in gender role performance in light of the dislocations caused by travel. As with Bonnie Bremser, Kyger embarks on Beat travels for and with a better-known Beat man; her *Japan and India Journals*, written in the early 1960s, published in 1981, and reissued in 2000 and again in 2016, records her negotiation of domestic, artistic, and sexual elements of her position as a trailing spouse and apprentice writer. Like Bremser, Kyger feels very visible as a "beatnik" American in an unfamiliar land, but, unlike Bremser, she is not at all sure she wants to be "Beat."

The "Joanne Kyger" who emerges in the *Journals* develops an increasingly confident investment in exchange and mutability as strategies by which to formulate "a whole new way of using language" (*JIJ* 242). And, where weiss's poetics of consociation produces her revision of the masculinist model of Beat, Kyger's revision of male-centered Beat culture seems in large part to underwrite her emerging poetics of female identity. Chapter 5 extends its investigation of Kyger's life-writing to her experimentation with language, gender, and creativity in her first collection of poetry, *The Tapestry and the Web* (1965). The poems in this text, composed for the most part during the same period as the *Journals,* articulate identities at "the verge" (*JIJ* 254) of transformation. Like weiss's work, Kyger's poetry subverts discourses of separation and binary opposition. A shifting palimpsest of myth, autobiography, and poetry, her work undoes hegemonic categories of gender, reconstituting identity as a fluid and ever-shifting mosaic of both established and evolving associations.

Joyce Johnson also expresses ambivalence about her affiliation with "the Beat Generation" and its writers. In *Minor Characters* (1983) and *Door Wide Open* (2000), she represents herself as a part of the New York Beat community and a fellow traveler in the sense that she shares its members' artistic aspirations and worldviews. But as a woman who never travels with her famous companions, she views herself as differently Beat. An autobiographer writing about her Beat experience during a period of revival of interest in the Beat Generation, Johnson confronts herself as a character created by other writers, a cipher in the index of Beat history. Chapter 6, "Cross-Textuality," investigates the intertextual strategies she deploys to pry herself and other Beat-associated women from reified index positions.

In her use of quotation and citation, Johnson, in Marko Juvan's words, "exerts influence upon the past, changing established ideas about older texts, conventions, and discourses." She deploys "techniques of intertextual representation to reform the system of tradition" (153–54) that underwrites the male-focused Beat mythos. For Johnson, self-representation very often becomes a matter of comparison, both explicit and implicit, coupled with speculation and projection. *Minor Characters* and *Door Wide Open* are texts full of terms such as "probably," "maybe," "seems to," and "must have," in which Johnson's life and the lives of others materialize at intersections of documentary history, authorial imagination, and collective and individual memory. Both of her autobiographical texts examine the rewards and the costs of rejecting mainstream U.S. norms for female identity, as well as the limits of that rejection in Beat contexts that define women "almost exclusively by their relationship to men" (Savran 44), in communities that simultaneously demand and deride female self-sacrifice and service.

Johnson's life-writing and Hettie Jones's *How I Became Hettie Jones* (1990) are centered in New York Beat communities of the late 1950s. Both women situate their excavations of their past selves in relation to better-known Beat men and what has been already-said about those relationships. Where Johnson draws primarily on texts by other Beats in her intertextual construction of identity, Jones references wider discourses, ideologies, and events to frame her experience in Beat bohemia. Writing in the late 1980s, Jones incorporates social and cultural citations meant to contextualize the Beat period and to account for the forces brought to bear in the formation of American identities in the 1950s. Her use of comparative allusions facilitates her assembly of an intertextual authorial position imbued with the authority that comes with historical knowledge and insight. This position both enables and illustrates her self-representation as a woman for whom there is "no precedent" (*H* 44), for whom no defining labels apply.

Chapter 7, "Contextuality," considers Jones's analysis of her social, cultural, and historical contexts as an autobiographical strategy, exploring the relationship of the "Hettie Joneses" of her narrative to national discourses of gender, class, and race, as well as to vocabularies defining Beat identity and establishing principles of literary merit. *How I Became Hettie Jones* posits a contested yet flexible relation between the individual and her contexts, representing a Hettie Jones always striving to "make her own self up" (32). Chapter 7 ends with an examination of *Drive,* Jones's 1998 collection of poetry, with particular emphasis on her continuing search for a vocabulary capable of fully articulating the meaning and value of female difference in contexts that prioritize male authority, artistry, and independence.

The brief coda to *Women Writers of the Beat Era: Autobiography and*

Intertextuality, "Rerouting Beat Nowheres," offers one last illustration of Beat-associated women writers' intertextual practices by focusing on their use of travel-related tropes and road metaphors as discursive tools to reframe the "Beat woman." Their road references bring them into revisionary dialogue with the dominant Beat Generation narrative and reflect their sense of the hazards and the pleasures of being both differently Beat and differently female. Drawing on the connotations of openness, freedom, and newness associated with travel, Beat-associated women autobiographers gesture toward the revolutionary transformations involved in remaking empty Beat nowheres as sites of productive alternatives. Their travel metaphors illuminate the extent to which the "Beat woman" label sticks but also provide occasion for intertextual improvisation and re-presentation of "Beat."

Finally, a word about the illustrations included in *Women Writers of the Beat Era.* Reproduced book covers serve as visual markers of the intertextual complexities that imbue every level of Beat-associated women writers' autobiographical texts. A book's cover conveys messages about its content, but cover materials such as images and photographs are generally not produced or controlled by the author. Instead, cover content reflects the perceptions and marketing priorities of the publication apparatus, its sense of what the reading public is likely to find resonant and appealing about the book and its author. Gillian Whitlock maintains that "paratexts"—the "features that surround and cover the text," including cover art, blurbs, and titles—reveal the "textual cultures" of life-writing, the "material processes and ideological formations surrounding the production, transmission, and reception of autobiographical texts" (14).[7] Readers can and do judge books by their covers.

The paratexts surrounding Beat-associated women's autobiographies often mirror the "textual culture" of the Beat Generation mythos, in which women (dis)appear as blurred, shadowy figures or as thinly delineated stereotypes. Many texts included in this study incompletely or dissonantly fulfill the promises their covers seem to make about women writers as Beats or beatniks, girls or women, lovers, wives, whores, or muses. Since Beat-associated women writers tend to approach such designations as "potential site[s] of experimentation rather than contractual sign[s] of identity" (Gilmore 42), friction between the identity inscribed on the outside and crafted on the inside of their texts is not uncommon.

As intertextual constructs, book covers simultaneously highlight and unsettle what Paul Jay describes as "the relationship between image and identity" (199). Photographs and other art chosen as paratexts for Beat-associated women's life-writing "represent forces that have helped define the identity of the writer" (191) in the American national consciousness, forces these autobiographers seem determined to reframe and redeploy. Since paratextual elements shape readers' receptions of and approaches to autobiographies, encouraging us to view their subjects from predetermined angles and through specific lenses, *Women Writers of the Beat Era* attends to the outside of Beat women writers' texts as intertextual sites where autobiographical conflicts are announced, where models of identity collide, and where the insistent stickiness of the "Beat woman" label becomes apparent. At the very least, these covers remind readers that for Beat-associated women writers, intertextuality is a site of both restraint and possibility.

1 INTERTEXTUAL LIVES
Reading the Autobiographical Texts of Women Writers of the Beat Era

We knew we had done something brave, practically historic. We were the ones who had dared to leave home.
—JOYCE JOHNSON, *MINOR CHARACTERS*

Life is made up of stories. And it is all autobiographical narrative.
—JOANNE KYGER, "PLACES TO GO"

You had to believe, as a woman, that stirring things up in general would eventually define a new life for you in particular. You had to believe in the transformative power of art, in the word, and you had to believe yourself part of that process.
—HETTIE JONES, "BABES IN BOYLAND"

Women's qualified, contingent positions vis-à-vis the Beat movement are both product and expression of intertextual exchange—the discourses, dialogues, and debates out of which "Beat" materializes as an intelligible category of identification. Male voices defined the Beat Generation in the public arena, and the images and texts that brought Beats into American national consciousness featured and foregrounded men—most notably Jack Kerouac, Allen Ginsberg, William S. Burroughs, Gregory Corso, and John Clellon Holmes. In a 1958 essay, Kerouac describes the Beat Generation as "a swinging group of new American men . . . intent on joy" and equipped with "wild selfbelieving individuality." Beats, he writes, are a "generation of crazy, illuminated hipsters suddenly rising and roaming America, serious, curious, bumming and hitchhiking everywhere, ragged, beatific," a generation "down and out but full of intense conviction" (qtd. in Charters, "Introduction: What" xv, xxix). Holmes's 1952 article "This Is the Beat Generation" defines Beat as "a sort of nakedness of mind, and, ultimately, of soul; a feeling of being reduced to the bedrock of consciousness. In short, it means being undramatically pushed up against the wall of oneself" (629). He characterizes Beats as "wild boys" who affirm "the life within [them] in the only way [they know] how, at the extreme" (630).[1]

In these oft-quoted definitions, the Beat subject is clearly and emphatically a "he." The Beat ethos espoused by its most visible practitioners and enshrined in popular and academic accounts of the Beat movement valorizes, as Barbara Ehrenreich has observed, enactments of "defiant masculinity" often expressed through "rejection of women and their demands for responsibility" (57, 54). It is hardly surprising, then, that men have stood out most vividly in the Beat Generation narrative and that Beat's trademark iconoclastic individualism has been perceived as a specifically male disposition.[2] Taking up vocabularies imbued with pervasive and enduring associative links between Beat and masculinity, women writers who lived within Beat communities endeavor to represent their Beat lives in and through what often seems an unwieldy, incomplete, and, at points, foreign language. As a result, their differently and ambiguously Beat stories bear the tracks and traces of intertextual dissonance and dislocation.

While some women writers associated with the Beat movement embrace it as a formative aspect of their life trajectories, others argue with its presuppositions or question its relevance. Many perceive "Beat" as something of a mis-fit classification, an identification they feel impelled to resist or to modify. In one way or another, all of the writers considered in *Women Writers of the Beat Era* approach the "Beat woman" label as a site of ambivalence, tension, inquiry, and challenge.[3] At some moments, this label becomes an occasion for fantasy and experimentation, and at others it serves as an impetus for the production of revisionary counternarratives and alternative histories. The writers examined here find that regardless of individual preference or self-perception, the "Beat woman" label sticks, carrying with it associations and implications I will describe as both pre-textual (generated by prior texts) and pretextual (constituted by stereotypes and clichés).

To more fully comprehend the cultural and literary positions occupied by women within the Beat movement, readers must recognize and reckon with the intertextual networks pervading their public and private lives. And nowhere are the repercussions of this constitutive intertextuality clearer than in their autobiographical narratives. Their life-writing engages and incorporates, quotes and references, acknowledges and disputes the narratives of others—in terms of published texts and in terms of more amorphous cultural discourses linked to the Beat Generation. Some of these narratives purport to tell women's stories through specific (though selective) biographical detail, while others rely on generalizations about what their authors think they know about the wives, friends, and lovers of Beat Generation men. Still others fall back on trite, reassuring clichés that reinforce both Beat and "straight" status quos by reducing bohemian women to, in Kerouac's terms, "girls" who "say nothing and wear black" (qtd. in Johnson and Grace, "Visions" 6). Why would readers seek any further understanding or meaning in such uncomplicated, unoriginal lives?

While all self-representation involves some level of intertextual negotiation, for Beat-associated women the intertextual composition of memory, truth-telling, and self-reference is particularly visible, tangibly present in the seemingly inexhaustible reservoir of texts, images, and ideas related to the Beat movement, its gendered sociolect, and its legendary writers, storied hipsters, and "minor characters." I use the terms "pre-text" and "pretext" to articulate a sense of the subtle distinctions and nuances that women writers must sort through as they encounter and process these overlapping categories and contexts of intertextual orientation. "Pre-texts" include any of the wide and deep body of publications that make up the already-known story of the Beat Generation: texts including Beat and Beat-inspired novels, articles, biographies, literary criticism, newspaper and magazine commentary, and so on. The term "pretext" plays on the idea of something alleged, ostensible, or false to indicate the less tangible yet often more forceful and pervasive impressions about Beats and Beat women conveyed in the form of oversimplification and caricature; these impressions may be proposed and perpetuated within particular texts and sets of texts but are also inextricable from commonly held cultural constructs of "the Beat Generation." My use of "pre-text" and "pretext" is intended to reference the status afforded prior utterances and already-known stories and to evoke the densely permeated discursive matrices in and through which Beat-associated women writers conceptualize and articulate identity.[4]

As an example, Joyce Johnson's intricate weaving together of material extracted from others' texts in her memoir *Minor Characters* (1983) indicates not only the degree to which her narrative intersects with others' stories but the extent to which it has been prewritten by them. *Minor Characters* incorporates and comments on representations of Johnson's younger bohemian self as she finds them in well-known pre-texts — publications including Kerouac's *Desolation Angels* and volumes of literary biography. Johnson also measures her sense of self against more general sketches of Beat "girls" appearing in John Clellon Holmes's novel *Go* and the Beat movie *Pull My Daisy* (1959). At the same time, she engages with broader caricatures—pretexts circulating in others' writing and in the cultural air—that dismiss her and other women of her New York circle as "chicks"—silent, sexualized, and unimaginative, at best secondary members of Beat communities, and "Beat" primarily through their links to men. In *Minor Characters,* Johnson attempts to reconcile the often reductive ways others have described her—their comments on her physical appearance, her ambition, her conformity, her relationships—with her view of herself as multifaceted and innovative. She cannot exactly hold that the voices of others are wrong—she acknowledges that they have been formative of her sense of self. But, she insists, in their lack of depth, complexity, and imagination, they are not entirely right, either.

Through her usage of strategic quotation and allusion, Johnson writes a self that is part of and partaking of the stories of multiple others. *Minor Characters* is like the famous pie—Ecstasy Pie—Johnson made with Cessa Carr on the evening before her twenty-second birthday. Aware of "Ecstasy Pie" as an already-told story, Johnson corrects previous un-"nuanced" (197) accounts of both the name and the pie: "Blind intuition guided me that night as I went through Cessa's spice shelves . . . sprinkling a little of this and reckless amounts of that on my sliced apples. 'How about cloves, Cessa?' She'd laugh and say, 'Why not?'" (196). It was, Johnson reports, the best pie she ever tasted, and Kerouac and Lucien Carr dubbed it—and her—"Ecstasy Pie." She observes: "Since the measurements of its ingredients were unrecorded, ecstasy pie turned out to be unduplicatable" (197). Like the pie, Johnson's Beat life is unscripted and communal. Attempting to account for it in her memoir, Johnson combines various and varying discursive ingredients to record an identity that cannot be fully or accurately duplicated, an identity subject to cooptation by others, an identity assembled out of improvisation and collaboration.

Beat-associated women's life-writing can be understood as recursive auto/biographies: texts that circle back to revisit already-known Beat "biographies," often using intervening cultural, historical, and literary discourses to craft improvisational models of femaleness and of Beatness. Encountering themselves from multiple perspectives, women writers affiliated with the Beat movement join already-formed conversations about their roles, their lifestyle choices, their interpersonal associations, their literary work, and their places in history. As they negotiate various and multiple representations of their lives, pre-textual and pretextual implications of the "Beat woman" label, and shifting social, cultural, and historical discourses of gender, the autobiographers considered in this study write their individual identities as sites of intertextual exchange.

"We Were the Ones Who Had Dared to Leave Home": Women and Beat Iconoclasm

The "Beat woman writer" category encompasses a diverse and varied set of figures with diverse and varied views of the Beat movement.

Beat-associated women's autobiographical texts, too, are very different, as are their motivations for composing them. I will not attempt, therefore, to posit a one-size-fits-all accounting of their methods and strategies of self-representation; I will, however, propose that the pressure of the already-known Beat narrative, coupled with the stickiness of the "Beat woman" label, encourages similar autobiographical priorities and concerns.

Perhaps most visible of the impulses shared by women included in *Women Writers of the Beat Era* is their tendency to rescript the roles reserved for them as set dressing in the passion play of Beat men's epic iconoclasms. Virtually without exception, Beat-associated women autobiographers recast Beat iconoclasm as a gendered construct rooted in social norms regulating male and female behaviors and desires. Their texts usually imply, and at points outright state, that their male compatriots' performances of "defiant masculinity" and enactments of "wild selfbelieving individuality" adhere to the dominant cultural logic of the United States, which easily accommodates male lives "at the extreme." In contrast, they observe, Beat women have access to no ready vocabulary through which to express female iconoclasm. Mulling over in *Minor Characters* Allen Ginsberg's declaration that "the social organization which is most true of itself to the artist is the boy gang," Johnson attempts a revision: "*The social organization which is most true of itself to the artist is the girl gang.*" She concludes: "Why, everyone would agree, that's absolutely absurd!" (79, 81).[5] Even as I write in the second decade of the twenty-first century, "defiant masculinity" makes considerably more sense than "defiant femininity," which sounds like an incongruous combination of opposed ideals.

Each of the autobiographical texts examined in this study situates its subject as a female iconoclast while simultaneously exploring the limits and contradictions of this position. These narratives convey the idea that if "iconoclast" is understood to mean a person who smashes through beliefs and practices established as normative, then girls who "dared to leave home" for Beat bohemia merit inclusion in this category. In their life-writing, Beat-associated women (quite deliberately, for the most part) highlight their attempts to break through the gender role expectations limiting female aspiration in the United States of the 1950s and early 1960s. Betty Friedan famously classified these expectations as a "mystique of feminine fulfillment" in which women's most cherished "dream" was to attain the position of "suburban housewife" (12, 11).[6] Women who chose Beat lives, their autobiographies maintain, did so with the pursuit of other kinds of dreams in mind.

Beat-associated women's life-writing insists on the radical and risky implications of rejecting middle-class housewifery in favor of the "deliberate downward mobility" of Beat bohemia (Douglas xxv). In *Recollections of My Life as a Woman: The New York Years* (2001), Diane di Prima remembers when she left home, she became an "outlaw," "barred from family life" (8). Choosing to live as "an artist . . . in the world of the 40s and early 50s," she asserts, meant "choosing as completely as possible for those times the life of the renunciant" (101). Renouncing both the restriction and the security of traditionally configured home and family, Beat-associated women mis-placed themselves into social nowheres and lived in states of cultural dislocation.

"Everyone knew in the 1950s why a girl from a nice family left home," Johnson remarks in *Minor Characters*. "The meaning of her theft of herself from her parents was clear to all—as well as what she'd be up to in that room of her own" (102). To others, Johnson stresses, her abandonment of the safe respectability of her parents' home incontrovertibly indicated she had gone "bad" (102). In the America of the mid-twentieth century, girls who ventured out into the world to write or to feel free or to live on their own terms were viewed as immoral and unnatural, if not insane and criminal. "Independence," Johnson asserts, "could be punishable by death" (*MC* 107). Di Prima similarly comments that for "women on the Beat scene," the "threat of incarceration or early death in one form or another was very real" (qtd. in Friedman, "Being" 238). Hettie Jones does not remember any woman among her Beat friends and acquaintances "who, if she was still in touch with her parents, was on good terms with them. Many had just left home and disappeared" ("D" 159–60). To illustrate the consequences of defiant femininity and Beat downward mobility, commentators often evoke the figure of Elise Cowen, Johnson's close friend and lover/companion of Ginsberg, who was institutionalized by her parents and committed suicide at the age of twenty-eight.[7]

In Johnson's *Minor Characters,* Elise—a girl who left her parents' home but could find no comfortable "room of her own"—emblemizes the potentially deadly dilemmas of the female iconoclast. On the one hand, Johnson admires Elise's "courage" in striking out to "live free" (63); she describes Elise immersing herself in New York's Beat bohemia, entering into intimate relations with men she does not intend to marry, and secretly writing poetry. On the other hand, Johnson enumerates the terrible costs of Elise's freedom, including the mutilation of an abortion/hysterectomy, the "wither[ing]" effects of drug use, and the alienation of a life spent "drift[ing] from one sunless pad to another, her possessions in shopping bags" (257). Johnson portrays Elise as a perpetual outsider, "tormented by speechlessness" and beset with "self-loathing and despair" (74, 77). Her difference and unbelonging, her sensitivity to the judgmental disgust of parents, employers, landlords, and friends, remind Johnson—and her readers—that violations of culturally permissible scripts of femininity endanger women, no matter the context, even in Beat bohemia.

What is more, Johnson shows that Elise is recontained within more normative female positions by the Beat community itself, where "suicide made [her] mythic briefly" (258). Noting Elise's reduction to "a bit player" (145) in texts by Kerouac, Ginsberg, Leo Skir, and Lucien Carr, Johnson draws on others' representations of Elise to point to her nowhere position as a woman overshadowed and contained within the Beat mythos. In *Minor Characters,* Elise represents the limits of female iconoclasm and its susceptibility to recuperation by discourses—both traditional and countercultural—that push women to the margins of male-centered stories and make "defiant femininity" a contradiction in terms.[8]

In addition to challenging and complicating the gendered terms of Beat iconoclasm, the autobiographical texts examined in *Women Writers of the Beat Era* point to ways in which Beats have become emblems of cultural difference and thus figures of social projection and fantasy. They offer critical responses to thin, one-dimensional portraits of the culturally fabricated "Beat woman," and seem especially intent on resisting the "Beat chick" caricature of "the attractive, young, sexually available and above all silent ('dumb') female" (McNeil 189). The "Beat chick" pretext looms in the background of Beat-associated women writers' self-representation— their attention to "women's struggle as wives, lovers, mothers, artists, breadwinners" (Waldman 259) appears in large part intended to drive her away by filling the space she takes up in the American national imagination with complex and nuanced portraits of female Beats.

Around and against simplistic "Beat chick" caricatures, Beat-associated women writers describe their occupation of multifaceted and diverse positions within Beat cultures. Their texts document their "struggles" and their achievements as—among other things and sometimes all at once— artists, lovers, rebels, muses, philosophers, providers, mothers, friends, and daredevils. They recount the adventure of taking on hybrid combinations of roles coded male and female and the uncertainties of inventing subversive, even defiant female identities.

Their texts often focus on creative endeavors (their own and others'), exploring Beat-affiliated women's priorities as self-motivated but often frustrated artists—writers, painters, dancers, actors, musicians, and photographers. Hettie Jones's autobiography returns again and again to her dissatisfaction with poems produced between household tasks and on lunch hours. Entries in Joanne Kyger's journals frequently focus on her yearning for a writing life unencumbered by gender role expectations. In *Minor Characters,* Johnson stresses her project to develop her own voice as a writer and expresses respect for the "heroic" Mary Frank, a sculptor who cares for a family and maintains a household while remaining "as fierce about her work as a man" (243). Additionally, autobiographers included in *Women Writers of the Beat Era* describe functioning as housekeepers, financial providers, and/or unpaid secretaries to Beat husbands and boyfriends while simultaneously re-creating themselves as nascent feminists, independent-minded activists, and/or originators of alternative family structures. Given this complexity and multiplicity, it is perhaps understandable that commentators fall back on the ready-made and readily available "Beat chick" caricature rather than attempting to sort through the rewards and conflicts experienced by women living productive but overly full Beat lives, lives unaccounted for in dominant cultural scripts of identity and belonging.

The life-writing of Beat-associated women frequently emphasizes their agency in crafting and maintaining Beat communities that welcome off-script ways of life. Early in *Minor Characters,* Johnson points to the importance of women in the formation of Beat groups in New York in the late 1940s, characterizing Joan Vollmer Burroughs's 115th Street apartment as "an early prototype of what a later generation called a pad" (*MC* 3). In *Recollections of My Life as a Woman,* di Prima describes her own "pads" as communal spaces in which she was empowered to wholeheartedly pursue her art, to write with "joy and abandon" (114). Hettie Jones devotes considerable attention in her autobiography to her construction (with her husband, LeRoi Jones/Amiri Baraka) of salon-like environments that fostered Beat creative community and answered her own need for alternative ways of life, rooms "alive with a din that satisf[ied] every emptiness [she'd] ever felt" (76). Whereas Beat men reject domestic realms as locales of conformity and repression, women writers of the Beat era tend to represent their bohemian homes as sites of freedom and experimentation. In these self-made spaces, they found new and exciting, if often hidden, possibilities that enabled and informed their art. "Subjected to the larger Beat paradox of gender inequity," Ronna Johnson argues, "women Beat writers have created their own paradox: their implementation of beat within and by their use of the domestic sphere has instantiated a Beat literary discourse made of materials that male-authored Beat literature has precisely defined itself in reaction against" ("Mapping" 26).[9] The incubators of Beat women's bohemian households, their autobiographies demonstrate, gave life to both artistic and social transformations.

All of the authors examined in this study construct modes of self-creation in which they improvise on available models of accepted and expected femininity and Beatness to construct their own "life forms" (di Prima, *M* 45). Many of these life forms could be understood as both compliant and transgressive, tentative and bold—as in Bonnie Bremser's depiction of her experience as a prostitute. Their life-writing revises and supplements incomplete and often unflattering versions of their stories—as in Joanne Kyger's and Hettie Jones's references to their famous author-husbands' references to them, as well as to others' depictions of their marriages. Beat-associated women writers intervene in media portrayals of the Beat Generation in which they appear as stock characters flickering in and out of sight within male-centered stories—as in di Prima's exaggerated rendering of her younger self as a voraciously oversexed proponent of free love in *Memoirs of a Beatnik* (1969). Where di Prima undermines cultural ideas about Beat chicks in parodic intertextual play that calls into question the gender dynamics imbuing the already-known Beat story, Kyger's wry mentions of her "beatnik" appearance (*JIJ* 195) and Jones's defense of her "blackest black tights" (*H* 129) challenge similar "Beat woman" caricatures by exploring their roots in everyday bohemian life.[10]

Jones's three-line poem "Self-Portrait" in *Drive* might half-jokingly reference her intertextual bind:

There it is:

I sulk all day
in various mirrors (75)

All of the autobiographers included in *Women Writers of the Beat Era* fashion self-portraits that reflect and refract the selves looking back at them from innumerable textual "mirrors." As a result, their life-writing often feels crowded, thickly plotted, and loudly imbued with others' defining voices and visions. Their texts are characterized by ongoing negotiation of pre-scripted expectations, careful unknotting of already-heard certainties, and self-conscious interrogation of the interpolative functions of both intimate social groups and larger cultural structures and social institutions. Narrating their intertextual lives, Beat-associated women autobiographers generate shifting and layered modes of self-representation that almost constitute the writing of multiple identities.[11]

"Life Is Made Up of Stories": Autobiography and Intertextuality

Multiplicity, a word I use frequently in this chapter, is (not coincidently) a central characteristic of intertextuality, a concept that accounts for a text's relationship to the myriad discursive realms from which it emerges, realms that flow in and through it. Intertextuality refers to the "productive" character of the text, in the sense that its meanings are fundamentally dynamic, in play between writer, reader, and literary/cultural/historical contexts. Every text, Julia Kristeva argues, constitutes "a permutation of texts, an intertextuality: in the space of a given text, several utterances, taken from other texts, intersect and neutralize one another" (36). Literary texts are sites of exchange with other printed texts, with social and cultural discourses and ideologies, and with language itself.[12] In this sense, any text—including autobiography—more closely resembles an expansive set of ongoing conversations than a singular, bounded, and immobile artifact.

Kristeva's poststructuralist articulation of intertextuality—"any text is constructed as a mosaic of quotations; any text is the absorption and transformation of another" (66)—is aligned with Mikhail Bakhtin's notion of dialogism, which holds that the meaning and function of words and phrases rest in previous utterances of those words and phrases, in the ways they have been used and understood by others. "Any concrete discourse," he theorizes,

> finds the object at which it was directed already . . . overlain with qualification, open to dispute, charged with value. . . . It is entangled, shot through with shared thoughts, points of view, alien value judgments and accents. The word, directed toward its object, enters a dialogically agitated and tension-filled environment of alien words, value-judgments and accents, and weaves in and out of complex interrelationships, merges with some, recoils from others, intersects with a third group; and all this may crucially shape discourse, may leave a trace in all its semantic layers, may complicate its expression and influence its entire stylistic profile. (276)

Like dialogism, intertextuality asserts the coincidence of "the life experience of the self with that of otherness" (Juvan 87). Intertextuality insists on the self's inevitable, unavoidable imbrication in others' modes and structures of expression. Language and its products construct meaning beyond an individual's intent and consent; "generated in relation to *an-*

other structure," the word constitutes "an *intersection of textual surfaces* rather than a *point* (a fixed meaning)" (Kristeva 64–65). Therefore, as Graham Allen observes, our texts necessarily encode "conflict over the meaning of words. If a novelist, for example, uses the words 'natural' or 'artificial' or 'God' or 'justice' they cannot help but incorporate into their novel society's conflict over the meanings of those words" (36). All words and their referents are always-already qualified and occupied by others, but words such as "Beat," "woman," and "writer"—especially in combination—occupy particularly fraught "tension-filled environments."

"Intertextuality," which derives from the Latin *intertexo* (to intermingle while weaving), has come to designate a wide range of signification, from the unconscious semiotics of everyday speech to deliberate deployments of literary conventions such as allusion and imitation.[13] Critical articulations and explorations of this concept come from a number of perspectives. They explore differentiations between overt and implicit intertextuality; enumerate narrative, generic, and cultural permutations of texts; and address the question of authorial agency versus authorial irrelevance. The prominent French critic Gérard Genette offers an "open structuralist" (399) model in which he renames intertextuality "transtextuality" in order to focus on "the textual transcendence of the text," or "all that sets the text in a relationship, whether obvious or concealed, with other texts" (1). This "terminological swap," Marko Juvan observes, indicates Genette's interest "not in the sociohistorical *inter*action between texts, which the concept of intertextuality implies, but in the moves by which a text . . . *trans*forms a pre-text" (126). Sorting through a taxonomy of relationships (including parody, pastiche, imitation, continuation, and versification) to examine ways in which texts intersect with and comment on other texts, Genette proposes that literature always exists "in the second degree" (9). Writing, he contends, is rewriting.

Other structuralists, such as Michael Riffaterre, hold that texts refer not to an outside world, "but to other texts, other signs" (Allen 115). Riffaterre identifies intertextuality as the primary "mechanism" of "literary reading. It alone, in fact, produces significance, while linear reading . . . produces only meaning" (qtd. in Genette 2). Charles Givet follows Riffaterre in viewing reading as "an 'act of intertextualization' and 'reworking of the implicit in a text'" (Juvan 118). Givet understands a text as a "variation of paradigms from 'cultural memory' and a serial phenomenon" that either "reinforces social systems of representation" or, "by a dissimilating entry to a series[,] . . . activates what the prevailing social discourse has marginalized and submerged" (118). Jonathan Culler, Paul de Man, Nancy K.

Miller, Monika Kaup, and others debate the functions of readers' and authors' "literary competence" in decoding and responding to textual signs in different cultural and historical contexts, from varying social and political positions, and within the constraints and possibilities accompanying raced and gendered subjectivities.[14]

At present, the term "intertextuality" tends to be used quite broadly to indicate a range of interrelations between texts and/or cultural materials; it encompasses discursive strategies, events, accidents, and phenomena including citation, allusion, affiliation, adaptation, influence, imitation, pastiche, irony, continuation, paraphrase, parody, quotation, collage, transposition, translation, and supplementation. Confronting the porous, indistinguishable border between citation and intertextuality, Juvan observes that "what we actually face is a ladder of changing gradations, a border zone that historically and culturally keeps reshaping itself." Intertextuality, he asserts, "depends on countless variables in literary fields" (145).[15] I will draw on contemporary theories of intertextuality—and develop some additional, related terms and applications—to explore the variables underpinning Beat-associated autobiographers' "absorption and transformation" of the social, ideological, and literary pre-texts and pretexts that have shaped not only the "Beat woman" label but also their own evolving conceptualizations of themselves, their communities, and their art. *Women Writers of the Beat Era: Autobiography and Intertextuality* examines strategies of self-expression crafted by self-conscious authors who engage with the overdetermined models of gendered Beat identity already-written in the published narratives of others and in ideals of Beatness and femininity circulating in literature and popular culture, in Beat and national discourses, in multiple and varied historical contexts. These deliberate forms of address often enfold less deliberate adaptations and improvisations that reveal ambivalent and ambiguous reformulations of Beat and female identity.

While theorists of intertextuality have not for the most part considered the unique "variables" intertextual reference and literary competence take on in the "literary field" of autobiography—the sort of textual interminglings and interweavings that take place when writers attempt to account for who they are and who they have been "in the second degree"—theorists of autobiography have long been engaged with structuralist and poststructuralist thought about the relationship of language and identity. This is not unexpected, given that concepts such as intertextuality dispute the "originality, uniqueness, singularity and autonomy" readers tend to attribute to authors and their texts (Allen 6). Intertextuality raises obvious questions about the nature of autobiographical writing, calling into question the autobiographer's implied promise to grant the reader access to the unique truth of her being by telling her own story in her own words. Our words, it turns out, are not entirely ours, nor do our paragraphs and pages stand alone as pure distillations of self-generated meaning. Writers inherit autobiographical forms and formulas from their predecessors and frame their perceptions within preexisting social and cultural parameters. In this sense, no one's story can be exclusively her own.

Judith Butler, in *Giving an Account of Oneself,* points out that the ways in which human beings "make ourselves intelligible to ourselves and to others . . . are social in character, and . . . establish social norms, a domain of unfreedom and substitutability within which our 'singular' stories are told" (21). If one's story is to be intelligible, it cannot be particularly original, nor can it be entirely iconoclastic. And, because individual experience is understood and conveyed though discursive filters that encode social norms, there can be no direct or unmediated access to the unique truth of another's life, or even to one's own, for that matter. Truth necessarily resides, to one extent or another, in the already-said and already-known.

Autobiographers depend on the already-said for intelligible lexicons of self-expression; the already-said provides the discursive structures that enable individuals to make sense of experience, channel instinct and desire, and conceptualize communality and difference. As individuals construct a "sustaining sense of self," Paul John Eakin observes, we inevitably "draw on models of identity provided by the cultures we inhabit." These models are thus "centrally implicated in the way we live and write about our lives" (*How* 46). In her work on women's autobiography, Sidonie Smith argues that the female autobiographer recalls past experiences and describes the self-concept shaped by those experiences through shared "interpretive figures"—"tropes, myths, metaphors"—that constitute "cultural scripts of signification." These intertextual and gender-specific figures "reflect privileged stories and character types that the prevailing culture, through its discourse, names as 'real' and therefore 'readable'" (*Poetics* 47).[16]

The emphasis in autobiography studies on the formation of subjectivity in and through culturally produced templates (such as interpretive figures and models of identity) might seem to indicate that identity is pre-scripted, configured by social and cultural norms over which the individual holds little sway. But, as Smith and Julia Watson contend, "autobiographical subjects oscillate between the narratives that write them and those they reconfigure in their local and strategic interventions" (*Getting* 21). Theoretical conceptualizations of autobiographical self-fashioning out of available discursive resources offer a vision of human beings as inherently intertextual, mosaics of experience, desire, and discourse continually under assemblage and subject to culturally and historically specific modes of accountability. Because selves and social domains are intertextual—dialogic, dynamic, and permeable—autobiographers find considerable space within the "dialogically agitated and tension-filled environments" of cultural discourse to improvise, to fill in and manipulate cultural models, stories, and scripts. In other words, while templates of identity may coerce and limit, they simultaneously function as cooperative locales for ongoing productions of identity.[17]

"Stirring Things Up": The "Transformative Power of Art" in Beat-Associated Women's Life-Writing

Like other female autobiographers, Beat-associated women writers invoke familiar social scripts to express female self-concept and to account for their experience in Beat contexts; in the process, however, they defamiliarize prevailing notions of both femininity and Beatness. They necessarily and inevitably call on inherited interpretive figures—such as mother, wife, whore, and muse—to narrate their lives, but the "readability" of their stories is often disrupted by their violations of social expectations for mothers, wives, whores, and muses in both Beat and mainstream discourses. Many Beat-associated women autobiographers script their life experiences around culturally "privileged stories" for women such as the heterosexual romance plot and its outcomes in marriage and family—stories that undergo change over time but remain coded as particularly female preoccupations and priorities. But Beat women mis-tell these stories in depictions of, among other scenarios, love without marriage, sex without love, open marriage, homosexual love and sex, marriage-related prostitution, and so on. In addition, they mis-apply female-coded scripts to Beat situations and contexts. The male-centered Beat ethos regards the attachments of romantic love, the obligations of marriage, and the bonds of family as repressive social constructs antithetical to the sovereign and defiant individualism characterizing the Beat subject, who, of course, is assumed to be male.

As Beat-associated autobiographers craft what amounts to paradoxical, contradictory, even impossible identities as simultaneously Beats, women, and writers, their absorption and transformation of others' texts and discourses produce formulations of identity that often resemble palimpsests. A palimpsest (the word derives from the Greek term for "rubbed away" or "scraped again") is a manuscript (parchment, tablet, vellum, scroll, etc.) used multiple times—earlier writing is erased or scraped off to accommodate new text. One narrative is overwritten by another, but its tracks and traces remain in irregularly discernable forms as previous writings emerge from beneath the textual surface. The foreground of a palimpsest shifts and changes because its "content has been subject to different temporal accretions, to deliberate erasures and emendations, to overwritings and inadvertent survivals" (Eakin, *Touching* 67). Beat-associated women's autobiographical texts feature similar effects: their life-writing is infused with intertextual strata produced by their rewriting of others' stories and by their revisions of Beat and mainstream models of femininity, as well as by their recourse to varied and evolving vocabularies of self-representation, social expectation, and cultural critique.[18]

Autobiographical palimpsests reveal the "self" as, in Eakin's terms, "a social reality, constituted in no small part by the others who surround it" (*Touching* 104). Others' voices may emerge and retreat in response to the discursive circumstances in which the autobiographer works to describe and define herself but cannot be disentangled from the autobiographical "I" that speaks in her text. Beat-associated women's autobiographical projects involve rubbing away caricatures of themselves as silent chicks, literary copycats, and repressed spoilsports; however, the ideas and implications underwriting those caricatures persist, seeping up to confront the writers' accounts of Beat parties, literary communities, journeys, and pads, shadowing and occasionally overshadowing the "I"s they want to write.

Some of these intertextual negotiations are more visible than others. Palimpsests are clearly discernible when Beat-associated women attempt to overwrite already-known versions of periods, interactions, and events—such as in Hettie Jones's retelling of her first encounter with LeRoi Jones/Amiri Baraka, a story previously told in his autobiography, among other places. Casting her younger self as independent and adventurous, resistant to culturally pervasive models of female identity, Jones contests her ex-husband's portrayal of her as passive and fearful. Nevertheless, his textual portrait clearly colors her recollection and articulation of how she "became Hettie Jones." Similarly, as Joyce Johnson cites previous accounts of her relationship with Kerouac, she essentially conarrates her Beat experience, borrowing others' descriptive words and phrases to reconstruct the life of a young woman she at points struggles to recognize.

Even in the relative privacy of her journal, Joanne Kyger's account of her 1962 trip to India with Gary Snyder, Allen Ginsberg, and Peter Orlovsky is shaped and infiltrated by her awareness of how this pilgrimage was being described and interpreted back in the States. Poetry written during the same period as her *Japan and India Journals* merges her Beat experience with mythic themes, allowing her to simultaneously inhabit the positions of the celebrated male traveler and the obscured female artist. Other Beat-associated women construct palimpsestic textual structures when they take up with crucial differences already-known genres and narrative formulas—such as Bonnie Bremser's Beat road story and ruth weiss's jazz poetry.

Beat-associated women writers create palimpsests in other ways when they deploy vocabularies formulated in other historical moments to account for their experience in the Beat era. For example, di Prima composed *Memoirs of a Beatnik* in the late 1960s using terminologies of "beatnik" identification that, she asserts, she was not aware of during her Beat years and that had nothing to do with her experience as an independent artist in the underground bohemias of early 1950s New York. Johnson's *Minor Characters* and *Door Wide Open* (2000) fuse multiple discourses and lexicons, including second-wave feminist critiques of traditional gender/power arrangements; post–World War II models of submissive femininity; principles of bohemian rebellion and gender difference formulated by 1950s New York intellectuals; revisionist ideals articulated within Beat revival narratives of the 1980s and 1990s; and Beat ethics and aesthetics enumerated in Beat communities and in texts by Cowen, Ginsberg, Kerouac, Holmes, and others. Such hybridity lends layers of complexity and difference to the already-known and creates fluctuating narrative and interpretive positions that unsettle fixed, singular articulations of identity. Instead, selves appear porous and prismatic, and autobiographical "I"s often seem to speak with more than one voice.

Because Beat-associated women's autobiographical "I"s bear traces of others' texts and residue of cultural expectations predominant in different historical and social contexts, their self-representation at points seems discordant, contradictory, or otherwise uncomfortable. Genette argues that the entry of a text into relationship with a previous text always "entails some kind of game, at least to the extent that it processes and uses an object in an unforeseen, unprogrammed, and thus 'unlawful' manner." And "true play," he observes, "always entails some degree of perversion" (399). Games played with one's identity have high stakes, and often involve unclear rules, unspoken bargains, and unexpected forfeitures. Perverse, playful, unlawful exchanges—"palimpsestuous" relations between narratives, utterances, texts, and discourses[19]—generate textual pressure points, fault lines, and incoherencies. These unsettled moments reveal configurations of defiant femininity groping toward or shying away from articulation under the surface of Beat-associated women's "second degree" life-writing.

Palimpsestic identities might seem incomplete or indeterminate, lacking authority and cohesiveness, obscured by uneven erasures and ambiguous rewritings. Built on unstable discursive ground, palimpsestic selves contend with competing textual materials and risk usurpation by others' narratives. At the same time, autobiography-as-palimpsest opens opportunities for creative transformations. Because palimpsestic life-writing offers possibility rather than certainty, it prevents identity from settling into one easily quantifiable model or script and offers an inherent challenge to already-known stories of all sorts.

2   TRUTHINESS
Diane di Prima's *Memoirs of a Beatnik* and
Recollections of My Life as a Woman

Reading [Memoirs of a Beatnik*] now, there's much that I don't remember, that I read like someone else's story.*
— DIANE DI PRIMA, AFTERWORD, *MEMOIRS OF A BEATNIK*

Close as I can, this is how I remember it. I could be wrong about some things. Most everybody is.
— DIANE DI PRIMA, *RECOLLECTIONS OF MY LIFE AS A WOMAN*

That an autobiography is a story created out of the author's memory in terms of his or her private mythologies suggests that autobiography is, in some ways, similar to mythology in the larger sense. Like the mythology of a community, or of a nation, autobiography seeks to refine the self's folk stories.
— TIMOTHY DOW ADAMS, *TELLING LIES IN MODERN AMERICAN AUTOBIOGRAPHY*

The title of Diane di Prima's *Memoirs of a Beatnik* (1969) invites a set of specific, if contradictory expectations. Its first word—"memoirs"— extends the twin promises of significance and truthfulness. Memoirs are autobiographies written (until fairly recently) by public figures and "pointed toward history and fact" (Cox 124); readers expect them to proffer an inside glimpse into important events, moments, or movements. At the time di Prima was writing, the genre was "associated with the stories of great men . . . stories deemed worthy of telling because their male subjects have performed noticeably and meritoriously" (Grace, "Snapshots" 141). Thomas Jefferson wrote a memoir.[1] So did Ulysses S. Grant. "The memoir," Gillian Whitlock notes, was "a genre for those who are authorized and who have acquired cultural legitimacy and influence" (20).[2] *Memoirs of a Beatnik* adheres to none of these conventions. Di Prima is neither male nor a noted public figure, and she tells outright lies in the guise of autobiographical reminiscence. What is more, most of these lies involve sex and sexuality, topics typically avoided by memoirists who have achieved positions of cultural significance.

Further, the title's labeling of di Prima as "a beatnik" conflicts with the implications of "memoir," given that the term "beatnik," which conveys a caricatured, reductive version of Beat identity, connotes illegitimacy and lack of influence. "The Russian-sounding suffix," Joyce Johnson points out, "hint[s] at free love and a little communism (not enough to be threatening), as well as a general oafishness." She further observes that "beatnik" suggests something fake or put on; the phrase "Beat Generation" carries "an implied history, some process of development," but "with the right accessories 'beatniks' could be created on the spot" (*MC* 188).[3] While "beatnik" would have been a term familiar to readers in 1969, when *Memoirs of a Beatnik* was first published, it seems odd to find this "sneering diminutive" (Holmes, "Game" 636) attached to the life-writing of a serious poet, a woman deeply invested in the Beat arts scene.

With these inconsistencies in mind, I will suggest that much of *Memoirs of a Beatnik* is more "truthy" than true, to borrow a term from Stephen Colbert. Di Prima's memoir plays with and on ideas that people expect to be true, challenging concepts readers might believe they know "intuitively or 'from the gut'" (Meyer).[4] Turning the mirror of truthiness on commonly held expectations about beatniks, di Prima caricatures the caricature. Her representations of her intertextual life comprise a kind of *contra*textual life-writing—her contrarian address to Beat pre-texts (prior texts and discourses) and pretexts (stereotypes and clichés), expressed as she weaves together fiction and memoir, compels the reader to participate in the production of a mosaic-self, to piece together contingent, incomplete, and evolving redefinitions of "Diane di Prima."

Memoirs of a Beatnik is generally recognized as a fictionalized autobiographical narrative—Last Gasp of San Francisco, publisher of the 1988 edition, designated it "Ficto-Biography; Erotica," while Penguin Books categorized its 1998 edition flat-out "Fiction." Commentators have identified the text as a "campy self-representational take on Beat mythology" (Grace, "Snapshots" 141), "for hire pornography" (Quinn 177), and "countercultural biography" melded with "pornographic improvisation" (Libby 46). The autobiographical claims of di Prima's 2001 *Recollections of My Life as a Woman: The New York Years*, on the other hand, have not been called into question. Composed primarily of her recollections of her life as an artist, *Recollections of My Life as a Woman* offers a portrait of the Diane di Prima informed readers would recognize as cofounder of the Poet's Press and the New York Poet's Theatre, cofounder and editor of the Beat literary periodical the *Floating Bear*, and author of texts including *Dinners and Nightmares* (1961), *Revolutionary Letters* (1971), and *Loba* (1978). In fact, reviewers of *Recollections of My Life as a Woman* applaud di Prima's "commitment to truth and accuracy," describing the memoir as "an unflinching portrait of the life of a Beat woman writer of the 1950s and early 1960s" (Gillan 297, 299) and as a record of her "struggle for truth" (Foley 350). I will argue that *Recollections* poses its own questions of autobiographical authenticity and, like *Memoirs of a Beatnik,* offers readers a contratextual truthiness that unsettles what they think they know about Beats and about Diane di Prima.

Di Prima composed her second, apparently more truthful autobiography during the late twentieth-century revival of public interest in the Beat Generation following the twenty-fifth-anniversary publication of *On the Road.* Writing in 1999, Ronna Johnson and Maria Damon point to the proliferation during the 1990s of "academic conferences, museum exhibitions, and literary anthologies" focused on Jack Kerouac, Allen Ginsberg, and William Burroughs (B4). In 2001, the year of *Recollections'* publication, a *New York Times* article on the auction of Kerouac's scroll manuscript of *On the Road* observed that the novel was "continu[ing] to sell at a rate of 110,000 to 130,000 copies a year," up slightly from 1991, "when steady annual sales of 25,000 quadrupled in one year" (Shattuck E1). Di Prima's "recollections" of the Beat era in New York City undermine the mythos built on narratives like *On the Road,* which the *Times* characterizes as "one of the elemental texts of the Beat generation" (E1). In this and other texts by Beat men, male characters' "defiant masculinity" (Ehrenreich 57) stands in stark contrast to female characters' conformity to traditional gender expectations. *Recollections of My Life as a Woman: The New York Years* seems to counterpose di Prima against those unremarkable and conventional girls, presenting her "life as a woman" in the Beat era through an almost mythically defiant femininity. According to the "private mythology" constructed in *Recollections* (Adams 168), the young di Prima effortlessly shrugs off the expectations and obligations that restrict other women, rejecting available models of gendered identity to "[carve] her own path" (*R* 224). Di Prima's portrait of a life unencumbered by social norms situates her as a uniquely iconoclastic woman— and as something of a cultural and historical anomaly.

In both *Recollections of My Life as a Woman* and *Memoirs of a Beatnik,* di Prima's "conscious and unconscious misrepresentations" (Adams 16) exploit one of "intertextuality's most practical functions . . . (re-)evaluation by means of comparison, counter-position, and contrast" (Orr 7). Di Prima's reevaluations make contratextual demands on readers, forcing us to view the Beat Generation through an oppositional, revisionary lens. Her manipulations of preconceptions about Beat women demand that readers process prismatic and layered figurations of "Diane di Prima." *Memoirs of a Beatnik* and *Recollections of My Life as a Woman* may "ring true" (Adams 16) in different ways and in different contexts, but the texts' sometimes playful, sometimes confrontational truthiness distances di Prima from her readers and leaves unsatisfied their desire for the truth of Beat life.

Locations of Truth in *Memoirs of a Beatnik*

To account for di Prima's deliberate misrepresentations in *Memoirs of a Beatnik,* I will examine the narrative along the lines Timothy Dow Adams proposes in his discussion of the American author Sherwood Anderson's conflicting accounts of his life story. In *Telling Lies in Modern American Autobiography,* Adams explores Anderson's "cavalier way with facts" and "predilection for story over history" as elements that "combine to present a truer picture of Anderson than a straightforward, factual biography could" (45). Anderson, he argues, "is not as interested in literalness about his life as he is in authenticity about its myths" (52). In *Memoirs of a Beatnik,* di Prima provides a form of truthy literalness about beatnik myths that reflects cultural fantasies about Beat-associated women; the memoir, as Nancy Grace points out, does not so much report di Prima's Beat experience as "perform" ideas about Beat chicks ("Snapshots" 160). The particulars of di Prima's performance, however, serve to draw into question the truth value of those ideas.

The shared cover art of the 1988 Last Gasp and 1998 Penguin editions of *Memoirs of a Beatnik* features a photograph of a young di Prima sitting on a rumpled bed—quite deliberately invoking sexualized stereotypes about female beatniks (figs. 1 and 2). The Last Gasp cover contains a picture of two naked women sprawled on another rumpled bed, which has been blacked out by the more mainstream Penguin.[5] Of course, this sexualized imagery does reflect much of what occurs on the surface of *Memoirs of a Beatnik,* a narrative originally written for publication as part of Olympia Press's "for Adult Readers" series. In fact, di Prima's afterword to the 1988 edition attributes the text at least in part to her editor's request for erotica. She explains that she had previously composed "sex scenes for a couple of dull and innocuous novels [her editor] had purchased as skeleton plots to which the prurient interest had to be added, like oregano to tomato sauce." The editor encouraged her to "write one [her]self," and when money became "scarce" she "quickly whipped out enough pages for an advance" (136–37). She reports that much of the book's sexual content came from

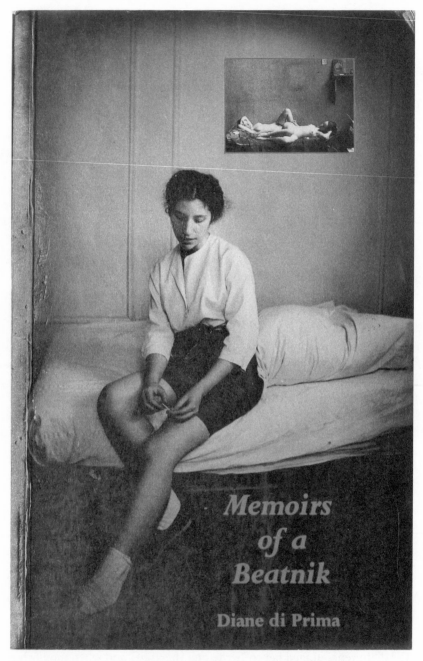

Fig. 1. Last Gasp 1988 *Memoirs of a Beatnik* front cover. (Cover photograph by
James O. Mitchell)

"A rare opportunity to view the Beat Generation . . . through a woman's eyes."
—*The New York Times*

DIANE DI PRIMA
MEMOIRS OF A BEATNIK
By the author of *LOBA*

Fig. 2. Penguin 1998 *Memoirs of a Beatnik* front cover. (Cover photograph by James O. Mitchell)

her editor's demands: "Gobs of words would go off to New York whenever the rent was due, and come back with 'MORE SEX' scrawled across the top page in Maurice's inimitable hand, and I would dream up odd angles of bodies or weird combinations of humans and cram them in and send it off again" (137).[6] It probably goes without saying that this process is not typical for the production of memoir.

However, *Memoirs of a Beatnik* is about considerably more than imagined sex. Di Prima refers to the material she wrote to spice up her "potboiler" of a book as "reminiscences" (137), and her narrative demonstrates clear emotional investment in the life she describes. Her afterword, tellingly entitled "Writing Memoirs," discusses the process by which she worked to retrieve her past, her ways of "remembering and recreating . . . that earlier time, those early fifties in The City" (137). While some critics view *Memoirs* primarily as fiction, I take the "memoir" claim of di Prima's title seriously. To do otherwise would ignore its truthiness, its self-conscious manipulation of pretextual cultural assumptions about beatniks and Beats, and fail to acknowledge di Prima's "responsibility to [her] own truth" (Adams 51), a truth located at least partially in the lies she tells. To do otherwise would mean overlooking the "Diane di Prima" who emerges as an ambiguous figure of difference in a palimpsestic memoir that repeatedly erects models for understanding female and beatnik identity, only to overwrite them at the next turn.

Structured around her movements in and out of "pads" and to and from lovers, *Memoirs of a Beatnik* covers aspects of di Prima's life from 1953 through 1956—compressed, altered, at points fabricated. Its fourteen brief chapters equate beatnik experience with the freest of free love. The narrative opens with di Prima's first heterosexual intercourse, which she positions as the inaugural event of her new and, the reader seems invited to assume, beatnik life. Dispensing with her virginity at the age of seventeen, she "enter[s] the world of the living" (15); she quite literally awakens in a new world, with the realization that "this is only the first of many strange apartments I'd be waking up in" (2). Di Prima presents her sexual encounter with a young man named Ivan not only as fairly random in and of itself, but as the beginning of an anticipated chain of similarly random couplings. As if to prove the point, she next recounts having sex with Ivan's roommate when he happens to arrive at the apartment. But after appearing to establish heterosexual sex in the one-night stand as the basis of di Prima's new life, the text offers another new beginning in a detailed exploration of a homosexual relationship.

Deeply in love with a girl named Tomi, di Prima agrees to abandon her college career to move in with Tomi and Tomi's lover, Susan O'Reilley (36). This relationship propels her "out of the safe, closed world of 'school' and into the hectic life of the city," where she searches for a "place in which to shape [her] own life form" (45). Di Prima embeds this relationship, as the presence of Susan O'Reilley might suggest, in a larger context of female bi- and homosexuality, portraying herself as part of a group of young women who provide each other with intellectual, social, and sexual alternatives to the deadening Swarthmore "college scene" (42), with its "male and female stereotypes in cashmere sweaters" (33). When di Prima locates an apartment for herself, Tomi, and Susan, she exults that she has found "a new scene, our scene" (36). But her plan to live with the two women falls apart when Tomi allows herself to be ensnared by her deeply dysfunctional family, leaving di Prima to move on alone to her "haven" (54) on the Lower East Side.

Following this abortive episode with Tomi, di Prima portrays her relationships as primarily heterosexual, shifting to a discussion of her "country scene" (71) as "a woman to . . . three men" (72), a scene in which, despite its transgressive multiplicity, she adheres to conventional expectations for women. She "loses" herself in her "new-found woman's role, the position defined and revealed by [her] sex: the baking and mending, the mothering and fucking, the girls' parts in the plays," and is "content" (79). She muses: "Yes, it was good, being a chick to three men, and each of them on his own trip . . . so that the world filled out, and interplay, like a triple-exposed photo, made infinite space" (77). Di Prima contrasts this unfixed "interplay" with the "claustrophobic and deadening . . . regular one-to-one relationship," which, she contends, is "OK for a weekend, or a month in the mountains, but not OK for a long-time thing, not OK once you have both told yourselves that this is to be the form of your lives" (77–78). Without a hint of irony, she follows these remarks on the dangers of monogamy with an account of her intense "one-to-one relationship" with Luke, a "supercool" heroin junkie whose lovemaking provokes her "utter surrender" (89). Reporting that she "belong[s] to him totally" and "want[s] him to mark [her] permanently with some mark that proclaimed [her] his" (89), she articulates a yearning for fulfillment consistent with the expectations underwriting the most conventional of romance stories.

But di Prima quickly sets aside the vocabulary of romantic thralldom characterizing her relationship with Luke to narrate her entry into what she calls "the simplest, kindest, and most devoted life I have ever managed to live" (96). Having moved into a "cold-water flat uptown on 60th Street" (96), she and Susan O'Reilley acquire a motley group of roommates of various sexual inclinations. They form "a tight little family with a life-style, a form and jargon of [their] own" (101). Within her new family life, sex comes to mean "fucking [her] comrades" (123). *Memoirs of a Beatnik* ends with the "little family's" preparations to move on to new scenes, and with di Prima's pregnancy. The afterword contains rather startling references to a husband.[7]

This overview of the intimate relationships within *Memoirs of a Beatnik* demonstrates that sexuality—the text's supposed foundation in erotica—fails to constitute a solid ground for the beatnik identity proposed in its title. Di Prima's sexuality will not stay still—she appears as simultaneously heterosexual and homosexual, dominant and submissive, tender and callous, detached and invested. Her movement from sexual scene to sexual scene prevents sure or stable characterization of her identity as a beatnik or as a woman. Instead, "like a triple-exposed photo," identity emerges as a palimpsest of associative claims constructed, reconstructed, and revised through play and experimentation.

Di Prima's life might appear to be one long orgy, but her portrayal of her Beat experience as a continuous sexual adventure persistently undermines itself and reveals its truthy misrepresentations. Her uncanny recall of the minute details of many, many long-past sexual scenes invites skepticism, and her accounts of multiple, effortless orgasms—each and every time, no matter the circumstance—strain credulity. Di Prima also gives readers other reasons to doubt her presentation of Beat-life as sex-life. Chapter 7, "Some Ways to Make a Living," recounts jobs simulating sex for money—a kind of parable, a cynic might say, for the memoir itself. Chapter 12 contains a section entitled "A Night by the Fire: What You Would Like to Hear," detailing prodigious group sex. Di Prima follows this section with another entitled "A Night by the Fire: What Actually Happened," in which her exhausted friends try to get some sleep in a freezing, overcrowded cold-water flat—a reversal that throws the verisimilitude of other, similar scenes into question.

As for the memoir's more imaginative sexual acts, in her afterword di Prima reports having posed friends in order to determine "if a particular contortion was viable." She adds, pointedly, that participants in these experiments were "completely not turned on" (138). This aside raises an obvious question: What if the reader is turned on? Di Prima's play with sex, with the stability of sexual identity, and, in Grace's terms, with "the cultural myth of . . . Beatnik life" that "promotes sexual excess as a major theme" (163) implicates the reader in the politics of the text's production. Even as readers are provided with what di Prima suspects they "would like to hear," they are forced to recognize prevailing notions about beatnik deviance as stereotypes. Evoking beatnik caricatures with a vengeance, di Prima overwhelms the reader with contratextual excess that undoes its own foundation.

In addition to parodying ideas about oversexed beatniks, di Prima's sexual lies mount a subtle critique of larger cultural tropes of sexuality organized around male desire. For example, she narrates being raped by Tomi's father through the terms of pornographic nonconsent plots—she struggles at first, but then derives satisfaction from the act. But she simultaneously mocks such plots and those who enjoy them, undermining the erotics of male dominance that provide pleasure in phallocentric fantasy: "This was Serge, poor silly Serge, who never got to screw his wife, and if he wanted to throw a fuck into me, why I might as well let him" (48–49). No one comes out of this scenario well; she describes Serge himself, her own "fear and horror" (48), and the satisfaction she achieves—her "abstract mechanical finale"—as "ridiculous" (49). Similarly, while she serves up titillating doses of college girl group sex in the Tomi section, her choice of descriptors does not quite adhere to male-oriented conceptions of desirable female sexuality; one young woman resembles "a large crescent moon" (43), while another "[comes] like a great, alien mammal" (44). As Anthony Libby suggests, "the empathy of the body on which pornography depends . . . can easily be compromised by . . . derivation from the most conventional metaphors, especially when great alien mammals disrupt the erotic theatre of the mind" (55). Di Prima's unconventional metaphors and revisions of common pornographic tropes prevent the reader from settling into a comfortable vantage point through which to conceptualize her beatnik life.

More disruptive of the male-dominant "theatre of the mind" typical of both pornography and the Beat mythos is the memoir's emphasis on female choice, agency, and freedom. Di Prima's in-your-face narratives of sexual exploits describe in detail men's bodies and their lovemaking, comparing and contrasting them, offering them up for judgment, making them objects of the reader's gaze. Chapter 13, "Organs and Orgasms—An Appreciation," recounts qualities she likes and dislikes in her male lovers, men including Ivan, other friends and roommates, and assorted "comrades." Di Prima characterizes individual men as "only a fair lay" (118) or "an easy lover who took you apart when you least expected it" (122). Their bodies are "slight," "pale and smooth" (116), or heavy and hairy, "solid and manly" (118). Penises are circumcised or not, "not terribly big" (116), or "big enough to meet all [her] requirements" (120). Sex is "passionate, but briefly so" (116), or "a bit like taking an exam" (118), or "more tantalizing than satisfying" (119). Most of *Memoirs of a Beatnik*'s sexual content, presented from a female point of view, dismantles conventional male and female power positions within the heterosexual scene.

In her accounts of sexual activity, di Prima consistently refuses the passivity and submissiveness commonly attributed to American women of the 1950s. Presenting her various relationships as expressions of her will and desire, she crafts a sexually defiant femininity. She often appears dominant and aggressive with her male lovers, marking their bodies with teeth and fingernails, "fully in control of the situation" (20), calculatingly giving pleasure and "wielding" power (23). Di Prima describes herself as a "vampire" intent on conquest and subjugation (20) and as a musician playing the male body "like an instrument" (21). In their female-focused multiplicity and variation, the sexual scenes represented in *Memoirs* come unmoored from Beat pre-texts as well as from cultural scripts for female identity.

Di Prima's tales of sexual freedom both invoke and threaten the ubiquitous "Beat chick" stereotype of the silent yet sexually accessible woman who "serves male freedom and narrative while herself remaining a cipher, a 'girl' who wears black and says nothing" (R. Johnson, "And then" 80). Despite all of the sex in *Memoirs of a Beatnik,* di Prima cannot be slotted into the "Beat chick" model of femininity conceptualized in terms of service to men. In *Memoirs,* di Prima's male lovers are silent, defined and represented through the forceful voice of a woman who exults in her robust and heterogeneous sexuality, gleefully claiming the subject position most usually afforded to male Beats narrating their conquest of chicks. In Beat pre-texts, as Helen McNeil points out, "the 'chick category' does not violate any existing gender codes" (189); fulfilling male desires while apparently having none of her own, the Beat chick validates male supremacy and upholds the primacy of male desire. Di Prima's (mis)performance of the chick script—her confident taking of "six or seven" lovers at a time (115), her aggressive pursuit of pleasure, and her dismissal of romantic dependence—violates the gender codes underwriting the dominant Beat narrative.

So if the reader is turned on, it is by something that does not adhere to cultural scripts or to Beat pre-texts.[8] In *Memoirs of a Beatnik,* the shifting seam between autobiography and pornography functions as a site for experimentation with gendered identity. Di Prima's ambiguous authorial intentions, her tendency to "play fast and loose with both the form and the content of life writing" (Grace, "Snapshots" 160), and the "calculated shocks" (Libby 49) provoked by her defiantly female-directed erotica serve to reorganize the relation of gender to Beatness. The narrative enacts a beatnik parody that contests, in Judith Butler's terms, "the very notion of an original" (*Gender* 138).

Di Prima's life-writing also undermines other notions of Beat life that have frozen into masculinist stereotype, especially its self-conscious "cool." In all interactions, "the game," di Prima remarks, is "Cool" (10), and she describes it with ambivalence. On the one hand, the "code of coolness in effect at that time" (82) discourages spontaneous expressions of emotion and at points erects walls around desire. Di Prima dislikes the "blasé professional quality" affected by some would-be lovers (18) and feels that "our code, our eternal, tiresome rule of Cool" constrains her from expressing her feelings for Luke (94). On the other hand, her narrative shows that coolness enables detachment from outmoded social expectations, cumbersome personal attachments, and binding familial and workplace responsibilities.

Critics almost unanimously accept the notion that "coolness and the cool mode of rebellion were at the time primarily masculine attributes" (Libby 47) and agree that these attributes served to "duplicat[e] female powerlessness and objectification, the gendered silence under the reign of which the majority of women of the 1950s suffered politically and socially, individually and as a caste" (Johnson and Grace, "Visions" 8). But in *Memoirs of a Beatnik*, di Prima transforms "cool" into something she can use. Her enactment of cool enables her to avoid hegemonic valuations of femininity along with the snares that lead women to shoulder the burdens of others' lives. And, at the same time that being cool empowers her to evade traditionally formulated models of femininity, it also allows her to alter and inhabit the most traditional of female roles—motherhood.[9]

Early in her narrative, di Prima discusses her younger self's refusal to accept the position of "breeding animal" within her patriarchal Italian American family and community (35). But she sees motherhood itself much differently. A section of *Memoirs* entitled "Fuck the Pill: A Digression" encourages readers to eschew all forms of birth control as unnatural and dangerous, not to mention a "drag" (75). In the process, di Prima manages to make motherhood countercultural: "Get welfare, quit working, stay home, stay stoned, and fuck" (76). While di Prima never quite follows her own advice, she does construct alternate "households" (99) through a form of free and cool mothering.

An unconventionally sexual woman experimenting with spontaneous and heterogeneous relationships, di Prima enjoys a "life form" that evades the constraints that force bourgeois mothers into singular, exclusive roles defined by service and submission. Instead, exercising her "sexual and maternal skills" (63), she ranges across gender roles, functioning as breadwinner *and* cook, protector *and* nurturer. She works for rent, prepares meals from the food family members scrape together, and reads new books aloud to her group, finding pleasure and satisfaction in her in-between position. "It was a good feeling," she recalls, "to settle down for the night with a full wood box and a book, keeping watch while the rest of the 'family' slept sung and content" (105). In households without hierarchies and families without preset parameters, di Prima's maternity nurtures both beloved others and the valued self.

She creates the households to which members of her "little family" (101) return from Broadway and the Art Students' League, the Ballet Theatre and the Museum of Modern Art. Acting as lover and comrade, di Prima constructs spaces in which she and her family "hole up and practice [their] art" (97) and where friends and associates "eat and talk and plan enormous projects" (110). She improvises, as Ann Charters observes, "her own domestic space so that she could function as an artist" (Foreword xii). Di Prima's Sixtieth Street pad facilitates "serious work," supporting the study of Homeric Greek along with the production of "poems and drawings" (102). Interspersed throughout depictions of lovers and descriptions of sexual scenes, readers catch glimpses of di Prima reading, studying, and "writing in large grey notebooks" (66).

Submerged under the sexual detail, literary and artistic experimentation abound in *Memoirs of a Beatnik*. Di Prima makes quick reference to "little magazines for which we couldn't raise any bread" and "theatre projects in gigantic lofts" (125). She briefly mentions *"This Kind of Bird Flies Backward,* [her] first book of poems" (125). At other points, di Prima proffers snippets of the arts scene in Greenwich Village, when "jazz was . . . the most important, happening art" (93), tantalizing glimpses of a bohemian environment imbued with creative energy that "seemed to spring from the fiery core of the planet and burst like a thousand boiling volcanoes in the music and painting, the dancing and the poetry of this magic city" (94). *Memoirs'* focus on sex overwrites a serious and passionate artistic life and protects a valued community that cannot be accounted for through beatnik pretexts or through the dominant Beat Generation narrative.

Emphasizing "there was no 'beat poetry' as yet" (85) and "the word 'beatnik' had not yet been coined" (84), di Prima situates her younger self at the beginning of a new literary and social movement. "As far as we knew," she explains, "there was only a small handful of us . . . who knew what we knew: who raced about in Levis and work shirts, made art, smoked dope, dug the new jazz." Their isolation, she insists, "was total and impenetrable" (126). Her "tight little family" and circle of artists and writers comprise their own movement and their own "world" (103). Their "chief concern," she reports, "was to keep our integrity . . . and to keep our cool: a hard, clean edge and definition in the midst of the terrifying indifference and sentimentality around us—'media mush.' We looked to each other for comfort, for praise, for love, and shut out the rest of the world" (126). In opposition to the "blasé" kind of cool that prevents honest and productive relationship, di Prima and her group "keep [their] cool" in artistic honesty and collaborative creativity.

Di Prima's discussion of artistic cool might serve as a contratextual mirror held up to shut out readers who have gained their understanding of Beat through "media mush" caricatures. *Memoirs of a Beatnik* challenges readers' confidence in the value of such pretexts as it presents di Prima as an empowered, creative, and fully participatory founder of what would come to be known as the Beat movement. As if to emphasize the gap between di Prima's experience and readers' expectations, well-known Beat men are notably absent from *Memoirs of a Beatnik* until its final section, when Kerouac and Ginsberg appear for a "strange, nondescript kind of orgy" (131). Their late entry into the narrative serves to highlight di Prima's difference, her displacement within the dominant Beat Generation story. *Memoirs* insists that for her there is no history or model of Beatness, no leaders to worship or emulate. It is only when she happens upon "Howl" that she becomes aware of "all the people who, like [her], had hidden and skulked, writing down what they knew for a small handful of friends" (127). "Howl" shows her that these people—her "brothers and sisters"—stand poised to "speak out," to emerge onto the national scene and create "a new era" (127).

It is at this break-out moment that di Prima "decide[s] that [she] want[s] to have a baby" (130). She relates her desire for motherhood simultaneously to bodily impulse and to her sensitivity to shifting social landscapes: "It was nothing that I decided with my head, just a vague stirring and impulse in my body, some will to flower, to come to fruition—and something in my cells whispering that the scene as I knew it had gone on long enough, that there were many other states of being to explore" (130). Asserting that her awareness of her "scene" grows organically from her female body, di Prima links her maternal "will to flower" with the flowering of the Beat movement. This claim recalls her role as a free and cool mother of alternative families and installs motherhood as a principle of Beat creativity. Di Prima's comments on motherhood offer a subtle regendering of Beat, positioning her younger self both at its birth and as its origin.

Memoirs of a Beatnik culminates in di Prima's pregnancy, achieved at the moment the people and the art she has nurtured are also about to "come to fruition," ready to be named and recognized in and as history. However, they will enter the U.S. cultural narrative not as she knows them but rather through caricatures that deny their artistic innovation and transformative influence. The title *Memoirs of a Beatnik* thus reveals itself as false in ways that exceed the problems of its truth claims—rather than performing a coherent script of "beatnik" identity, the memoir experiments with Beat and female subjectivity, producing shifting and layered portraits of Diane di Prima that defy simple or easy classification.

As di Prima gives the reading public what it thinks it wants, she proposes different Beat truths in the lies she tells, the expectations she deconstructs, and the alternatives she creates. Superimposing "beatnik" discourses over her experimental life forms, di Prima compels readers to reconsider the intertextual frameworks we bring to her memoir. Playing a palimpsestic game of hide-and-seek with elements of pornography and autobiography, sexuality and creativity, womanhood and Beatness, fantasy and lived reality, *Memoirs of a Beatnik* forces its readers to question all of the labels available to define Diane di Prima. What *do* we want to hear from her? And why?

Locations of Myth in *Recollections of My Life as a Woman*

Thirty-two years later, in *Recollections of My Life as a Woman: The New York Years,* di Prima tells us what *she* would like us to hear, foregrounding aspects of identity submerged and pushed to the margins of *Memoirs of a Beatnik.* The redirected focus and revised priorities of this second memoir are immediately evident on its cover, which features a photograph of a young di Prima seated not on an unmade bed but atop an upright piano, preparing to read from her first poetry collection (fig. 3). A sign behind her establishes a distinctly literary context: "Poetry Reading/Gas Light Café," and a copy of *This Kind of Bird Flies Backward* sits propped beside her. Almost a corrective to *Memoirs of a Beatnik, Recollections* contains little explicit sexual detail, instead lavishing attention on di Prima's self-directed life as a poet.[10]

The title *Recollections of My Life as a Woman* emphasizes the processes of recall assumed to motivate and direct autobiographical writing; di Prima's author's note—"Close as I can, this is how I remember

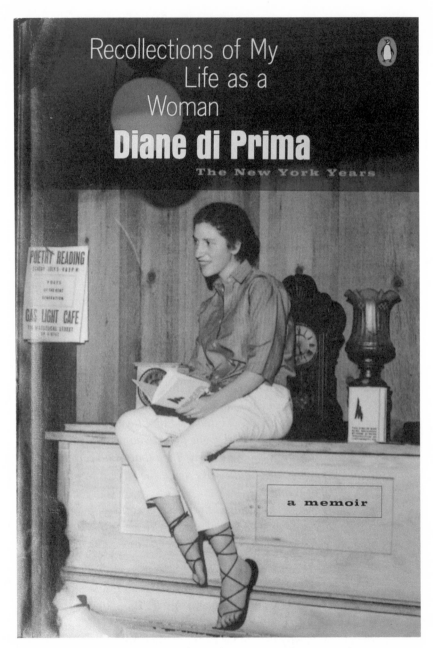

The New York Years

Diane di Prima

Recollections of My Life as a Woman

a memoir

Fig. 3. Penguin 2001 *Recollections of My Life as a Woman* front cover. (Cover photograph © Fred McDarrah/Getty Images)

it"—promises an accurate account of the past while at the same time acknowledging the slipperiness and selectiveness of memory. "What we remember," Adams suggests, "is a mysterious amalgam of what we choose, what we really want, what actually happened, and what we are forced to remember." As autobiographers convert this material "into language and [write it] down," it "becomes [their] personal truth without much consideration for its literal accuracy" (171). In its unconventional, mosaic-like structure, di Prima's autobiography reflects and enacts the complexities associated with locating and conveying truth with "literal accuracy." *Recollections* is something of an "amalgam" shaped by multifaceted strategies of self-representation: interspersed with chronological detail documenting di Prima's "New York years," readers encounter dreams, Zen proverbs, impressionistic "memory shards" (*R* 12), material extracted from her journals, and italicized meditations on her experience.

For example, her discussion of her parents' punitive and reductive focus on her appearance and their relentless enforcement of "a certain image" of "nice" correctness (33) leads to the following reflection on vision and self-perception:

Better not see who you are. My houses have always had a paucity of mirrors . . .

My whole life I have been nearsighted, a child in pink plastic-framed glasses, an adult whose love of landscape . . . made her long to see farther. One day in the 1970s . . . I dreamed that I was closeted in a very small room with a huge and vague figure who was very dangerous. . . . [Y]ou had to stay out of its way. Then that small cowering person took a psychic turn, and I woke up on the fervent words "I will see it," repeated over and over.

For the next two weeks I walked through the world with the gift of perfect sight. My eyes alive and awake as they've never been. . . . My vision slowly faded, but to this day I can bring more seeing by repeating that dream phrase.

So perhaps there was more that I would not, could not see, but the hardest is not to see one's own face and body. "The sequence of exchange starts with oneself" says a Buddhist text.

Perhaps that is why I spent years of my life working as a model. . . . I can "see" art. I was looking for myself in it. (36–37)

This passage from chapter 3 of *Recollections* illustrates di Prima's tendency to create personal "folk stories" (Adams 169) out of multiple modes of self-expression. In this instance, as she supplements childhood memories with intensely focused self-analysis, she excavates the residue of her younger self's felt inadequacies in order to convey the enduring psychic effects of oppressive familial dynamics, of "unspeakable barters made in the dark. . . . That [her] father's wrath be appeased, that [her] mother be left in peace with her griefs" (36). At the same time, di Prima's ability to speak the unspeakable and to assert her own way of seeing, her own clarity, establishes her sense of internal agency and her impulse toward resistant, defiant self-definition. Her claim to have achieved "perfect sight" adds an element of mysticism, perhaps of fantasy, that elevates her capacity for self-determination above everyday impediments and difficulties; not even physical limitations can restrict her possibilities, and she is able to construct out of fear and powerlessness a means of initiating meaningful "exchange" with a wider, more welcoming world. While the "private mythology" (Adams 168) di Prima crafts in *Recollections of My Life as a Woman* does not push the limits of credulity to the extent of the staged sex in *Memoirs*, it does raise related questions about communicating and understanding the intertextual lives both referenced and obscured by the "Beat woman" label.

In his investigation of Sherwood Anderson's "private mythology," Adams argues that Anderson "meant for his life . . . to stand as a mythic expression of the true artist in America" (68). A similar claim could be made about di Prima, whose autobiographical "I" in *Recollections* seems intended to stand as a mythic expression of artistic integrity. Unlike Anderson, who drew on hospitable literary and cultural models to craft his mythic persona—he "identified himself as a sort of modern Whitman" who embodied "the American man striving to become . . . conscious of himself" (Adams 68)—di Prima represents her writer-self in and around oppositional, often antagonistic pre-texts and pretexts. *Recollections of My Life as a Woman* forcefully declares di Prima's independence from hegemonic categories of gendered identity, presenting her as daring, innovative, and free—the embodiment of defiant female iconoclasm.

The Diane di Prima of *Recollections of My Life as a Woman* is never not a rebel and nonconformist. At the tender age of three, she reports, she feels "contempt," "impatience," and "an unchildlike sense of pity" for her parents. Perceiving them as "sad, intimidated people, and, [she] suspect[s] even then, somewhat stupid," toddler di Prima realizes she is "on [her] own from here on out" (19). Throughout her childhood and adolescence, her self-sufficiency and critical detachment enable her to preserve her "maverick inner world" (72) in the face of her father's abuse and her mother's tears.[11] Believing against all cultural evidence to the contrary that "no one [has] the right to a minute of [her] life" (99), she refuses her parents' demands for daughterly submission and affirms her "Will," her "fierce, silent love of Self" (78), as her guiding principle. Essentially, the adult di Prima remembers her younger self as a new, unquantifiable sort of girl-child, one who fits no preestablished models of identity and submits to no familial or cultural restrictions.

Di Prima finds in this unprecedented child-self the origins of her identity as an artist. Remarking that her first poem (composed in her "first-grade Catholic-school hand" at the age of six) "still works," the adult autobiographer designates it a "gift of memory. Mnemosyne. Mother" (15). This movement from "Mnemosyne"—the Titan goddess of memory and mother of the nine muses—to "Mother" proposes a kind of closed circuit of identity in which di Prima recognizes in her younger poet-self the mother of the poet she is and always was. At fourteen years of age and in full awareness that doing so would mean exempting herself from the "simple comforts of the regular human world," she claims poetry as "the shape" of her life and resolves to "liv[e] in the Vision of art to be achieved," sure that "no matter what I will be a poet. Be great, whatever that means. Fulfill the dream" (78). Although her pursuit of this dream is largely deferred during her "deadly [dull] . . . college life" (93), her desire for a writing life never wanes. It therefore seems "inevitable and right" (97) when she strikes out on her own.

Di Prima describes easily and eagerly giving up school, family, and material security to plunge into bohemian New York. She joins communities composed of outlaw artists and of actual outlaws, in whose company her "self-identity" as a "maverick" and an "outrider" feels "natural and easy" (114). Rejecting familial expectations that she do "better for herself" (110) by advancing her socioeconomic status, the young di Prima embraces "deliberate downward mobility" (Douglas xxv) as a primary vehicle of the alternative forms of success for which she believes herself destined. The "rawness" and "harshness" of city life, di Prima observes, "suit" her younger self, "fit [her] high energy and spirits, as [she] match[es] [her] self against various privations" (126). In her renunciation of "the regular human world" and immersion in subterranean bohemia, she affirms her innate difference from her parents and from the world in which she was raised. Di Prima's portrayals of her younger self's unflinching independence and refusal to perform the role of proper young lady contribute to a "private mythology" in which Diane di Prima stands aloof from and immune to the regulatory demands of 1950s America.

She "come[s] into [her] own" (126) among artists who enjoy an un-structured way of life they call "Swinging"—or "being at the right place at the right time to run into the right people for the right adventure" (138). This principle might appear to echo the Beat tendency to privi-lege "trust in spontaneous action," to disregard "preestablished patterns" and "encounter each moment as though for the first time" (Mortenson 34). However, *Recollections* presents di Prima's unfettered approach to the world as the natural outcome and expression of her "Will"—not as a Beat phenomenon. More explicitly than *Memoirs of a Beatnik, Recollections of My Life as a Woman* shows di Prima living a Beat life independent of an identifiable "Beat Generation." Rather than joining already-established Beat communities, she gravitates toward others who open themselves to life without predetermined plans or parameters; for her, it is a matter of course that she creates community with artists and writers who value pure, unregulated experience as "*the ultimate good*" (154). In this free-form lifestyle, di Prima and her friends "[carry] a world in [their] hearts" and learn "what art really [is]" (147). Her "Vision of art," di Prima stresses, arises organically from her experience—discovered and lived rather than adopted from Beat models or mentors.

Recollections' emphasis on di Prima's full-hearted commitment to po-etry adds flesh to the "skeleton plot" of artistic self-determination all but obscured by sexual scenes in *Memoirs of a Beatnik*. In *Recollections,* di Prima focuses on her passionate immersion in the New York Poet's The-atre and devotes attention to her work on *This Kind of Bird Flies Back-ward* and other texts. Recalling her development of poems with "longer lines and almost deadly certainty," she relays the joy of "finding . . . on the page . . . a world without shame, beyond good and evil. A world where things, in all their intensities, just *were* whatever they were. Where I could be who I was, without pulling punches, where there was room for my cynicism, my bitterness and my strength, as well as for the vision and the passion" (222). In her portrait of herself as a developing poet, di Prima emerges as a self-created artist in full control of language, "shaping . . . words to [her] Will" (136). Her poetry enacts her iconoclastic self-concept and expresses personal truths that exceed the binary categories (good/evil) underwriting dominant cultural worldviews and discourses of iden-tity and belonging.

Not only does di Prima demonstrate that she did not adopt her individ-ualistic personal aesthetic from an already-formed Beat literary culture, but she also establishes her formative role in the development of Beat literary principles. As coeditor of the *Floating Bear,* she lives a "continuous and seemingly endless rhythm of editing, typing, proofing, printing, collating, stapling, labeling and mailing" (251). Her literary labors keep "the energy moving," bringing together writers associated with the New York School, the Black Mountain poets, and the Beat Generation. Immersing herself in the work of others, she stands at the center of shifting circles of artistic production, disseminating experimental literature to "a hundred and fifty artists, many of them . . . friends," who might "answer in their work—incorporate some innovation of line or syntax, and build on that. Like we were all in one big jam session" (254). This "jam session" account of Beat creativity—which highlights collaboration and creative exchange—subtly contests the Beat Generation mythos and its hierarchical model of literary community—in which influence and inspiration flow from primary, iconic male figures downward to lesser, secondary artists.

At other moments, *Recollections of My Life as a Woman* mounts markedly less subtle critiques of Beat pre-texts. Di Prima debunks in specific detail a "story . . . told by [Robert] Creeley in a documentary about the Beats" (201), a story that incorporates her as a character in ways that misrepresent the lived realities of her Beat experience. In his version of events, a group of men persuade a young di Prima to remain at Ginsberg's apartment rather than leave at the time she promised a friend who had agreed to watch her daughter. According to Creeley, she "quickly forgot about the babysitter" and stayed to take part in an orgy (202). Di Prima contradicts him, insisting that even though Kerouac had warned her "in a stentorian voice" that "UNLESS YOU FORGET ABOUT YOUR BABYSITTER, YOU'RE NEVER GOING TO BE A WRITER," she chose to keep her "word" to her friend (202). Creeley, she supposes, got "mix[ed] . . . up no doubt with the orgy at the end of *Memoirs of a Beatnik,* or the eternal Beat Orgy that will live forever in the minds of all guys who were around for the second half of the twentieth century" (202). Beyond this skewering of the male-centered Beat mythos, di Prima further deflates the mystique surrounding its main figures with her description of an uninspired gathering dominated by a "pontificating" Kerouac and "lots of important intense talk about writing you don't remember later" (201). Not only is there no orgy at this particular meeting of Beat icons, it also lacks meaningful literary insight or artistic inspiration.

Di Prima finds Creeley's account—narrated, she notes, "as a man would want to have it happen" (201)—"destructive" (202) because it offers a misleading view of her "life as a woman" and demeans her priorities as a poet. She argues:

If I had, as he put it, so "charmingly" opted to stay for the orgy, there
would be no poems. That is, the person who would have left a
friend hanging who had done her a favor, also wouldn't have stuck
through thick and thin to the business of making poems. It is the
same discipline throughout—what Pound called "a 'man' [read
'woman'] standing by [her] Word." (202; brackets di Prima's)[12]

Revising Creeley's story to declare a female-centered alternative to author-
itarian and masculinized definitions of artistic integrity, di Prima points
to the gendered exclusions of Beat Generation pre-texts. She supplements
those narratives with her ethical and aesthetic stance as a woman "standing by her Word," a stance that she understands as both the fundamental
principle underwriting her Beat life and the fundamental principle marking her out as differently Beat.

Di Prima's personal mythology, in which her younger self both di-
verges from and coincides with male-dominated Beat cultures, offers
a series of self-portraits of her "life as a woman" in company with Beat
men that carry different and at points contradictory implications. On
the one hand, she characterizes the "determinedly male community of
writers" she interacted with during her New York years as a "male cabal:
self-satisfied, competitive, glorying in small acclaims" (107). Male poets
"[hold] forth pompously," "come on to [her] condescendingly," and labor
under inflated self-images as "teachers, or rabbis, or revolutionaries, or
god knows what" (246). Beat men maintain their "self-satisfied" privilege,
she suggests, through a myopic egotism that limits the community's potential for innovation. They claim artistry as an inherently male property
and protect their status by denying entry to women. Despite her centrality
to Beat literary circles, she is "not asked to literary events" and left out
of Donald Allen's important *New American Poetry* anthology (237, 238).[13]

Watching another woman artist contend with the "chaos" of "overflowing" art "beyond anything that could be sorted out, anything that was
called for by the world," she identifies the creation of "great work without
outlet" and without "*articulation* as to its meaning, its actual intent," as a
"particularly female syndrome" (197–98). This dis-ease appears to be both
self-inflicted—rooted in an inability to "articulate" artistic purpose—and
imposed by external conditions and circumstances. Considering the "dilemma" confronted by "women artists," di Prima asks: "How to carve a
niche . . . if one doesn't have access to galleries, to publishing houses? How
make a place if one doesn't speak the language of the critic?" (198). At
such moments, *Recollections of My Life as a Woman* genders Beat male

and argues that masculinized Beat contexts deny women full freedom to pursue and achieve their visions of art.

On the other hand, di Prima maintains that gender does not actually limit *her*. As a young woman, she writes, she views the "male cabal" of Beat Generation writers "as artists simply." For her, men are "fellow companions" who walk with her "on the roads of Art. Roads of our dreaming." She further asserts that "seeing it thus [makes] it possible for [her] to walk among these men mostly un-hit-on, generally unscathed" (107). Her commitment to art, she claims, enables her transcendence of gender-coded social norms and thus of the "particularly female syndrome" of art "without outlet." Di Prima's account of "walk[ing] the Dreamtime," the "eternal world of the Poem," not with men but "with companions" (107) implies that her worldview changes or overcomes the external conditions that lead to the dis-ease of the female artist. She credits her way of "seeing" with essentially ungendering her interactions with men and enabling her to remain "unscathed" by the sexist perceptions and expectations pervading Beat social and literary contexts. As with the heroes of more traditional mythologies, the Diane di Prima of *Recollections* transforms her world through force of Will.

She also exerts her Will, her "fierce, silent love of Self," to revise the cultural norms organizing more intimate forms of male/female relationship. Emphatically rejecting dominant scripts for female fulfillment, she holds that no man "by 'providing' . . . would buy the right to tell [her] what to do" (157). The young di Prima "scorn[s]" gender role arrangements based in male ownership and "control" (157) and dispenses with culturally mandated performances of female identity. Di Prima enacts defiant femininity in her conscious decision "not to be beautiful" (114), drawing on the reserves of independence she manifested as a child "who had never given a damn: about clothes, appearance, walking gracefully[,] . . . [w]hose choices in clothing had been laughed at, or beaten out of her" (115). Free from familial judgment and social regulation, she unleashes her "rough-and-tumble self," "the tomboy . . . who had never had room at home," and "let the forthright, cruel truthsayer out of the shadows" (115). Her rejection of available templates of femininity, di Prima contends, uniquely positions her to articulate truths others find "cruel," the kind of direct truths young ladies are counseled to avoid in favor of tactful niceties. In the process, she claims for herself characteristics commonly associated with men, especially confident self-sufficiency and individualistic self-focus.

The young di Prima renders herself essentially unidentifiable, "tromp[ing] through the city as some strange hybrid: neither gay nor straight, neither butch nor femme." An unquantifiable figure of difference, she "clear[s] some kind of path, cut[s] a swath" (116). Her self-willed androgyny exempts her from the limitations of cultural femininity. And, as in her ungendered travels on "roads of Art," her strange hybridity affects others' behaviors—she "[is] rarely stopped, or hassled" (116). Although di Prima entitles her memoir *Recollections of My Life as a Woman,* the text makes a forceful claim that in her self-willed separateness she constructs and inhabits a defiant, individualized gender outside and beyond prevailing norms and intelligible models of mid-twentieth-century American womanhood.

In a further contradictory layer of palimpsestic self-identification, she insists on a fundamental grounding of her identity in an essential, embodied femininity. As in *Memoirs, Recollections of My Life as a Woman* identifies the maternal "will to flower" as di Prima's destiny as a woman. Because she understands "woman" and "poet" as interchangeable terms for her being, di Prima commits herself to experiencing everything she "could possibly experience, as a human in a female body." She views this mandate as "obviously just part of the job, part of what one as a writer set out to do." Therefore, it is both "inevitable" and necessary that she take the "next step" and "become a mother" (161). Doing so, however, causes one of the central conflicts of her New York years.

One aspect of this conflict is external: while di Prima sees "no quarrel between these two aims: to have a baby and to be a poet" (162), friends and colleagues perceive her "desire to have a baby" as "a form of insanity" (165). Her childbearing decisions provoke her community's incredulity, resentment, and anger. Another aspect of the conflict caused by her desire to be a mother is internal: even as she asserts a natural correspondence between poetry and pregnancy, she fears motherhood will endanger her identity as an artist (162). Despite her articulation of a female-centered aesthetic, she codes art male, personifying "Poetry" in the figure of John Keats, who acts as her "mentor and guide" (162). And the Keats in her head takes sides in the pregnancy debate, accusing her of "breaking a sacred vow" (162) to art:

> He told me I was taking a terrible risk. That I might lose Poetry forever by giving another being a claim on my life. He told me if I did this thing, he could no longer promise to come when I summoned him. . . .
> He told me, as he often had before, that it was hard enough for a woman. That women didn't do it right, the art thing, we wanted too

much of the human world besides. That no one had done the thing
I wanted to do. At least in hundreds, if not thousands, of years. That
I probably wouldn't succeed. (164)

Despite these daunting odds, di Prima accomplishes both motherhood
and "the art thing" by "simply follow[ing] [her] Will" (267). She portrays
motherhood, like poetry, as a product of her truth to herself.[14] Ultimately,
her daughter and her art are "inextricably one"; her commitment to her
daughter "echo[es] and double[s]" her "commitment to writing" (224).
Making pregnancy an enactment of defiant femininity, di Prima declares
victory in an arena in which generations of women—spanning "hundreds, if not thousands, of years"—have failed.

This claim to a unique and self-willed experience of motherhood highlights and reinforces di Prima's difference from other women of her time.
In *Recollections,* di Prima separates herself from the wives and daughters
of the U.S. mainstream but also distinguishes herself from women inhabiting alternative Beat communities. Attempting to "define" her younger
artist-self—asking, "who was she, this young woman, so fierce, so certain,
so swept away?"—di Prima uses the third person to articulate her distance from her female acquaintances.

> Among her peers, her immediate friends, there were no women
> with her certainty. No women writers who were *artists first,* who
> held to their work as to their very souls. There were writers and
> would-be writers among the women, but they held other, alien
> priorities, assumptions. The assumption that Art . . . was compat-
> ible with comfort, a nice house in the suburbs; all this poverty and
> struggle was a kind of a trial period, something you passed through
> on your way to better things. . . . The assumption that there truly
> *were* better things.
>
> These women were present and articulate, and friendship with
> them was possible, though bewildering. (223)

Even in Beat bohemia, di Prima finds, women lack true commitment to
art and "[throw] themselves away" for men in the false belief "that *there
was something a man could do for them* that they couldn't do for themselves" (224). Di Prima suffers under no such delusion, certain in her conviction there is nothing she cannot accomplish by and for herself.

In *Recollections,* di Prima can locate no meaningful common ground
with other women, leaving them mired in the dream of upward mobility,
the feminine mystique of the 1950s. Identifying herself as the only truly

"self-defined" (226) woman she knows, di Prima effectively narrows a revised "Beat woman" category to a single figure—Diane di Prima. Ironically, she answers the male-dominant Beat mythos with a myth of defiant femininity that might serve to reinforce the already-known Beat narrative by making herself the exception that proves the "Beat chick" rule.

Rejecting both the Beat chick caricature and the dominant model of American womanhood, di Prima writes an autobiographical "I" that shares very little with other female "I"s. This detachment of di Prima's "life as a woman" from the lives of other women emphasizes (again) her defiant individualism, but at a cost—her narrative offers readers only the slightest means of connecting with her or relating to her story. Faced with her adamant and uniquely self-determined difference, readers might be inclined to empathize with figures such as Joan McCarthy, whom di Prima rejects as a "normal" woman with "a straight job" and "no imagination" (149). An uncool outsider, Joan is "fascinated" by di Prima but is "not like" her (149), a condition likely shared by virtually all di Prima's twenty-first-century readers.[15]

An Unlocatable Woman

Di Prima's life-writing reworks the masculinized Beat mythos, constructing other, more personal myths that propose alternatives to the Beat already-known. *Memoirs of a Beatnik* and *Recollections of My Life as a Woman: The New York Years* critique the dominant Beat Generation story, pointing to its gendered exclusions and exposing it as a distracting pretext incompletely superimposed over her own story. In addition, in their unpredictable incorporation of lies, facts, and fantasy, both of di Prima's autobiographies challenge expectations about the genre itself, forcing readers to question the extent to which the "truth" of another's life can be known.

In *Memoirs of a Beatnik,* parodic play and truthy representations of beatnik sex seduce readers toward di Prima's alternative truths without articulating what those truths might be. As the text traces—in blurred, submerged lines—the places she occupied in Beat bohemia, it offers only sporadic and fleeting glimpses of di Prima as an artist. *Recollections of My Life as a Woman,* for all of its specific autobiographical detail and depth of self-examination, locates di Prima's New York experience somewhere outside shared discourses of Beatness and of femininity. Her insistence on her transcendence of all familial and cultural limitations and on her ability to remain "self-defined in the midst of it all" (226) distances her from readers unable or unwilling to imagine or accomplish such radical disconnection from their social contexts.

Both memoirs compel readers to search for the truth of di Prima's experience as a Beat-associated woman but withhold definitive answers and refuse real connection. As they fashion a personal mythos of difference, *Memoirs of a Beatnik* and *Recollections of My Life as a Woman* leave di Prima essentially unlocatable. The aggressively sexual persona assembled in *Memoirs* and the impossibly individualistic claims to "existential self-reliance" (*R* 236) characterizing *Recollections* push readers (and other Beats) away and show us we cannot know her. Projected outside the bounds of available models and scripts of identity, "Diane di Prima" incompletely materializes as the ungraspable embodiment of a "dream of openness and freedom" (*R* 228) that seems hers alone.

3 DIVERSIFICATION
Bonnie Bremser's *Troia: Mexican Memoirs* and *Beat Chronicles*

I have somehow figured out . . . that if I . . . collect all the pieces of my travel-worn memory that I will find the truth.
—BONNIE BREMSER, *TROIA*

There were . . . no female Kerouacs because to go on the road [brought] the "chick" rhetoric into play, and ruinously.
—HELEN MCNEIL, "THE ARCHEOLOGY OF GENDER IN THE BEAT MOVEMENT"

Certain people, those positioned off-center from the dominant group, those claiming or assigned nonhegemonic identities, find themselves partitioned in their bodies, culturally embodied.
—SIDONIE SMITH, "IDENTITY'S BODY"

Like *Memoirs of a Beatnik*, Bonnie Bremser's *Troia: Mexican Memoirs* (1969) is an odd, off-kilter kind of autobiography. But in contrast to di Prima's confident challenge to the already-known Beat narrative, Bremser's life-writing manifests more ambivalent Beat identifications and dis-identifications, due in large part to her troubled relationship with a Beat man. Where di Prima caricatures "Beat chick" rhetoric, Bremser finds herself enmeshed in its expectations of female silence and sexual service. *Troia* recounts Bremser's "fugitive" (54) life in Mexico in 1961, on the run from U.S. authorities seeking to arrest her husband, the Beat poet Ray Bremser. During this time, she worked as a prostitute at Ray's behest, gave up her infant daughter, and endured violence, destitution, and paralyzing anxiety, conditions that produced profoundly disorienting dislocations of self-concept.

Bremser articulates her sense of dislocation early in *Troia*: "How to be myself in such a different place? Put it all in a sieve and squash your personality through into a new diversified you" (20–21). A term often applied to business or corporate endeavors, to "diversify" is to make various or multiple, to change and extend in different directions. Despite or perhaps because of its association with systems of economic exchange, Bremser's "diversified you" proves an apt metaphor for her intertextual life—her diversification results from the give-and-take of her negotiation of cultural scripts and interpretive figures and her reckoning with expectations related to Beat pre-texts (preexisting texts) and pretexts (stereotypical preconceptions). Piecing together an identity out of a cacophony of competing models of female embodiment and Beat affect, Bremser writes a "diversified" self that almost necessarily diversifies available categories of identity—including wife, mother, muse, chick, whore, writer, and Beat. She does so, however, with considerable difficulty, dissonance, and risk. After all, things squashed through sieves come out in pieces.

First published in 1969 by Croton Press, *Troia: Mexican Memoirs* was released in the United Kingdom in 1971 by London Magazine Editions under the title *For Love of Ray*. After decades out of print, it was reissued in 2007 by Dalkey Archive Press. Michael Perkins, who edited the original text, describes the narrative as "searingly romantic" (34). The Croton Press cover art (reproduced on *For Love of Ray*), featuring a blurry photograph of a dreamy Bremser, her face pressed against a man's flannel-clad chest, echoes this characterization (fig. 4). In contrast, Dalkey Press appears attuned to interpretations of *Troia* as more wrenching than romantic; design elements of its 2007 edition seem intended to reference the discomforts and dangers of Bremser's "off-center" positions as a Beat woman and a prostitute (fig. 5).

The front cover of the Dalkey edition is taken up by a drawing of a haggard Bremser, rendered in dark, harsh lines. Portrait-Bremser's mouth appears set, almost twisted; her unfocused eyes stare past the viewer, and her hands are pressed against her face in a pose indicative of anguish or desperation. This portrait, complete with disheveled hair and tattered black turtleneck, conveys the impression of a woman "pushed up against the wall of [her]self," to invoke John Clellon Holmes's definition of Beat. A cover blurb from Ann Charters's introduction to *Troia* announces its Beat context, proclaiming the narrative "the most extraordinary memoir ever written by a woman in the Beat circle." But the drawing—which lacks the directness and referential authority of a photograph—and the title "Troia"—which is not an English word or a term connected to Beat pre-texts—inject a sense of difference and distance into Bremser's affiliation with Beat.

Inside the Dalkey edition, adjacent to the title page, readers encounter a nude photograph of Bremser; readers of the Croton edition and the 1971 edition of *For Love of Ray* see an abbreviated version of this picture (missing the head) on the back cover of the dust jacket. The full photograph features Bremser seated with her back and side toward the camera,

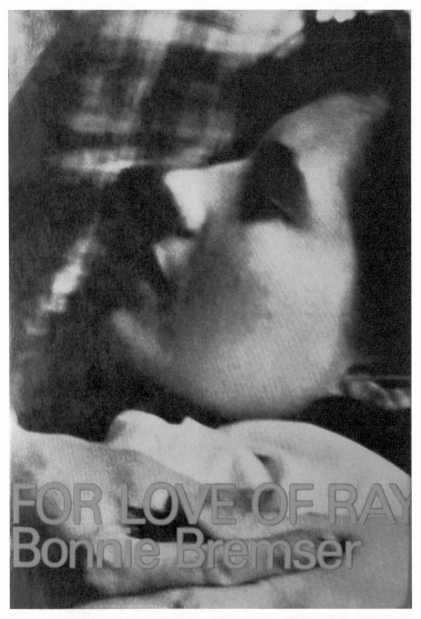

FOR LOVE OF RAY
Bonnie Bremser

Fig. 4. London Magazine Editions 1971 *For Love of Ray* front cover, with cover art from the Croton 1969 edition.

bonnie bremser

TROIA

mexican memoirs

"The most extraordinary memoir ever written
by a woman in the Beat circle."
Ann Charters, from the Introduction

Fig. 5. Dalkey 2007 *Troia: Mexican Memoirs* front cover. (Alice Neel, *Bonnie Bremser*, 1963, ink on paper, 29½ × 22 inches)

head turned to meet the viewer's gaze, chin tucked behind her shoulder in a guarded, defensive position. She appears to be frowning. While her nudity might seem to promise a certain intimate access (to both her body and her story), photograph-Bremser's expression and posture do not appear particularly welcoming, again conveying distance and difference. As noted in the introduction to this study, "specific photographs are often used in autobiography precisely because they have come to represent forces that have helped define the identity of the writer" (Jay 191). The nude photograph of Bremser, with its long expanse of bare skin, gestures toward her "off-center" identity. As a Beat woman and as a prostitute, she is irregular and aberrant, object of a regulatory cultural gaze—a woman out of bounds, a woman "partitioned" in her body (Smith, "Identity's Body" 269).

References to Bremser's off-center status continue on Dalkey's back cover, where a brief biographical note identifies *Troia*'s author as "Brenda Frazer (a.k.a. Bonnie Bremser)." Brenda Frazer is Bremser's birth name and the name she resumed after her divorce from Ray Bremser, but Dalkey does not offer this (or any other) explanation for the two names.[1] The "a.k.a.," an acronym frequently used in APBs and wanted posters, implies a suspect kind of difference—as in an alias or disguise. Ironically, given Bremser's avowed desire to "find the truth" of her experience (*T* 17), the Dalkey paratexts present an overall impression of an autobiographical subject at a remove, exposed yet unknowable.

Paratextual distance and disguise also characterize the memoir's title, which originated with Ray Bremser. In her introduction, Charters explains Ray "suggested the title [*Troia*], which he roughly translated for her as 'courtesan.' Ray . . . told Bonnie that he associated the word 'Troia' with the ancient city of Troy, and that he thought of his beautiful wife as a powerful temptress like Helen of Troy" (iii). But "troia" is also Italian slang for "slut" or "whore," terms loaded with connotations of abjectness and powerlessness.[2] Although Bremser mentions her "trouble" determining what "to call" her acts of prostitution (*T* 30), she never uses the word "troia" to describe herself. Further, the positioning of "Troia" as the main title of the memoir dislocates "Bonnie Bremser" as its author and subject; visually, "TROIA" (rendered in capital letters) overshadows "bonnie bremser" (rendered in all lowercase letters) on the front cover of the Dalkey edition. The London Magazine Editions title, *For Love of Ray,* accomplishes its own form of overshadowing, attributing the impetus for Bremser's life-writing and for the events it covers to her husband.

This overshadowing, which encodes the force of others' defining claims, reflects the process through which the text came to print. Bremser composed the material comprising her *Mexican Memoirs* in 1963 as a series of letters to Ray, who was in prison in New Jersey, having been arrested after their return to the United States.[3] The original format of Bremser's life-writing cannot be discerned in the published text because her letters were edited and their content reorganized by Perkins, a writer/critic/editor and acquaintance of Ray's. In a 1999 interview, she explains Perkins "put [*Troia*] together," "pick[ing] and choos[ing] among the pieces" of her letters to construct the book. "Ray kind of turned it over," she remarks, "and I hardened myself to it because there was so much vulnerability for me" ("A" 120, 122). *Troia* owes its existence to Bremser's loss of control over her story, yet retains—as in a palimpsest, or perhaps a cubist painting—her priorities in writing her remembered experience, producing a doubled, dislocated narrative with competing narrative structures and authorial intentions.

Troia is a fragmented and disjointed text, riddled with gaps, understatements, and contradictions; at points, it is impossible to follow with any real degree of certainty.[4] Its tone fluctuates wildly, veering from defiant to mournful to flip and hip—sometimes within the course of a single sentence. In addition, *Troia* is a radically diversified narrative—letter and memoir, travelogue and Beat performance piece, directed to Ray and mindful of a wider potential readership.[5] At moments, it privileges autobiographical truth and realism, while at others it prefers the poetic lyricism of the unleashed imagination or the hallucinogenic transformations of drug-induced fantasy. The memoir explores (at points simultaneously) the heartbreaking vagaries of love, the mundane details of family maintenance, the risky and repetitive routines of sex work, the painful privations of poverty, and the expansive discoveries of foreign travel. *Troia* addresses Bremser's volatile relationship with her husband, poet and pimp; her struggles and failures as a mother, and the pain of losing her child; her activities as a prostitute, a role that brings her both shame and pride; her adventures in Mexico, that mythic mecca of Beat journeying; her displacement as a cultural outlaw and an actual outlaw, dodging U.S. and Mexican authorities; and her uncomfortable public embodiment as an American in Mexico, a woman partitioned in her body and in violation of prevailing gender norms on both sides of the border. These diversified locales of identity push Bremser "up against the wall of [her]self," but she finds that wall porous and indeterminate.

Attempting, it seems likely, to manage and control the "scariness" and "pain" of "writ[ing]" (43) the diversified self formed and re-formed in

Mexico, Bremser narrates her experience using economic concepts and metaphorical terms related to gain and loss, buying and selling, risk and reward. Most events in her Mexican experience involve some exchange of assets, actual or imaginary. Even her loss of her daughter Rachel constitutes a kind of trade: "Shameless Mexico, I am your child, and you have my child as the token" (13). For the most part, however, Bremser cannot manage to balance her diversified roles and relations or to impose order on their conflicts and contradictions.

In *Travel as Metaphor*, Georges Van Den Abbeele argues that "the exchange of objects that defines commercial activity implies by its back-and-forth movement some kind of travel." He suggests that travel "models the structure of investment itself, the *transfer* of assets that institutes an economy, be it political or libidinal, 'restricted' or 'general.'" Like economic exchange, travel extends "the possibility of gain" tempered by the "insecurity associated with the menace of irreparable loss" (xvii). As she struggles with the slippery and unstable outcomes of gain/loss equations of identity, Bremser's economic metaphors expose the "ruinous" potential for specifically gendered losses put "into play" by her travel as a Beat "chick" (McNeil 193). She describes herself variously as a wistful observer of commercial activities, a predatory merchant leveraging her body for pesos, and an exploited patsy ensnared in physical and psychological con games. Her experience in Mexico, she claims, "heighten[s] [her] abilities of calculation," making her akin to "a gem appraiser" (55). In *Troia*, however, Bremser functions more like a beleaguered and uncertain accountant, anxiously tracking gains and losses, tallying the cost/benefit ratio of diversification, seeking a kind of bottom line of identity.

Textual Exchanges

Of course, *Troia* itself is a product of exchange, originating in correspondence between Bremser and Ray. She undertook the epistolary life-writing that culminated in *Troia: Mexican Memoirs*, she explains, in large part "to make things okay" with her husband ("A" 122). Her intention was "to communicate with Ray over the difficult experiences in Mexico" and "try and get our relationship back on a level after I'd had so many of these sexual experiences . . . many of which had been required . . . by the situation and by him" ("A" 113, 121). Beyond repairing her damaged marriage, she also wrote to accomplish some sort of repair to herself. Life-writing, she remembers, "was therapy for me" ("A" 121), "a liberating experience" and a "way to stand on my own feet," to "[be] myself in my own space, which I hadn't done before" ("A" 123). In *Women of the Beat Generation,* she asserts: "I defined myself when I sat down to write. It was a rebellion against my most immediate authority figure, my husband" (Knight 271). Writing to define herself, Bremser undertakes a deliberately intertextual project aimed at revising others' definitions of her and others' versions of her story.

Bremser's autobiographical writing seeks to accomplish various and diverse forms of intertextual exchange. Having rejoined the Beat scene in New York, she composed her letters to Ray in the midst of a community she refers to in the narrative as "friends" (181) and "you who know me" (4). Given this context, it is not surprising that her life-writing reveals her desire to craft an identity as a Beat writer. Bremser was familiar with *On the Road* and *The Subterraneans,* and was reading Kerouac as she composed her letters; she has acknowledged that she "modeled" her life-writing on *Doctor Sax,* a text that combines autobiographical detail with elements of fantasy (Charters, "Introduction" v). "If I sound like Kerouac," she states, "it's because I tried to" ("A" 115). Feeling the judgment of the Beat literary circle in the person of Ray Bremser the Beat poet "on the other end always reading what [she] wrote every day," she strove "to measure up" to Beat literary standards ("A" 115).

Critics find that *Troia* does indeed "measure up," noting its adherence to "Beat aesthetics of immersion in memory and imagination enhanced by sensory deformation" and to "certain political impulses of the Beat avant-garde, especially the belief that writing must be freed from market pressures" (Grace and Johnson 110). Perkins remarks that "like many of the major works produced during . . . the Beat literary moment, *Troia* is rough-hewn and defiantly unconventional and true to the experience of the author" (35). The memoir embraces Beat philosophies and worldviews, chronicling Bremser's enthusiastic drug use, open sexuality, and search for transcendence and "clearer vision" (54). Bremser laments that parts of Mexico have been "monsterized by capitalism" (81), seeks "food for the soul" (13), and demands "life as it is," unsullied by "smelly rules" (127). She deems her lifestyle choices more authentic than those of her respectability-seeking sister (56) and emphatically rejects the bourgeois morality and "cop atmosphere" of the United States (81). Characterizing herself as "a rebel . . . still investigating just the outmost bounds of [her] self" (3), Bremser aligns her self-concept with Beat self-seeking and defiant individualism. She also aligns her life-writing with Beat road narratives.

Troia, which is structured into four "books" with titles such as "Mexico

City to Veracruz and Back to Texas," has been characterized as the first Beat road tale authored by a woman. Perkins, for instance, describes the memoir as "a picaresque tale that relates a series of adventures that rival in excitement the adventures in Jack Kerouac's works" (34). But, even as Bremser strives for acknowledgment as a Beat writer, she critiques the Beat travel ethos established in work by Kerouac and other male writers. The "Mexican Memoirs" subtitle might evoke the storied Beat journeys chronicled in texts including *On the Road* and *Desolation Angels*. But *Troia* highlights, as Ronna Johnson has argued, "the unrecognized gendered premises" underwriting those and other Beat Generation narratives. Bremser's "simultaneous multiple subjectivities as wife, mother, daughter, sister, whore . . . shape the text's hipster account of sex, drugs, marriage, maternity, vision, and travel . . . exposing aesthetics and forms of Beat writing as gendered, rather than generic, 'beat'" ("Beat Transnationalism" 52, 53).[6] Because Bremser quite literally pays the price for her husband's freedom, her story confronts the Beat mythos with the gender/ power arrangements upholding its assumptions about both the causes and the effects of male independence and artistry.

Positioning herself as a Beat traveler, Bremser draws the reader into uncomfortable exchanges with the dominant Beat Generation narrative, in which the freedom of the road enables escape from the demands of a constraining social order. *Troia* clearly demonstrates that because Bremser is a woman, Beat road life actually heightens the demands of her socially mandated roles. She might be living outside the restrictions of the U.S. mainstream, but her caretaking obligations have become all the more urgent and onerous as a result. Bremser experiences the intersection of Beat traveling adventure with her "service" "responsibilit[ies]"—her obligations to "keep Rachel healthy, or at least not crying," and "to satisfy Ray"—as a "very lonely thing" (9), uncomfortable, anxiety-ridden, and alienating. Traveling by bus with Rachel and Ray, she holds "the baby on [her] lap" and feels "broken-hearted at every spell of crying," but nevertheless "[tries] to groove under the circumstances" (9).[7] As the Beat call to "groove" and the "service" duties of mother- and wifehood rewrite and overwrite each other, Bremser's travel creates identity paradoxes, situations in which she occupies overlapping but conflicting categories of Beat and gendered identity.

One such situation occurs when Ray "decides" his wife "look[s] so good [she] ought to walk out and try to sell it." Bremser writes: "I walk out, but don't try to sell it, wander streets looking up, senselessly waiting for some vision, trying to force a vision" (142). As Charters notes, being "receptive to" visions figures highly in the Beat ethos ("Introduction: What" xxiii). In *On the Road*, that urtext of Beat travel, Sal Paradise hits the road anticipating "girls, visions, everything," confident that "somewhere along the line the pearl would be handed to [him]" (11). But Bremser discovers that the necessity of earning money by selling her body, "the horror of being the breadwinner" (33), impedes her access to the sorts of transcendent treasures awaiting male travelers. As a woman and a "breadwinner," she is differently Beat and must "force" Beat identifications and experiences.

Although Bremser assumes the role of breadwinner for her traveling household, she does not assume the power and authority that come with the provider function; she lacks control over her breadwinning activities and over the bread she wins. This paradox comes painfully clear to her when Ray hits the road to Tehuacán, taking with him the funds she raised through prostitution and leaving her behind to "pay the hotel bill" and earn enough money to follow him. "It took four days . . . to get the money," she recalls. "I was really bugged, thought Ray was turning cold on me in weird ways" (145). Rather than freeing her, Beat travel partitions Bremser in her body, a body understood as a commodity and used as a vehicle of male independence. The longer she remains on the road with Ray, the more she becomes subject to "Beat chick" expectations, her sexuality deployed in service of his needs, her voice muted by his demands.

So many texts by Beat men portray women as interchangeable and easily replaceable—commodities that, when possessed however briefly, provide returns of pleasure and power.[8] Bremser's account of Beat travel in her capacity as an object of exchange confronts the readers (and the writers) of Beat travel narratives with their displacement of women into Beat nowheres of silence and objectification. Her life-writing maneuvers her readers—Ray Bremser and members of the larger Beat community—into an encounter with the Beat Generation narrative through the perspective of the commodity.

In addition to offering an off-center view of Beat travel, *Troia* decenters the priorities of its first and primary reader—Ray Bremser—in life-writing that thwarts his desires even as it appears to fulfill them. Ray lays out his expectations for his wife's self-expression in a letter he composed and mailed to her during a previous stay in jail. This letter, which appears between books 1 and 2 of *Troia*, directs Bremser to "*tell me some sexual items.*" Ray dictates the "*plot*" of the sexual story he wants his wife to write; he tells her to "*start alone, self-sex, then me, then he, then he or she and so on,*" and instructs her to "*make your flesh delirious for me, but unperformed*" *without me!"* (77).[9] In this scenario, Bremser's sex and her story seem to exist for his benefit alone.

Bremser's account of her Mexican travels does on the one hand seem to observe Ray's epistolary mandate; she tells "sexual items" from her life in Mexico in a textual exchange that substitutes for the sexual exchange deferred due to his incarceration. Thus, this autobiographical transaction carries the potential to continue a service pattern in which Ray controls his wife's pleasure and purpose in self-representation. On the other hand, the bulk of the "sexual items" Bremser offers in *Troia* are rendered in fairly dry, undetailed, and undelirious prose.[10] Many contain more anger and revulsion than titillating sensuality. Interspersed with sexual acts, Bremser records her loneliness and fear, often dwelling on the anxiety and "disgust" attending sex work (158). Additionally, like a set of earlier letters that are reproduced in *Troia*, Bremser's "sexual items" frequently emphasize economic concerns over erotic possibilities.

Bremser composed the longest prior series of letters included in the memoir in Mexico City, where she had gone alone to raise money while Ray remained in Veracruz. These letters, which she characterizes as a "chronicle" of "gains" (57), provide detailed accounts of her earnings and offer tentative instruction about how Ray might use the pesos she encloses to right their dire financial situation. She conveys love and money in interrelated terms: "*Spend all my time on the streets except to sleep a little—so lonely for you but the growing stash brings us closer together*" (58). However, as she later discovers, she and Ray have actually moved farther apart—he had been taken into custody and was being held in Laredo, Texas, as she directed letters, love, and money to him in Veracruz.

Letters sent but not received provide a fitting metaphor for the dislocated modes of exchange that develop between Bremser and Ray; her references to misdirected correspondence demonstrate her cognizance that the letters she writes in New York, the letters comprising *Troia*, might not reach her husband (in the sense of failing to produce their intended effects). Writing to "communicate with Ray over the difficult experiences in Mexico" ("A" 113), Bremser seeks his acknowledgment of her side of their story and his acceptance of the "Bonnie Bremser" she constructs in the retelling. But the memoir manifests considerable anxiety about the reliability of letter writing as a means of conveying truth. Bremser stresses that their Mexican sojourn ends in large part due to "inaccurate information" (187) conveyed in a letter from a newspaper reporter who had "chronicled Ray as a beat (beatific) poet" (175); "it was that letter," she exclaims, "that did us in" (176). The possibility for "miscarriage" (188) of notes and letters meant to perpetuate meaningful interpersonal relations haunts the narrative written, as Bremser states, to "explain" (1) and assert herself.[11]

Troia's economies of exchange do frequently miscarry, a fact Bremser ignores in the memoir's brief introduction. In this section, which largely contradicts the transactional dynamics chronicled in the text as a whole, Bremser announces: "My mind is on my needs" (1). She couches these needs in explicitly economic terms of exchange that serve to verify that others value her. "I like to think of other people helping me," she observes. "It occurs to me that everything will be O.K. because there will always be someone to help me get the things that I want" (1). But Bremser's confidence in others' willingness to fulfill her needs is not borne out in *Troia*; for the most part, people do little to help her get the things she needs without exacting a price.

The introduction also links pleasure to exchanges of money and goods: Bremser remarks that just "looking at money pleases" her and claims that when she has no money herself she nonetheless feels "pleased to see people buying things" that she does not "have the money to buy" (2). The very sight of economic interaction provides satisfaction—"a green bill passing hands," she comments, "is especially beautiful to me" (2)—despite her position of lack. Indeed, she identifies lack as a crucial element in her pleasure: "Walking by a wholesale jewelry store I am called into a dream by the fairy-tale beauty of diamond bracelets, and moreover, I think of the people I could have buy me those things; . . . the moment passes, but leaves its impression of a completed sensual experience. I decide that I will go without money more often to enjoy this feeling" (2). Her narrative, however, expresses a continual yearning for money and documents an anything but pleasurable quest to find "someone" to provide it. In her account of her travels in Mexico, being without money is a constant source of worry and leads to the loss of her daughter, the intensification of conflict with her husband, the horror of breadwinning, and the depletion of her sense of personal worth.

These seemingly incongruent comments linking pleasurable self-concept to economic exchange likely reflect Bremser's anxiety about deserving others' approval and regard, an anxiety she expresses over and over again in her life-writing. For example, aware of her apprentice status as a Beat writer, she apologizes "for [her] emotional outbursts" (29) and "timeless sentences" (42). Judging herself inadequate in her maternal and wifely capacities, she regrets "not being a very good mother really" (9) and fears her love is not enough to "satisfy" Ray, who often "leaves [her] behind" to "set his eye on something that [doesn't] include [her]" (15). Her letters report her dread of being treated "casually" and without appreciation by her customers (69), of being "put down" in "some way that will hurt" her (162). In this context, the economic scenarios Bremser imagines in New York and reconstructs in her letters to her husband might be understood as a kind of parable indicating the acceptance she seeks from her reader.

Notably, the "fairy-tale" she constructs outside the jewelry store mimics the traditional heterosexual romance plot—in her imagined exchange, she is found worthy of being gifted with expensive tokens (diamonds!) and enjoys a final payoff akin to a "completed sensual experience." The satisfaction provided by this imaginary episode parallels Ray's letter-fantasy of "sexual items" provided by his absent wife, written and read from a position of lack, "unperformed." In Bremser's version, the transaction is "completed." For a moment, at least, pleasure, consumer goods, and love converge in a fantasy transaction that provides completeness, acceptance, and recognition. These rewards, which are notably withheld from Bremser during her Mexican sojourn, closely echo the often elusive aims of life-writing.

Sex/Text Exchanges

A discordant vocabulary of lack also shapes Bremser's insistence on Ray's centrality to her sense of identity. In another claim situated in *Troia*'s introductory section, she draws on the familiar interpretive figure of a woman in love to "explain" herself. She declares: "Here is the way I really am: I HAVE GOT PLENTY OF NOTHING, if you will excuse my banality. My heart belonged to Ray since the day I met him . . . that is the basis of my life" (1). Using the "banal" terminology of romantic thralldom to account for a self with "nothing," Bremser again merges economic and erotic lexicons of identity but in the process raises the possibility of loss and impoverishment.[12]

In a literal sense, Bremser really does have "nothing" in Mexico because she gives everything she earns to Ray, who determines she is "capable of walking the streets" and demands she do so (31–32). The primary beneficiary of her trade, Ray arranges for her first paid sexual encounters, watches her having sex with other men, and occasionally records her exchanges of sex for money, "writing notes and digging from various angles of the room" (144). She prostitutes herself while he writes; she prostitutes herself so that he can write. "The object," she explains, "is to . . . keep the money coming in and us fed and Ray writing poems frantically" (157). Bremser trades her body for other men's money, money that Ray "always holds" and that serves as a means of communication between them: after one particularly violent argument, she signals they are "together again" by returning pesos he had given her (155).[13]

Although she gains capital—carefully recorded numbers of pesos—through her work as a prostitute, her narrative insists she loses more intangible forms of personal capital in these exchanges. At the end of book 2, after days of desperate hustling that seem to accomplish no worthwhile end, she feels utterly depleted—"a useless wife who was so tired out" she did not "dare to enjoy anything anymore" (114). She "complain[s] to Ray" that hustling is "killing" her and becomes "so depressed about the whole thing" that she "starts[s] getting sick" (140). Her Mexican sojourn, she concludes, leaves her with "half of [her]self fucked to the winds" (175); prostitution costs her her health, her "close[ness] to Ray" (149), and her composure and ease in her body. She considers suicide more than once.

Bremser's narrative suggests but does not overtly state that the personal capital she spends acting as a prostitute goes unreciprocated by a similar expenditure on Ray's part. In other words, there is little to indicate a fair or even transaction. Throughout her time in Mexico, Bremser struggles to balance her interests with Ray's; she wants to "preserve [her]self" but knows her husband's priorities lie elsewhere: "Ray had a lot of time to be involved in other thoughts—and I found that he got tired of consoling me for my hard lot" (149–50). Of course, no economy of exchange—whether of goods, service, power, or desire—guarantees equal rewards for all parties involved, and in *Troia* the threat of being cheated is ever present. In fact, Bremser's first streetwalking endeavor proves profitless when she is cheated by a "little punk" who "never deliver[s] the money" he promises her (33)—an inauspicious beginning to an enterprise that provides uneven and uncertain returns at best. Her accounts of hustling are pervaded with fear about the very real possibility of being "taken," swindled, undervalued.

Not surprisingly, this anxiety extends to her interactions with her husband. The Bonnie Bremser represented in *Troia* appears to view Ray's love and validation as compensation for her breadwinning. But even this intangible and subjective return turns spotty and uncertain: "[Ray] takes to hanging out in all-night restaurants to write 'cause I am usually sick in bed or wanting to fuck or have some relief from the worry and monotonousness of paranoia and disgust at the apparently-permanent occupation of fucking a bunch of guys I don't like or have any interest in to get money for us to continue this way. It has no rewards for me; I am alone, lonely, bugged, feeling more and more unloved, as if each trick I turn is a negative score on the happiness list" (157–58). Loser in their uneven economy of give-and-take, Bremser watches as her balance sheet—the internal resources re-corded on her "happiness list"—dips further and further into the red. Her insistence she receives "no rewards" for her sex work implies Ray uses her much as her johns do. He disagrees, arguing that "fucking for money . . . is [her] own gig and [her] own problem" (159), denying his stake in her prostitution. In this context, her declaration that she has "plenty of noth-ing" because her heart belongs to Ray might carry a residue of resentment and bitterness, despite her avowal that he "has done [her] no harm" (17).

Kurt Hemmer notes that many male Beat writers "believed that their identities as artists entitled them to the sacrifices of non-artist women" (108). And, when pressed to account for her sacrifices, Bremser justifies "stay[ing] with Ray so long" despite his callous and violent "treatment" of her with "excuses about his being a poet and a beautiful soul" (186).[14] This explanation positions Ray as interior—soul and writer—while she remains exterior—body and beauty. As a poet, he trades in words; as a "chick," she trades in flesh. Both Bremser and Ray deem his the more valuable commodity.

However, even as Bremser appears to assent to the Beat hierarchy that assigns Ray greater worth, she entertains the possibility that poetry con-stitutes a kind of cheating, envisioning writing as "fun, a pleasure, a game that he was indulging in behind [her] back while [she] had to go out and get drunk and sick and fucked, and come back to loneliness, or quar-rels" (159). She points out that while others laud Ray Bremser the Beat writer, embracing him as "poetry's representative," she has become "too desperately frantic a picture of what poetry can do to the soul to be ac-cepted easily" (116). Having paid the price for Ray's creative autonomy, she plans to "distill" her "own poetry" so that she "can find a correspon-dence" (116) of her own. She adds: "And don't think this isn't an enormous drive, look at this book!" (116). Since things that correspond are alike, of a kind, Bremser may view her life-writing as a means of evening the score, of rehabilitating the "soul" devalued by Ray's superior status and denied in the body/spirit dichotomy structuring their unbalanced interpersonal economy of exchange.

Distilling her experience into a text that tells her "truth," an "enor-mous" (116) and daunting undertaking, Bremser resists Beat chick sta-tus as all-body, only-body, imagining her life-writing as a project of self-definition with the potential to alter the economics of personal worth that previously ordered her existence. As she builds a writing life in New York, she "pick[s] up a man" who could have provided money for rent, but does not close the deal—her "eye is on visions of writing it instead. What is the truth and how far does it go?" (57). Seeking her truths, and their limits, Bremser pursues the visions she failed to realize when Ray sent her out to "sell it," trading the service and silence he imposes—at points beating her into quiet acquiescence—for the unsure authority of authorship.

Bremser's accounts of the role personal narrative plays in her Mexican experience indicate her awareness of the potential for both redemptive and reductive outcomes of autobiographical expression. Multiple episodes in *Troia* pull together story and sex in ways that imbue both with exchange value. Personal narrative often plays a part in Bremser's transactions with customers; she notes their desire for detail about her life and reports speaking or not speaking to men with almost as much frequency as she reports having sex with them. One customer, she recalls, keeps "trying to get the informational goods" on her. However, she "remain[s] tight-lipped and unimpressed" (143), refusing to allow him to commodify and consume her story. She expresses her "[disgust]" with another sexual scene "long before it ends" by refusing to partake in conversation that would signal participation and acceptance (70). In these circumstances, a girl who says nothing "protect[s]" herself with "silence" (115) and retains some measure of autonomy.

When Bremser does choose to speak, she deploys her personal narrative to establish power and control. In times of crisis, she "coerce[s]" money from friends, acquaintances, and strangers alike by recounting her "story" (94). Telling her story sometimes increases her value, garnering the respect and acknowledgment of others; like sex, Bremser's story generates financial gains. After Ray's arrest, she "explain[s]" her situation to a male acquaintance, focusing on "the small facts of the tragedy and impress[ing] him with the expensiveness of [her] escape from Veracruz." In return, he "presents [her] with 200 pesos and wishes [her] good luck" (93). One of her more reliable customers, she boasts, is always "interested" in her "narratives," "ready and anxious to do [her] bidding" (62).

But the gains Bremser achieves through her "narratives" are more than offset by the losses she suffers when versions of her story circulate beyond her control. She expresses frustration that her "reputation" invests her interactions with unpredictable nuances that prevent genuine connection with others and "make [her] personality and [her] love a recluse" (94). Officials in Mexico have "heard" about her, her husband, and her activities; as a result, they define her solely in her role as a prostitute, restrict her freedom of movement, and hinder her attempts to reach Ray in jail (36). Finally, when "the word gets around" in Laredo "that there is a beautiful blonde American baby who needs a home, that there is a chance that some vagabond criminal poet and his wife have an eye to flee the country and are looking for someone to take proper care of their offspring" (121), she loses Rachel.[15]

As *Troia* draws to a close, Bremser has lost everything she values. Wandering alone in Mexico City without Rachel or Ray, she is utterly impoverished: "I have no muse to resort to, no sun to proclaim, no babies to worship, no steadfast love to defend myself with, no roads and mountains to climb with my eyes seeing freely, nothing but my own heart to search out in cold Mexcity" (187). Perhaps her life-writing has its roots in this moment of profound emptiness and lack, a condition that motivates her "search" for "something besides money" (187)—possibly the "heart" that had resided with Ray, and in his absence awaits recovery from its disbursement throughout the cold and foreign locale where she has left traces of her body and fragments of her story.

Writing to replenish the self degraded and impoverished by her Mexican experience, Bremser describes autobiographical expression as akin to both sexual completion and economic recovery—a way of "turn[ing] myself on in retrospect and regain[ing] what was lost, and I will, I *will*, as sure I am building up to another climax here, and you know what that means. I will make it" (117). Reaching a self-produced "climax," Bremser anticipates achieving satisfaction through autobiographical expression. At this moment, she sounds confident that rather than remaining "unperformed," this textual exchange will allow her to "regain" herself.

Indiscriminate Exchanges

Despite *Troia*'s (often imaginary) moments of fulfillment and satisfaction, Bremser consistently runs up against the lack of certainty inherent in all exchanges—sexual and/or textual—resulting in confusion that leaves her "indiscriminate":

I get indiscriminate to the point where I am not able to figure how love can exist in all of this turmoil of not considering any one person more worthy than another than by how much money he has or how easy it is to get it; and even that flies to the wind, meaningless, when I get fucked, dig the person, service him, get next to him, do the bit, and then get burned. That's one of the main ways my head got twisted, for then it all became a lie. The climax came when Ray himself starting digging people and saying that it had something to do with poetry. In other words he was doing the same thing as I was but on an intellectual, emotional plane that was, in his description, more interesting, more valid, than the straight hustle I had learned. (174)

At such moments, the logic supporting Bremser's economies of exchange implodes. The discourses she relies on to account for her diversified positions and to evaluate personal worth leak and bleed into and over each other. Finally, she is unable to attribute consistent value to the commodities she trades in—love, money, sex, story, service, poetry.

Lacking a consistent lexicon for self-representation, Bremser formulates shifting, palimpsestic, and paradoxical identity claims. She describes her role as a prostitute as a "character" (193) she plays, but she also comments that in acts of prostitution she "give[s] away" her "true nature" (50). She depicts sex acts with customers in terms ranging from cool sensuality to defiant "whorishness" (57) to traumatized victimization; her prostitution is a source of humiliation and, as "the money accumulates," of self-importance (140). She feels "proud," she avows, that she can "take care of the baby . . . independently of American law" but adds "the light and the dark still [haunt] me" (104). At some points, she asserts that her occasional pleasure with her customers is "natural" (140), yet at others reports feeling "ashamed at enjoying" acts of "paid for" sex (50). Bremser characterizes herself variously as "a con artist," "the mark in the crowd," and "the goods" (165, 172). She is a "pig" (31), a "deity being worshipped" (47), a "heifer to the slaughter" (33), and a precious, sought-after "beauty" (193). As a commodity without fixed value, Bremser lacks the discursive resources to construct a stable vantage point for self-recognition or to assemble a coherent autobiographical "I."

Bremser's performance of multiple roles distributes her intertextual life across at points overlapping, at points contending categories and contexts. Early in the memoir, as she prepares to recount Ray's "requirement" that she take up prostitution, she struggles with the question of how to refer to paid sex acts. "Usually," she explains, she uses the phrase "go out and get some money," trying "to be discreet and not mention the sex, or any love-coincidental relation in terming it for that would be too hard on [her] marriage" (30). Despite her sense that she ought to use different vocabularies to discuss matrimony and prostitution, terms associated with these conflicting modes of relationship frequently overlap. Bremser equates hustling *and* her role as Ray's wife with performing, repeatedly referring to acts of prostitution as "shows" and to her interactions with Ray as "acts." The dynamics of her paid sexual transactions leak into her exchanges with Ray; for instance, when she returns to their hotel after a successful evening of hustling, he "require[s] pornographic schemes . . . to satisfy his curiosity" (140). Bremser's use of the term "pornography" (which appears twice in the context of sex with her husband) links her marital relations with Ray to the business of sex work.

Her prostitution also overwrites her discursive dealings with her husband. Ray becomes angry when she speaks to him as she does "people on the street" (148), and discord over her occupation interferes with their marital agreement that "everything that was not business was supposed to be pleasure, sacred, necessary." Instead, "the moment any irritation comes up between us the whole story comes out in very personal glyphs and the arguments take longer and longer and it gets so that we both can't even stand to enter the argument anymore knowing the enormity of involvement beforehand, and begin to concentrate it" (150). Unable to hold separate the (theoretically) opposed categories of business/pleasure and prostitution/marriage, Bremser crosses and recrosses categories and layers of identity, finding boundaries between them unreliable and indiscriminate.[16]

A muted alternative for self-conceptualization emerges in book 3, which contains numerous references to Bremser's love of drawing and her experience of artistic creativity as both consolation and delight. She expresses her hope that drawing will "save" her "from the boredom brought on by . . . realities" she does not "want to be bugged by" and, faced with the necessity of returning to prostitution in Mexico City, comforts herself with the promise of art: "I can draw now, I can spend hours of just seeing things the way I want to and recording the best I can on paper" (138). She creates "Van Gough chairs, tilted rooms, shadows of cat ghosts in the mirror. Ray metamorphosed into a sitting-in-drawers portrait" (138). In addition to serving as a source of "satisfaction" (141), drawing offers Bremser a mechanism of control and a means of self-expression that counter her uncontrolled diversification. Art appears to ameliorate the reductions of her position as an intertextual object of exchange, fixed and defined in the narratives of others. "Seeing things the way [she] want[s] to" in art, she causes Ray to "metamorphose," skews "reality," and merges things that seem opposed. Creating in images rather than in already-used and over-determined words, she alters "the realities" that impoverish her.

Even in art, however, she cannot evade intertextual complications. Describing an attempt at self-portraiture, Bremser recounts trying to "dig the beauty of [her] face that had everyone so mystified." Unable "to see it exactly in the mirror," she dons "exaggerated" expressions, "striving, torturing [her] head with the inability to capture what was right there . . . to see" (193). This tortured attempt to understand others' perceptions reveals something of Bremser's diversified position as an autobiographer—seeking herself in multiple and shifting discursive contexts, she is "hardly" able to "believe that what I write is me" (141). Remaining "inscrutable . . . even to [her]self" (5), Bremser can offer no moral to her story, no redemptive message, no satisfying closure, no certainty in her account of a self "squashed through a sieve," a self in pieces. Instead, her overlapping and contestory performances of gender and her indiscriminate fusion of lexicons of identity produce a "savage self" (208), a jagged and jarring palimpsest layered with identifications and associations that cannot be called into order in such a way as to repair divisions and recoup losses.

Re-Exchanges

Unwilling, perhaps, to allow this "savage self" the last word, Bremser, now using the name Brenda Frazer, is composing a prequel and sequel to *Troia*, to be titled *Troia: Beat Chronicles*. Three excerpts of this work—"Poets and Odd Fellows," "Breaking out of D.C.," and "The Village Scene"—have been published in Beat anthologies. Writing at a distance from the Beat era, Bremser/Frazer continues to address Beat calculations of personal worth and to explore the dislocations of feeling oneself differently Beat. Like *Troia: Mexican Memoirs*, excerpts from *Troia: Beat Chronicles* draw into view the "gendered premises" (R. Johnson, "Beat Transnationalism" 52) underwriting Beat identifications. But at the same time, Frazer's *Beat Chronicles* also posits alternative forms of belonging that project Beat beyond gender-based classifications. In so doing, the new material promises further reevaluation of "Beat chick" pre-texts.

Frazer's recent life-writing offers more specific, though also diversified, appraisals of the fraught intersections of the categories "Beat" and "woman." On the one hand, Frazer believes Beat freed her younger self from normative standards of femininity. In "Poets and Odd Fellows," she reports that the night she attends her first Beat poetry reading is the "last time" she "put on a girdle or a bra" (18). Free from the restrictive trappings of middle-class American womanhood and immersed in the downward mobility of Beat bohemia, she does not "miss the things of normal life," she asserts, because she has "the better part of the deal in being Ray's wife" ("TV" 28). Being a Beat wife, she suggests, constitutes something entirely different from normative models of female identity.

On the other hand, Frazer is particularly attuned to gendered nuances of power in Beat communities. She contrasts Ray Bremser's commanding and influential position as a Beat poet with her secondary, supporting role as a "poet's muse" ("TV" 31). In New York, as she contends with "the impact of so many strangers, and so much hot concrete, the sense of no home, no place to hide, no rest except for nights when we [have] an invitation to someone's apartment," her "sense of security" comes to depend entirely on her relationship with Ray ("TV" 29). "I was completely helpless when he didn't give me all of his attention," she writes. "I needed him" (29). Her "need" for Ray is both material—his friends house and feed them—and ontological—she draws her sense of self from his status as a Beat writer. She feels "proud of him, proud of [her]self for being a part of his fame" (31). Due to his superior stature in Beat contexts, her life becomes an exercise in "fitting in" to his life ("P" 20; "TV" 30).

Throughout her work in progress, Frazer contrasts her younger self's silence with Ray's strong and imposing voice. "Breaking out of D.C." begins with her inability to ask Ray not to leave her behind to go to New York: "My words fail, my voice hangs just short of speech." In contrast, Ray and "his friends" are "loud": "Their talk is like single-celled animals, amoeba under glass, bumping into each other, patting each other on the back. . . . I'm the only serious one, going into my low cycle that prepares the heart for pain, closing everything off except for secret messages like this, low singing under my breath, inside ear echoing, who's to notice?" (60). In "The Village Scene," she reports Ray's success in "coerc[ing]" her into taking a job waitressing at "the Café Bizarre." He asks, "'How are we going to eat?' And I [can't] argue with that" (26). Not only does she not argue with Ray, she stands by while he speaks for her.

She reports that Ray "like[s]" her quietness and compares her favorably to women who "talk endlessly about nothing" ("P" 22). When he comments that "quiet people are usually writers," she vows to "be whatever he is, whatever he wants me to be" ("B" 60). In a way, Ray does make her into "what he wants" when he appropriates her body and their lovemaking as raw material for his poems. His assertions about who and what she is constitute the primary intertext of her identity. When Ray gets "imperious and use[s] words like love and poetry," she remarks, "there just [isn't] any way to argue. No one ever wanted to refute him" ("TV" 33). Ray, it seems, expresses everything worth knowing: "'You see, Bonnie?' he explained. 'It all works. It's all OK.' He made it OK. His voice, mesmerizing. The poetry imaginative, yet embellished with his experience of the courts of law, justice, life, civilization. And the understanding of it. Our love made it expansive and human palpitating with heart, the sharing of our life. The security I'd been missing was there in the poem, along with the reshaped understanding" (31). In Ray's poetry, her younger self finds refuge in a "reshaped" view of her place in the world; however, the "awe" inspired by his voice, she notes, "obliterat[es] independent thought" (33–34). As wife, muse, and chick, she accepts Ray's articulation of "the philosophy of [their] love" and accedes to his definitions of "[their] beatness" and "[their] identity" (34). She presents Ray as the embodiment of Beat, the gatekeeper admitting her to Beat life.

At other points, Frazer posits more generally inclusive forms of belonging based in a consociative ideal of Beat. Drawn into the beatific atmosphere of her first Beat poetry reading, she partakes in a "communication" that brings "all" present to "understand as one mind" ("P" 19). In "Breaking out of D.C.," she describes feeling "part of D.C.'s growing artists' scene," where even though she is "shy," she "communicate[s] with intuitive skills, sincerity in the eyes and heart." In this nonverbal communal exchange, "it's like we all mix in an elemental way, growing with connections, vibrating like leaves on a tree" (62). Positing an "elemental" unity of connected, vibrant being, Frazer gestures toward a Beat experience beyond the already-known, outside gendered hierarchies of presence and power.

A Beat-associated woman and second-time autobiographer, in *Troia: Beat Chronicles* Frazer reassesses the nuanced intertextuality of Beat pretexts, including her own *Mexican Memoirs*. Keeping the "Troia" of her original title but claiming the right to author a "Beat Chronicle," she assumes the authority of Beat identification her younger self reserved to Ray. And her commentary on the rewards and the risks of self-representation in *Troia: Mexican Memoirs* indicates her sense of the seriousness of this undertaking. Mulling over the power of life-writing, its ability to "awak[en] . . . that part of [her] that memory composed," she asserts: "As this story has grown I have grown. And what's more, the situation has grown around me, and I have shaped it with my eyes to take me more so back into other memories and as I shaped, it stayed that way. It has truly grown up around me. I say that everything I have written has become true, again, doubly true" (56). Because she writes from Beat nowheres, Bremser must "find" and articulate her own truths. Asserting the importance of an experience that exceeds already-known Beat stories and situations, she asks her readers to expand the parameters through which they understand and attribute validity and value to Beat lives. It will be worth the wait to discover what further truths grow in her ongoing *Beat Chronicles*.

4 CONSOCIATION

ruth weiss's *DESERT JOURNAL,*

FOR THESE WOMEN OF THE BEAT,

and *CAN'T STOP THE BEAT*

> *a new view of matter*
> *or an ancient one regained*
> *only a new view of what matters*
> *will break the trapped pattern*
>
> —RUTH WEISS, "TURNABOUT"

> *The men . . . have gotten most of the credit as the movers and shakers of*
> *the "Beat" literary movement. But here [*Women of the Beat Gener-*
> ation*] we may be privy to what else—what "other"—was going on at*
> *the same time, in parallel time, and how the various lives—of both men*
> *and women—interwove and dovetailed with one another. I've always*
> *appreciated ethnologist Clifford Geertz's notion of "consociates," a useful*
> *paradigm that touches on the interconnectedness of shared and experi-*
> *enced realities. It takes into consideration the influences of time, place,*
> *mutually informed circumstance on individuals existing in proxim-*
> *ity—yet not necessarily intimates—to create a larger cultural context for*
> *action and art.*
>
> —ANNE WALDMAN, FOREWORD TO
> *WOMEN OF THE BEAT GENERATION*

At some point in the 1960s (she cannot say exactly when), the San Francisco jazz poet ruth weiss began spelling her name in all lowercase letters
as an antiauthoritarian gesture of "rebellion against law and order" ("S"
69).[1] This stance, as Nancy Grace notes, "was not her only form of rebellion" in a "life devoted to art, self-definition, and cosmic liberation" ("ruth
weiss" 340). By any standard, weiss has lived a life far out of the ordinary,
and she applies her unique "view of what matters" to the Beat movement
in autobiographical prose poetry that challenges preset categories and
"trapped patterns" of all kinds.[2]

As a child, the German-born weiss fled with her parents from Nazi-
occupied Austria to live as a refugee in the United States. Her family returned to Europe in 1946, and weiss entered boarding school; she spent
little time studying, she has said, preferring to hitchhike and write. The

year 1948 found her in the Art Circle boardinghouse in Chicago, devoting herself to poetry and finding work as "a dice girl, a waitress, and a nude model" (Grace, "ruth weiss" 340). She lived in bohemian communities in New York and New Orleans before hitchhiking across the country and settling in North Beach in 1952. weiss found the San Francisco Renaissance in full swing and soon established herself in West Coast art communities, writing and performing poetry in bars and coffeehouses, and on the streets.

She honed her unique poetics in San Francisco's flourishing jazz scene. The poet Jack Hirschman describes weiss's work as "scores to be sounded with . . . riffy ellipses and open-formed phrasing swarming the senses. Verbal motion becoming harmonious with a universe of rhythm is what her work essentializes. Others read *to* jazz or write *from* jazz. ruth weiss *writes* jazz in words" (qtd. in Knight 247). weiss collaborated with other poets and participated in readings and literary events with San Francisco figures including her good friend Madeline Gleason. Like Gleason, weiss quickly emerged as a dynamic force in Beat-affiliated artistic circles. In addition to her innovative poetry performances, weiss published her work in Beat literary magazines, entered into haiku "dialogues" with Jack Kerouac, and formed productive relationships with Beat-associated figures including Philip Lamantia, Bob Kaufman, Lawrence Ferlinghetti, Jack Michelene, and Helen Adam ("S" 64, 74–76; Grace, "ruth weiss" 340–41).

An independent artist moving "in and out of all kinds of scenes" ("S" 62), weiss did not identify herself as Beat in the 1950s and 1960s. Nevertheless, she lived in "true Beat fashion," making "her own way as an artist, unencumbered by conventional boundaries . . . doing whatever she could to write poetry and plays, make films, and paint" (Grace, "ruth weiss" 341). Grace asserts that "few poets—male or female" more fully "embody Beat" ("ruth weiss's *DESERT JOURNAL*" 57); she hears in weiss's work a "Beat voice" that shares "Diane di Prima's tough wit and Kerouac's immigrant joy," and points out that "like her Beat contemporaries, weiss defines poetic language as a free-flowing force moving outward from the unconscious toward self and others" (Grace and Johnson 58, 55). Over the years, commentators have described weiss as a "Beat goddess" (*C* xix),[3] as "the Beat scene's matriarch," as "one of the most active poetry/jazz readers keeping the Beat alive in a besieged community" (French 25),[4] and as a reminder that "women Beats thrived as writers and artists in their own right" (Trigilio, "A New View" par. 3).

After initially rejecting the "Beat" label as a media caricature, weiss has "come to embrace" the term, believing "it has come to turn around . . .

to mean an alternative approach to life away from the materialism that exploded after World War II" ("S" 59). Her published work reflects this changing perception of the Beat movement and of her place within it; while early texts such as *STEPS* (1958) and *GALLERY OF WOMEN* (1959) largely eschew Beat Generation reference, later texts, including *FOR THESE WOMEN OF THE BEAT* (1997) and *CAN'T STOP THE BEAT: THE LIFE AND WORDS OF A BEAT POET* (2011), explicitly claim Beat as an essential element of her identity. In 2012, a cache of weiss's previously published poetry was reissued in English/German editions with highly visible paratextual elements—titles, photos, essays, interviews— framing her artistic career and personal ethos in Beat contexts. A blurb on the back cover of *ruth weiss: a fool's journey / die reise des narren* describes her as "indisputably . . . the feminine voice of the beat generation."[5] I will suggest that weiss's voice both intersects with and redirects other, more familiar "Beat Generation" voices. She confirms and extends Beat values while challenging the gender-coded distributions of freedom and artistry underwriting the already-known Beat story.

Before investigating work that explicitly engages with the dominant Beat mythos, I will attend to weiss's declaration of her consociative philosophy of identity in her seminal 1977 text *DESERT JOURNAL*. In this work, she presents interconnectedness and integration as the foundation of her sense of self and relation to the wider world. Asking "what is that face / of a whole human race / that gazes through one's eyes?" (53), weiss finds the universe within herself, and vice versa. She does not directly reference Beat pre-texts in *DESERT JOURNAL*, but this text clearly reflects Beat practices and priorities rooted in questing, nonconformist revision of post–World War II social, spiritual, and literary structures, expressed with a linguistic freedom that utterly disregards convention, sweeping it aside to make space for something new. Like other Beat work, *DESERT JOURNAL* stands as "a defense of the human spirit in the face of a civilization intent on destroying it" (Holmes, "Philosophy" 635).[6] weiss's "defense of the human spirit," however, proposes an alternative to Beat models of gender that reserve to men the capacity for the transformative clarity of vision and voice capable of achieving it. In her later work, weiss deploys the consociative view of human consciousness and creativity articulated in *DESERT JOURNAL* to interrogate the predominant image of the Beat movement as a single-generation "boy gang." weiss's Beat-claiming collections *FOR THESE WOMEN OF THE BEAT* and *CAN'T STOP THE BEAT* install consociation as a fundamental Beat principle, crafting intertextual forms of identification that unmoor the

Beat Generation story from its traditional "plot" and enable her Beat "story" to both intersect with the larger Beat narrative and "make it/on its own" (*DJ* 123).

"One Seeks the Nomad/to Find the Self": weiss's Mobile Poetics of Identity

weiss characterizes herself as a wanderer, a "natural" hitchhiker, a woman who "like[s] to move" ("S" 78). Her impulse toward journeying is among the characteristics she shares with other Beats for whom, as Allen Hibbard observes, "movement and pursuit of freedom . . . are inextricably linked conceptually, often in an antithetical relationship to stasis, boredom, oppression, and authoritarianism" (15). *DESERT JOUR-NAL* makes movement and freedom synonymous with self-discovery and self-expression. Encountering "the self" in nomadism, weiss constitutes identity in/as movement.

She expresses her mobile self-concept in autobiographical prose poetry shaped in "open circular form" ("S" 61) and imbued with fluidity and motion. weiss's nontraditional poems convey an overriding sense of flexibility and interconnection through cyclical lines, repeating anecdotes, flashes of recurring recollection, and playful free association. Her avoidance of standard punctuation ensures that "quests & discovery" do not "end at a period." Instead, "the line of the journey" continually "forms once more" (*DJ* 74).[7] *DESERT JOURNAL* constitutes an epic poetic journey through what weiss calls her "internal desert" (*DJ* 207).[8] In opposition to representations of the desert as empty, stark, and featureless, weiss's desert "has as many facets/as the human heart." In fact, "the desert is the squeeze/between each beat" (*DJ* 100). For weiss, the desert, with its infinite facets and shifting landscapes, functions as a metaphor for human consciousness. And, she asserts, "the way is always open/in the desert" (29).

DESERT JOURNAL is comprised of forty poems written between 1961 and 1968. Composing five pages "non-stop each day," weiss embraced "whatever surface[d]," "forget[ting] characters & plot" (*DJ* 207). The poems—titled in the sequence of their composition—are themselves mobile and shifting. They morph and slide between internal and external, here and there, self and other. Jokes and puns interact with snippets of memory and mystic insights into the nature of the universe, and weiss privileges no aspect of experience over others. She mixes "doggerel, contemporary slang, neologisms, and word inversions to track the free associations of the moving mind" (Grace and Johnson 56). The "mov-

ing mind" represented in *DESERT JOURNAL* wanders between states of
being—human, animal, geographic, and elemental. It knows no boundaries and accepts no restrictions—not of time or place, not of age, gender, or
race. While the poems sound repeated themes—the generative freedom
of the wandering mind, the simultaneous mutability and universality of
the human spirit, the creative potential inherent in language—the text's
refusal of poetic convention and of traditional "characters & plot" creates
space for the construction of open and fluid expressions of selfhood, community, and culture.

The poem that opens *DESERT JOURNAL* mounts an immediate challenge to already-written axioms held as self-evident truths:

one plus one is two
two plus two is four
four is no more
(singular of mores)
than now

the law is always behind
where it is safe
to have a behind
or vast past
do not wiggle
do not giggle
THIS IS SERIOUS! (12)

This "FIRST DAY" poem, which sets the tone for the collection as a
whole, offers a refutation of singular, authoritative modes of perception
and arrangements of knowledge. Its playful response to the big "behind"
on which "the law" sits asserts undervalued aspects of expression and
experience—whimsy, play, free associative vision—as relevant and authentic lenses through which to understand and interpret human being
in the world. Her "SECOND DAY" poem, which ends with the challenge
"who are you / to say / a or the?" (15), continues in this vein:

one has to throw it all away
notes—numbers
all the references
even the reverence of nothing
mirror—memory
all hinges
swinging doors to possibility (14)

Manipulating a medium filled with and constitutive of the already-known, weiss acknowledges that language creates and expresses the authority of singularity, but she also asserts and pursues the potential of language to open "possibilities" beyond "notes, "numbers," and "trapped patterns." She understands language as an endlessly flexible system of improvisation and transformation.

weiss views the free-flowing and experimental medium of language as a source of collaborative exchange in which the mobile self necessarily encounters and intersects with others. A later poem—"SOMETHING CURRENT," composed on her fiftieth birthday—offers "collage" as a model of collaborative self-representation:

> this is an i poem
> this is a look straight into the eye poem
> this is a you poem
> you
> we
> WXYZ
>
> we talked collage that night
> someone asked
> what is collage?
>
> you rip a piece of this
> you rip a piece of that
> fuck the facts
> come through the true story
> the core directed
> to its essence (128)

Seeking to reach the "essence" of self and other, the poet gathers various "pieces" of stories rather than delivering already-formed, complete "facts." For her, essential truths reside not in "facts" but in moments of connection, when the eyes of "i" and "you" meet.

DESERT JOURNAL situates these truths in the sensations and perceptions of the present moment; her poetics offers the immediacy of an unfiltered now.

> turn each & all
> from the moment of recall
> to the moment that IS NOW—
> the desert

that by its very barren-ness
holds all possibles (*DJ* 29)

The desert is barren in the sense that it "is always open" (29), but it is always and endlessly generative of "possibles" for the same reason, much like the human mind cleared of rules and restrictions, even of its own past. As a metaphor for the mind, weiss's desert leaves all "ways" open, all equally present and possible. Rather than a nowhere—a place of emptiness and nonbeing—the desert/mind is "the pure-point where all gathers," an expansive field for creativity with the capacity to "[conjure] all places" (33). On the "EIGHTH DAY," weiss writes:

the desert is all myth
and all true
as are you
whoever the you may be
at the moment of telling (45)

Defining both the truth and "the you" as the experience of the now and product of "the moment of telling," *DESERT JOURNAL* demolishes already-known plots to envision human selves as fluid and evolving, uncontainable and unquantifiable.

weiss's poetics thus critiques and reformulates models of identity based in binary opposition, in either/or organizations of being that demand and perpetuate separation and exclusion as ordering principles. In *DESERT JOURNAL*, identity, experience, and perception hover between associative markers, in both/and formulations that confound generally accepted expectations about the usefulness of discrete classifications for categorizing being in the world. This is a desert that "slake[s]" thirst (62), a desert that "is all living organism" (45). Because weiss eschews "characters & plot," the entities occupying her desert/mind do not remain still or separate— human figures morph from everyday normalcy to become transformative, even supernatural. They align themselves with topographical features of her imagined landscape and take on characteristics of birds and animals; they combine opposites, appearing, for instance, "quite blond / and black" (15). Entities flash between "look[ing] familiar" and "stranger" (33), appearing and reappearing, seeming "the same as before" yet "not the same" (56). Doors are both "open" and "locked" (45), and "blue" and "red" function simultaneously as "color" and "sound" (136). The poem's wandering speaker, as Grace notes, "is sometimes referred to as 'she,' sometimes as 'he' or 'we' or 'you,'" and the narrating voice shifts "from ambiguous first person to third person omniscient, from human to animal to bird" ("ruth weiss's *DESERT JOURNAL*" 63). The poet is "either sex / or both," with "no name to touch" (*DJ* 10)—undefinable and uncategorizable.

If selves are open and porous, best expressed through vocabularies of both/and rather than either/or, weiss suggests, self-discovery and possibilities for encountering the world are boundless. In fact, the final *DESERT JOURNAL* poem rejects the idea of finality itself, whether of a poem or a person:

how does one start
what one has to finish?

a hard line?
a fine line?
a blurred edge
into another self? (198)

Setting aside all the markers cultures devise to make distinctions between selves, weiss's poems represent self-discovery as mutable, multiple, and ongoing, a journey that intersects with the journeys of other selves. "Thus," she asserts, "you be in all places / and know the face that ALL FACES / and know the face that IS ALL FACES" (39). weiss's poetry consistently breaks down borders that restrict free exchanges of "you" and "all," conceptualizing freedom and connection as integral components of the same whole rather than as opposed principles.[9]

In weiss's later work, she extends the philosophy of consociative interconnection established in *DESERT JOURNAL* to Beat travel. Her 2011 collection of autobiographical poetry *CAN'T STOP THE BEAT: THE LIFE AND WORDS OF A BEAT POET* includes a poem entitled "POST-CARD 1995," which reaches out to Beat-associated men and women who spent time in Mexico, all of them, she observes, "mad to be reborn" (96). As the poem moves back and forth between her life and the lives of others, weiss links her experience to that of Kerouac, Lamantia, Neal Cassady, and others. Asserting she, too, "die[s] every time i go to MEXICO / and return reborn," she speaks directly to Beat figures who died or disappeared in Mexico, ponders the unknowable details of the ends of their lives, and asserts that their work continues to "live" (96). The poem concludes with weiss contemplating "patterns of self on the wall":

a movement of self
fire-works on the water
the eye a reflection of stars

what put us here
the self of course

the course is not always clear
the water is not always clear
the sky is not always clear

it is still—
a time for reflection (97–98)

weiss's "fire-works on the water" and references to friends "mad to be reborn" formulate subtle links to Kerouac's "mad ones," the "ones who are mad to live, mad to talk, mad to be saved, desirous of everything at the same time, the ones who never yawn or say a commonplace thing, but burn, burn, burn like fabulous yellow roman candles exploding like spiders across the stars" (*On the Road* 8). The "patterns of self" weiss records in "POST-CARD" partake in the lives of her Beat friends, aligned with both the sudden, fleeting beauty of fireworks and the eternal cadences of sky and water.[10] As in *DESERT JOURNAL*, the message conveyed by this postcard encourages the reader to look beyond finality, positing instead "a movement of self" that makes individual lives potentially limitless.

"POST-CARD 1995," with its focus on the Beat obsession with Mexico as a site of creative transformation, precedes a long poetic travelogue entitled *COMPASS*, which weiss wrote during a 1958 trip to Mexico with her first husband, Mel Weitsman, and her friends Anne McKeever (a poet and photographer) and the Beat poet Philip Lamantia. *COMPASS* presents their journey as an experience that breaks down certainties and already-known categories. Its free-flowing form—it is composed of brief phrases connected by ellipses—conveys a sense of constant motion and provokes continual readjustment of readers' frames of reference, as stances on and relationships to the world repeatedly coalesce, dissolve, and re-form. Rather than adopting the role of interpreter and situating herself as the source and focus of a coherent narrative arc recounting her road exploits, weiss opens herself and remains open, allowing the world to flow through her.

In Mexico, she is reborn as a child, "the center the connection of all out to in" (105). As a child, she becomes "a stringed instrument" sounding out endless "combinations" (105) that enable ongoing transformations. Not just in *COMPASS*, but consistently in the canon of her work, weiss describes herself as an "instrument" for the expression of human experience across time, distance, and either/or classifications.[11] Defining herself as a conduit of world truth, weiss rejects the individual genius model of artistry in favor of "a new view of what matters" that positions her mobile poetics as an instrument of community and connection. This "new view" also facilities her intertextual interventions into "the trapped pattern" of the already-known Beat story.

"OH HEAR THE WOMEN!": weiss's Beat-Claiming Poetry

weiss dedicates *DESERT JOURNAL* to "all artists who work from their inner truth / to keep the faith that their work will find / its way to be shared." As a street performer and jazz poet, weiss has been sharing her work since 1948. And, increasingly since the 1990s, she has been reaching out to the wider audiences generated by the late twentieth-century renewal of interest in Beat literature and culture. Two recent collections, *FOR THESE WOMEN OF THE BEAT* and *CAN'T STOP THE BEAT: THE LIFE AND WORDS OF A BEAT POET,* are characterized by layered, palimpsestic modes of address that refashion the self and the "Beat woman" label by engaging the narratives of others. Even as these texts indicate the degree to which weiss's self-representation comes bound up in the already-written story of "the Beat Generation," a story that includes her only as a footnoted anomaly, the two collections reassess female experience in ways that rewrite and extend Beat as a consociative phenomenon.

In the mid-1990s, weiss was commissioned to compose introductory poems for the audiotape version of Brenda Knight's *Women of the Beat Generation: The Writers, Artists, and Muses at the Heart of a Revolution,*[12] an anthology often credited with bringing Beat-associated women out of the shadows to receive long-overdue recognition as "revolutionaries" in their own right. As noted in the introduction to this study and repeated in the second epigraph to this chapter, Anne Waldman's foreword to *Women of the Beat Generation* suggests that the anthology offers a consociative model of Beat characterized by "interconnectedness of shared and experienced realities" that "takes into consideration the influences of time, place, mutually informed circumstance on individuals existing in proximity—yet not necessarily intimates—to create a larger cultural context for action and art" (xi). weiss's companion poems—a series of sharply focused mini-biographies published separately in 1997 as *FOR THESE WOMEN OF THE BEAT*—offer an overtly consociative intertextual take on the lives and creative energies of Beat-associated women.

Clearly, weiss's project in *FOR THESE WOMEN OF THE BEAT* involves supplementing the masculinized Beat mythos with the presence and contributions of women. In "DIANE di PRIMA," her poem for the best-known and most visibly prolific of the Beat women writers, weiss remarks, "it was said there was a break-through," and wryly asks "where were the women?" (18). *FOR THESE WOMEN* provides manifold answers to this question by breaking down and picking apart dominant categories structuring possibilities for Beat identity and for its representation. weiss's "women of the beat" are vibrantly present and creative figures of connection, "beating their hearts into shares" (7) and producing work that "grows" even after their deaths (5). Their "words rise from the flame" of pain and heartbreak (21), and when "the path is stones" and "the foot is blood," they nevertheless produce "blooms along the way" (32). weiss's portraits of Beat-associated women present a flexible and inclusive model of creative community as the foundation of her revised articulation of Beat ethics and aesthetics.

An early poem in the collection is named for weiss's friend Helen Adam, a poet known for her unique, magical voice. The poem makes Adam's "wild, witchy voice" ("S" 76) speak for a multitude of women both known and unknown in Beat histories.

HELEN ADAM

the beat the beat the beat
OH HEAR THE WOMEN!
SOME GONE, SOME OF US STILL HERE
ALL OF US STILL HERE (2)

Presenting Adam as representative of a group, "the women"—to whose voices she demands we attend—weiss contests their relegation to the silent nowhere of a distant and inaccessible past. The poem insists on their continued presence and influence, asserting the relevance of "all" their lives and work in the here and now. Her sustained use of capital letters in the body of the poem gives the impression of a shouting down of dismissive voices, or perhaps a shouting over the static of common wisdom that draws singular, exclusive, and masculine parameters around "the Beat Generation."

The poem bearing weiss's name identifies her (yet again) as an "instrument" of human truth:

ruth weiss

the beat the beat the beat
the poet to be instrument

to keep the instrument clear
sound a new view of matter
an ancient one regained (29)

The "view" she conveys—which makes "ancient" and "new" akin—resists models of history, identity, and Beat affiliation based in binary opposition. This poem, which closely echoes her earlier poem "TURNABOUT" and its assertion that "a new view of what matters / will break the trapped pattern," urges the reader to look past established Beat pre-texts and pretexts in order to perceive "the beat" that flows in and through "ruth weiss," the poet in and of the poem, and through each woman named in the collection.

The refrain "the beat the beat the beat" prefaces each poem in *FOR THESE WOMEN*, a device that both renders "the beat" familiar and reveals it as new; the word "beat" evokes the already-known Beat Generation narrative, while the lowercase *b* serves to distinguish weiss's sense of women's lived experience from the capital *B* Beat mythos. More significantly, the repeating echo "the beat the beat the beat" connects the women to each other within an enlarged, expansive Beat movement. This refrain also functions to illustrate and emphasize the ongoing pulse of women's "beat" lives and art, extracting them from the stasis of an already-known, finalized history by insisting on the unrelenting vitality of their beating hearts.

weiss's poem for Barbara Guest, who published in Beat literary outlets but is most usually associated with the New York School, references interconnection and reciprocal exchange as shared characteristics of Beat-identified women:

BARBARA GUEST

the beat the beat the beat
as some looked to the men for guidance
there were women who found women
whose words beat sparks upon the anvil (19)

This poem positions female community as a foundational site of productive creativity. The image of "words beat[ing] sparks upon the anvil" imbues women's texts with heat and light, energy and force, pounded out in "beat" rhythm. weiss's blacksmith metaphor aligns these women with the fiery productivity of Emily Dickinson's "soul at the white heat," rendering the literary expression of unsung craftswomen potent and powerful.

Guest appears only briefly (in a two-paragraph sidebar) in Knight's anthology, but weiss uses her "BARBARA GUEST" poem to make one of her strongest statements about unacknowledged yet vibrantly creative communities forged by women. Her poem for/about Aya Tarlow, another woman mentioned only in a sidebar in *Women of the Beat Generation*, draws attention to an unsung craftswoman and weiss's "heart sister" (*F,* foreword n.p.):

AYA TARLOW

the beat the beat the beat
"where have i been here before
look
there are my footprints on the shore" (30)

Tarlow is not regarded as a major figure in popular or academic accounts of the Beat movement; indeed, she barely appears at all. But weiss and others in their San Francisco community know that Tarlow's life as a poet, editor, and filmmaker, a Buddhist, astrologer, and feminist branched into many others', leaving her "footprints" on Beat literary and cultural geographies.

Of "ANNE WALDMAN," weiss observes: "some flowed easy into the stream/the influenced becomes the influential/a natural progression" (34). This statement challenges the "generational" view of Beat, which accepts only an exclusive cadre of male Beats as truly and fully Beat. weiss's poem reminds readers that not only did Waldman coalesce effortlessly with the New York Beat community, but she also altered its course. She developed a unique and innovative poetics, becoming a highly regarded writer and an educator at the Jack Kerouac School of Disembodied Poetics at Naropa. weiss's characterization of Waldman's "influence" as "a natural progression" indicates her "view" of "the beat" as an elastic social and literary context.

In *FOR THESE WOMEN OF THE BEAT,* weiss constructs flexible and consociative Beat communities using other strategies, as well. Many of the poems dedicated to individual women portray them as representative of a more general female Beat ethos and experience. In the Waldman poem, the assertion that "*some* flowed easy into the stream" proffers the possibility that others did the same. Similarly phrased "some" constructions and references to one woman as representative of many "women" appear throughout the collection—including the Adam and Guest poems quoted above, in which Adam appears as a representative "woman of the beat" and Guest as an exemplar of female creative community. These claims offer the possibility of more unsung women standing behind the named figures and further yet-unrecognized "streams" of Beat identification and artistic production.

Connecting her "women of the Beat" to each other, weiss breaks down the barriers commonly used to segregate them into separate categories, restrict their belonging in Beat contexts, and elide their relationships with each other. These barriers appear even in discourses and texts meant to challenge and critique male-focused Beat histories, including Knight's *Women of the Beat Generation*. The anthology reinforces pre-textual classifications by dividing the women it profiles into "The Precursors," "The Muses," "The Writers," and "The Artists." These classifications appear nowhere in *FOR THESE WOMEN OF THE BEAT*, and, in another inclusive move, weiss writes poems for women relegated to sidebars in Knight's anthology—women such as Guest, Tarlow, Helen Hinkle, and Gabrielle Kerouac. Inclusion of these figures, especially Kerouac's mother, who, as weiss notes, "does not want to hear it" (15), compels readers to recognize and reexamine their already-known definitions of Beat. Impelling us to ask in what ways Hinkle (Galatea Dunkel in *On the Road*), for example, is a "woman of the Beat," weiss pulls us in to join her in testing pre-textual limitations on Beat identification. *FOR THESE WOMEN OF THE BEAT* encourages readers to adopt weiss's view of "the Beat" as a creative context of consociative exchange—a community, in Brenda Frazer's words, "growing with connections, vibrating like leaves on a tree" ("B" 62), a community without boundaries or finalities.

As if to announce a new paradigm for reconceptualizing the "Beat woman" label, *FOR THESE WOMEN OF THE BEAT* begins with a poem for Brenda Knight:

the beat the beat the beat
she follows its lead
voices of women calling
the echo her heart (1)

Knight, editor of the 1996 anthology *Women of the Beat Generation*, is nowhere else considered a Beat herself. weiss's poem, however, claims her as a "woman of the beat" because she "follows its lead," the direction indicated by "voices of women." Significantly, the poem's last line—"the echo her heart"—complicates Knight's relationship to those voices, making it not simply or only a matter of following, but more of a spiritual kinship, a visceral heartfelt connection. In this sense, the poem posits consociative possibilities for ongoing manifestations of "the beat" in the lives and work of new generations of contemporary women, further unbinding "Beat" from the narrow confines of a single Generation.

weiss's handwritten inscription on my copy of FOR THESE WOMEN OF THE BEAT draws the reader's attention to already-known Beat histories in her directive to "meet again these ladies." Her poetic portraits assume an informed reader aware of the circumstances and contexts of her subjects' lives; for instance, her poem "ELISE COWEN" alludes to Cowen's troubled life and suicide with the observation "some flew the coop with broken wing/and crashed" (20). But the cryptic briefness of weiss's poetic mini-biographies of "women of the Beat" also invites readers to seek out further details and additional sources of information about their subjects. The poems refer the reader to the Knight anthology and to the women themselves, while gesturing toward the larger social, historical, and literary narratives in which "women of the Beat Generation" have been situated. Her readers thus find themselves in an intertextual position akin to weiss's—confronting and sifting through multiple discursive layers overwriting Beat-associated women's lives and art. weiss's often indirect references to historical and biographical materials readers are presumed to understand ask not only that we recall what we think we already know, but that we "meet again" that knowledge in light of her poetic reformulations of "the Beat" as an open, consociative field of identification.

Her 2011 CAN'T STOP THE BEAT: THE LIFE AND WORDS OF A BEAT POET, a mixed-genre text that pulls together autobiography, biography, literary criticism, poetry, and travelogue, invites a similar remeeting of the already-known in weiss's self-representation as "a Beat Poet" and "the Beat" who can't be stopped. The collection, which includes previously published work, identifies weiss as always-already Beat and situates her at/as the origin of the movement's West Coast incarnation. Early in CAN'T STOP THE BEAT, the reader encounters testimonials that seem intended to establish weiss's Beat credentials; the text opens with excerpts from Blows Like a Horn: Beat Writing, Jazz, Style, and Markets in the Transformation of U.S. Culture, in which the author, Preston Whaley, argues that weiss and the Beat street poet Bob Kaufman "wrote from the boundary, the very brink of selfhood" (n.p.). Next, an introduction—"ruth weiss and the American Beat Movement of the 50s and 60s," written by Horst Spandler—stresses that weiss "was there before the literary fireworks exploded, sparked off by the writers of the Beat Generation in San Francisco" (ix). He characterizes her as the poet who "connect[s] jazz and poetry more consequently and lastingly than any other writer" (xvi–xvii), but at the same time acknowledges her marginal position in the dominant Beat narrative, noting that "she obtained [her Beat] classification and the recognition that went along with it only subsequently" (xx).

CAN'T STOP THE BEAT rehearses the personal history behind weiss's claim to identity as "the Beat," and thus to the authority to rewrite already-known Beat histories. The opening poem, "TEN TEN," retraces in mythic terms the route she hitchhiked from Chicago to San Francisco as an epic journey undertaken by a "dragon":

cometh the dragon
skims on ten thousand feet
drumming remember
along the street of applause
pauses—

it was 1952
a dragon-year
at broadway & columbus
my last hitch from chicago
said this is where you belong (2)

Here, weiss is both herself—"hitching" to the place she "belongs"—and representative of a larger movement arriving on "ten thousand feet" to shake up 1950s America.

Multiple "dragon" references in "TEN TEN" echo other moments of self-representation in weiss's canon; her poems repeatedly use dragon/phoenix/bird imagery to convey a flexible and transformative model of selfhood. In "ALTAR-PIECE," for example, she asserts:

i am not a symbol
i am who i was & who i will be
i am the warrior of
the GOLDEN DRAGON
i fly I have flown i fly

it shall not be kept secret much longer
it is time for all to know
i am dying
to be reborn (44, 46)

This poem proclaims a sense of self that exceeds the symbolic structures of language and evades their power to order and control identity. Another poem, "FOR CAROL BERGÉ (1928–2006)," refers to the Beat-associated

Bergé as a "dragon-lady" and promises her a similar sort of rebirth. "Your phoenix is rising," weiss assures her; "you are bathed in multiple colors of light" (140). References to phoenix-figures abound in DESERT JOURNAL, in which weiss uses imagery related to birds, flight, and phoenix-burning to represent her self-seeking, a project she positions as of a piece with the larger search for meaning in human existence.

weiss's desert is inhabited by a "fire-bird perched" on the "peak" of a "pyramid," its "beak . . . open to soul-stars" (44), and by enigmatic "fig-ure[s]" and "stor[ies]" that "[go] up in smoke," "the ashes left . . . to do it again" (56–57).[13] She imbues her fire-birds with characteristics that flicker between male and female, and their repeating cycles of death and rebirth symbolize the regenerative qualities of mobile, unbounded selves. DES-ERT JOURNAL opens and closes with weiss's embodiment as a hybrid bird-figure—in "FIRST DAY" she identifies herself as a "hermaphroditic" "kangaroo-bird / carry[ing] my own pouch" (10), and "FORTIETH DAY" ends with the poet "sprout[ing] wings" and launching into flight:

> she touched one horn
> it was of the sea
> she touched the other
> it was of the land
>
> and twin-spirals propelled her
> lighter than light (200)

A heterogeneous figure of connection "blurred like a bird" (199), weiss combines and resolves opposites and binaries as her DESERT JOUR-NAL journey proceeds to its next cycle of discovery and regeneration. In CAN'T STOP THE BEAT, references to weiss's dragon/phoenix-self serve to align her with Beat friends "mad to be reborn," who "burn, burn, burn like fabulous yellow roman candles exploding like spiders across the stars" (On the Road 8), creating in intertextual reference a form of community beyond the already-known Beat narrative.

Emphasizing that weiss-the-dragon makes her way to a place she fits and that fits her during "a dragon-year," "TEN TEN" presents her advent in North Beach as destined and inevitable. Grace has noted that "consis-tent throughout [weiss's poetry] is the thread of her autobiography con-structed as a collage of idiosyncratic artifacts marking the terrain of her narrative as an archetypal experience" ("ruth weiss's DESERT JOURNAL" 59). "TEN TEN" renders weiss's experience as archetype while also con-veying in specific, intimate detail the depth of her "belonging" in North

Beach, referencing her "room on montgomery" (2), her work waiting tables, her love for the music played in "THE HOUSE OF BLUE LIGHTS" (4), her relationships with other rebels against Cold War America, and the publication of her "first book STEPS 1959" (4). Here and in subsequent work in the collection, these accumulating details flesh out an identity grounded in the particulars of a well-known and well-loved landscape, one familiar to readers conversant with Beat-affiliated San Francisco communities.

weiss's long form poem "I ALWAYS THOUGHT YOU BLACK," next in the collection, similarly dwells on her everyday interactions within North Beat jazz and literary scenes and incorporates figures including Kaufman, "in france known / as the black RIMBAUD. beat the system. beatitude. / attitude beatific" (48). The poem further reiterates weiss's pre- "Beat" history, a history already-told in "TEN TEN" and in Spandler's introduction:

> years before BEATNIK exploded through the media
> i arrive in north beach. 1952. thumbing from
> chicago. within hours i'm in THE BLACK CAT. a bar
> that is legend. marbles of memory pinged me there.
> mention san francisco and someone would say THE
> BLACK CAT. in chicago. in new orleans. even in
> new york. (55)

Telling and retelling the story of her arrival in San Francisco, a story she imbues with the resonance of legend, weiss situates her story as a Beat narrative of origin.

She gives similar treatment to her jazz poetry, evoking then reevoking its genesis and her role in the development of an art form that tends to be attributed solely to male Beats. Section 5 of "I AWAYS THOUGHT" mentions "THE CELLAR. san francisco / north beach. where i had started poetry & jazz" (17). In section 15, she repeats the story of her

> first night of poetry & jazz at
> THE CELLAR. my first time in public with poetry & jazz.
> other nights i carry beer & wine to the tables. but
> this is wednesday (60–61)

It should be noted that weiss intends her "I started" phrasing—which appears again in the final segment of the poem (75–76)—quite literally, as "nobody knows" that she "innovate[d] jazz and poetry in San Francisco in 1956 at The Cellar" ("S" 71). In "I ALWAYS THOUGHT," weiss does not retell well-known Cellar stories or invoke the names of well-known Beat men who congregated and performed there. Instead, she recounts moments that exemplify the communal and improvisational possibilities of the art form as she "innovated" and lived it. On one memorable evening, she finds someone new onstage at the Cellar, engaged in creating an "electric blue" sound that "sparks into blue flames" at the piano. "who are you i whisper. BOO PLEASANT she laughs never / missing a note. I jump in & off we go. The drum & the / bass thrum behind us. . . . what a set. what a night" (61). Occupying a storied landmark but ignoring Beat events associated with it, weiss both references and rewrites Beat history, pulling to its surface her contributions, filling Beat locales with her creative and collaborative energy.

In addition to repeated references to weiss's "first time in public with poetry & jazz," "I ALWAYS THOUGHT YOU BLACK" indelibly inscribes weiss's story on West Coast geographies associated with the Beat movement; the poem insists on her dynamic, long-standing presence in the "walking city" of San Francisco, tracing her movements back and forth "from north beach to the fillmore," fearlessly walking alone, "always wear[ing] black" and "melt[ing] into the night" (25). Incorporating the comments of friends and acquaintances accumulated over a fifty-year span, the poem establishes weiss as a fixture on North Beach streets and in its coffeehouses and bars. Always to be found "writing in the dark" with "a beer in one hand" and "a pen in the other" (30), she appears as a mythic figure, embodiment of the spirit of this storied time and place.

As "I ALWAYS THOUGHT" draws to a close, it points to weiss's ongoing function as a creator and nurturer of Beat-related art scenes. The long poem ends with a section entitled "ruth weiss," which describes her institution in 1971 of "the only open reading going on in San Francisco at the time," at Minnie's Can-Do Club on Fillmore Street. This series, which extended "the Beat" to new artists and audiences, empowered "anybody" to "read whatever." She recalls that "some poets combined with musical instruments" and others "did duets" (75–76). weiss and a fellow-organizer / poet "would have POET-TREE night. A word from the audience would become an improvised poem. It kept us quick; it kept us laughing" (76). She characterizes that "once-a-week poetry scene" as "the root of a tree" that "branch[ed] out" to include poets as far flung as New York and "even . . . Europe" (76, 75). It also branched into other social and artistic sites, influencing activities at "other clubs and coffee shops" and providing the seed for weiss's development of a new poetry theater in North Beach (77). Through these interconnections, weiss demonstrates that her "Beat" is not a function of a particular historical moment or the product of a handful of Beat Generation men but rather a shared spirit of innovation and collaboration.

Opinions vary regarding weiss's claim that she essentially created "poetry & jazz" as an art form in her Wednesday evening performances at the Cellar, but it is clear that she is at the very least, in Michael McClure's words, "an originator of the scene" who "made herself heard as a performing jazz poet" (37). It is also clear that until fairly recently, as she points out, Beat literary histories have not acknowledged her role in initiating the poetry/jazz connection immortalized in Beat legend and lore, in familiar photographs of male Beats on stage with jazz musicians, and in recordings including the LP *Poetry Readings in "the Cellar"* (1957), featuring Kenneth Rexroth and Lawrence Ferlinghetti.[14] In *CAN'T STOP THE BEAT,* weiss does not attribute this oversight to her standing as a woman operating on the periphery of an established "boy gang." But Spandler's introduction to the collection explicitly critiques her lack of recognition as function of her gender, quoting Joyce Johnson to reference the "minor character" standing of women within the Beat Generation narrative and pointing to weiss's designation as "the 'goddess of the Beats'" (xix). This label might seem to contradict assumptions about female absence and irrelevance (at least in weiss's case). But the term "goddess"—which implies some heightened manifestation of femininity—separates weiss from the mass of "the Beats," singling her out with/as a female stereotype.

In *CAN'T STOP THE BEAT* weiss does not directly address the "goddess" label, nor does she examine gender norms of the Beat period or recount (as she has in other contexts) issues and obstacles she encountered as a woman on the Beat scene.[15] However, the collection does include sixteen pages of photographs of weiss, many of which feature theatrical garb and stylized makeup that almost constitute female drag; the front cover is dominated by a photo of her heavily made-up face (fig. 6). Taken as a whole, the text's portrayals of weiss as a woman *and* as "the" representative "Beat" simultaneously evoke and deny the disjuncture between "Beat" and "woman" encoded in the dominant Beat mythos. This duality—gender is persistently present as paratext but largely ignored in the poetry itself—reflects the intertextual complexities of weiss's project of self-representation as a differently Beat woman. weiss's Beat-claiming text presents a "Beat" who fits neither the masculinized model of Beat individualism nor the "Beat chick" model of oversexed hipster femininity. Instead, she appears as something else altogether, a "dragon" who exceeds the already-known.

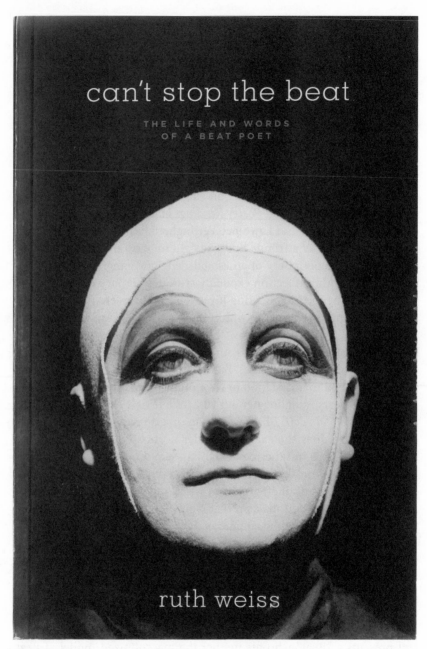

can't stop the beat

THE LIFE AND WORDS
OF A BEAT POET

ruth weiss

Fig. 6. Divine Arts 2011 *CAN'T STOP THE BEAT* front cover. (Cover photograph by Dennis Hearne)

weiss's later work calls for reformulated vocabularies not only to account for the experience of Beat women but to reaccount for "the Beat" as a consociative cultural phenomenon. At the end of "I ALWAYS THOUGHT" she observes:

> What happened back then is all part of now. It just reverberates and reverberates like a pebble tossed into a pond . . . just keeps going on in waves. This dot on the planet—no façade, nothing fancy, no frills was an exciting vortex—this wonderful mix of street people, of wanderers from high and low places. They brought their real selves there. They could not help but be real there as true poetry is real. (78; ellipsis weiss's)

Just as "the beat the beat the beat" echoes through the mini-biographies of *FOR THESE WOMEN OF THE BEAT,* the poetry collected in *CAN'T STOP THE BEAT* presents the "reverberations" of Beat as part of a continuously evolving and endlessly productive "now." The phrase "can't stop the beat" invokes multiple associations—including the rhythms of weiss's jazz poetry and her living presence in the here and now as "a Beat poet." "Can't stop the beat" might indicate not only that "the Beat" cannot be held back or prevented but that Beat does not end and is not restricted to the past. Joining disparate "wanderers" in creative community, weiss extends "the Beat" beyond narratives that have limited it in "trapped pattern," reaffirming consociation as a defining principle of "the Beat" and asserting as "real" people and places that have gone unmentioned and unrecognized in the dominant Beat narrative.

"It Just Reverberates and Reverberates": weiss's Beat Never Stops

To claim Beat as hers, weiss must alter the "Beat Generation" narrative, dislodge its singular and exclusive connotations, and posit a wider, deeper, and more welcoming Beat paradigm. She has been accused of attempting to cash in on the Beat revival, of revising her life to make it "Beat." But in essence she does nothing much different than what Beat figures have done from the moment "Beat" was proposed as a category of identity. Like Kerouac, Ginsberg, Holmes, and others, weiss puts forward a vision of Beat identification based in her experience and reflective of her self-concept. Just as men found ways to mold media representations of Beat in their images, weiss responds to and seeks to adjust a deeply intertextual field of Beat association. She does so by articulating Beat as a movement that cannot be contained within a "Generation" or limited to a few iconic figures and their already-known stories. Like a tree, her Beat community continues to grow.

In her foreword to *FOR THESE WOMEN OF THE BEAT*, weiss observes that as she read Brenda Knight's *Women of the Beat Generation* she encountered continuing possibilities for Beat community in the mid-1990s:

> Some of the women I never knew. Others I had met,
> did not connect. With some it's happening now—
> a sisterhood emerging (n.p.)

Knight's "search" for Beat women spurred weiss's process of Beat rediscovery and sparked her impulse to advocate for recognition of mobile, growing Beat communities and fluid networks of association and exchange in the present day. Beat itself, then, becomes an intertextual process of listening, responding, and creating out of the words and stories of others. weiss is convinced these processes will go on: "Many of my friends," she continues, "some here some gone, belong in one more book. And then another" (n.pag.).

5 DISPLACEMENTS

Joanne Kyger's *The Japan and India Journals* and *The Tapestry and the Web*

I don't yet know how to share parts of my life with the other parts—each clump of me wants to act independently and ignore the existence of anything else. No wonder my body is tense from that constant tug of war.
—JOANNE KYGER, THE JAPAN AND INDIA JOURNALS

If we require that someone be able to tell in story form the reasons why his or her life has taken the path it has, that is, to be a coherent autobiographer, we may be preferring the seamlessness of the story to something we might tentatively call the truth of the person, a truth that, to a certain degree . . . might well become more clear in moments of interruption, stoppage, open-endedness—in enigmatic articulations that cannot easily be translated into narrative form.
—JUDITH BUTLER, GIVING AN ACCOUNT OF ONESELF

In January 1960, Joanne Kyger sailed from San Francisco to join the Beat poet Gary Snyder in Kyoto, Japan, where he was studying Zen Buddhism. Having abandoned her college career three years earlier to establish herself as a "poet of the second San Francisco renaissance," when Kyger boarded that Japan-bound ship, she left behind a vital artistic community in which she had been honing her craft, defining herself as a writer, and developing an "independent, personal kind of poetry" (Berkson 324, 325). As with the North Beach arts community as a whole, Kyger's project of self-definition involved examining her aesthetic in relation to the practices and priorities espoused by the East Coast Beats who had become a formidable presence on the West Coast literary scene following the seismic 6 Gallery poetry reading, an event that connected San Francisco writers with their New York counterparts and led to fruitful (if sometimes combative) literary community (Murphy 288).

Before meeting Snyder, Kyger had joined a rigorous and challenging poetry group led by Robert Duncan and Jack Spicer. She immersed herself in the literary cultures of North Beach and formed friendships with Philip Whalen and Lew Welch, among other Beat-associated figures. Kyger began studying Zen Buddhism, living for a time at the East-West House, "a co-op begun by Snyder and other Zen students, where Kerouac, Lenore

Kandel, Lew Welch, and Philip Whalen were occasional residents" (Fried-man, "Joanne Kyger" 184). In 1958, Kyger began a relationship with Sny-der, a more established poet known for his participation in the 6 Gallery reading. His first collection of poems, entitled *Riprap*, came out in 1959, followed by *Myths & Texts* in 1960. Snyder was also known as a mentor to Kerouac, who based *The Dharma Bums* (1958) on their experience to-gether; it was no secret that Japhy Ryder, a "rucksack revolutionary" and "great new hero of American culture" (*Dharma Bums* 27), is a thinly veiled Gary Snyder.

When Snyder returned to Kyoto to resume his studies at the First Zen Institute of America, it was with the understanding Kyger would follow him. Embarking for Japan not "know[ing] what in god's name I am doing or *why,*" Kyger records her ambivalence about this plan in her journal: "I decide to stay only a short time in Japan and not marry" (*JIJ* 3). Never-theless, three days after her arrival, she and Snyder did get married, as ex-pected by his sponsor, Ruth Fuller Sasaki (founder of the First Zen Insti-tute and abbess of Ryosen-an Temple), who wanted the couple to observe the "fixed social customs" of the Institute (*JIJ* xii). For the four years the marriage lasted, Kyger studied Zen, learned flower-arranging techniques, kept house for Snyder, and wrote much of the poetry that would appear in her first published collection, *The Tapestry and the Web* (1965).

During this time, she kept detailed and wide-ranging journals, using daily life-writing to record her poetic insights and inspirations and to ex-amine her often disorienting positions as a new wife and a Beat-affiliated American in Japan. In *The Japan and India Journals: 1960–1964* (1981),[1] "Joanne Kyger" materializes as a palimpsest of intertextual associations, a fluctuating and multifaceted self assembled in and around internal "tug of wars" provoked in large part by external demands and expectations. Kyger's journals attest to her experience of "clumped" and contradictory selves—in different ways and in different contexts, she appears as Beat and not-Beat, a defiantly self-fashioned writer and an apprentice of es-tablished poets, a seeker after enlightenment and a resistant student, an independent woman and a dependent wife. As she reckons with various and contesting notions of artistry, spirituality, Beatness, and femininity, Kyger's life-writing registers the displacements of a divided self, but at the same time recasts and exploits contradiction and inconsistency as oppor-tunities for self-improvisation.

The shifting and displaced "I"s of Kyger's journals convey an open and fluid self-positioning that also characterizes the radically flexible "I"s of her poetry. Jane Falk notes that "because Kyger thought that the poem should be a direct transcription of the experiences of daily life and of the mind's movements, which made it somewhat like a journal entry, the journal, by bridging the gap between writing and life, provided her with both the substance and style of her poetry, and allowed for the following of the mind in the moment in its spontaneity" ("Journal" 997).[2] In her journals, Kyger constructs, as Linda Russo suggests, a "space in which to explore and challenge received notions of gender and poetic authority, particularly those notions of the feminine fostered by cold war culture and reinforced in poetry by the masculinist rhetoric of the New American poetry" (179). Both *The Japan and India Journals* and *The Tapestry and the Web* explore possibilities for *"shar*[ing] parts of . . . life with the other parts,"* disputing models of identity and affiliation shaped by opposition and separation. In its imaginative fusion of travelogue, diary, and poetry, Kyger's writing transforms "tug of war" positions into sites of creativity.

"A Real *Fear* of Being Submerged Not Heard"

Early in *The Japan and India Journals* (March 10, 1960) Kyger expresses her "fear" of "being over powered" by Snyder, "of being submerged not heard" (11). This fear hardly seems unfounded, given that she is overshadowed by her husband and the Beat Generation "boy gang" in virtually all aspects of her experience in Asia. Over the intervening decades, paratextual elements attached to her life-writing from that period have borne witness to her "submerged," partially visible condition. When Tombouctou Books released her *Japan and India Journals* in 1981, Kyger appeared on the front cover in submerged, indirect fashion, represented as the female half of a plastic wedding cake topper, her pallid bride-self overshadowed by other, more vibrant images referencing Asia and the journey itself (fig. 7).[3] The cover of the 2000 North Atlantic Books reissue entitled *Strange Big Moon: The Japan and India Journals* is considerably more indirect (fig. 8). It includes no visual representation of Kyger, featuring instead an image of a large full moon set over a repeating pattern of blurred ideograms. The phrase "strange big moon" echoes a poem that appears in her journal, as part of her entry of February 16, 1963:

MOON

refusing to move me at all
falling from the morning sky
and its strange bigness
at certain evening times. (234)

Fig. 7. Tombouctou Books 1981 *The Japan and Indian Journals* front cover. (Cover photograph by Ken Botto)

Fig. 8. North Atlantic Books 2000 *Strange Big Moon: The Japan and India Journals* front cover.

Use of this phrase as a title might constitute a gesture toward recognition of Kyger's standing as a poet, but neither the title itself nor any information included on the cover or in the front matter of *Strange Big Moon* references her as its source.

Only with the 2016 edition of the *Journals*, published about a year before Kyger's death and during a time of increased interest in women writers affiliated with the Beat movement, do readers encounter a cover image of the autobiographer herself (fig. 9). Nightboat Books chose for its cover art a well-known photograph of Kyger in Japan; taken in 1963 by Allen Ginsberg, it shows a smiling Kyger posed in front of a statue of the Buddha. The image is accompanied by Ginsberg's signature and his handwritten caption, which focuses predominantly on his interpretation of the statue's symbolic elements. Unlike most of Ginsberg's references to his experience traveling in India and Japan, the caption does at least mention Kyger, although glancingly.[4]

In her foreword to *Strange Big Moon: The Japan and India Journals,* Anne Waldman observes that Kyger "never seems to get her due" (ix). During her time in Asia, at least, Kyger attributes this lack of acknowledgment to being eclipsed by Snyder—his Beat celebrity, his status as a recognized poet, and his accomplishments as an advanced student of Zen Buddhism. In comparison, her position is notably secondary and subordinate; she records feeling directionless and lonely, sometimes miserable, occasionally "trapped" (10) in her "new existence" as a "housewife in Japan" (xii). While Snyder, secure in his familiarity with Japanese culture, moves about at will and spends long periods away from home, Kyger must rely upon him for navigation in a new locale and for help communicating in a new language. Snyder is accomplished in zazen, the practice at the heart of Zen. In contrast, Waldman points out, Kyger "struggles with the axiomatic truths of Buddhism and her own difficulty to sit still" (vii). In zazen—or seated meditation—practitioners focus on the breath, let go of the ego, and "settle [the] mind in its original state" of "purity and clarity" (Tri 5). Kyger's journals reflect the tension generated by her simultaneous desire to learn this disciplined art and to be free of the disciplinary pressure of others, especially Snyder, whom she describes as "a very committed person, very strict on himself, very disciplined" ("Particularizing").[5]

In her introductory note to the first edition of *The Japan and India Journals,* Kyger remarks: "Shortly after arriving in Japan ... Gary asked me, 'Don't you want to study Zen and lose your ego?' I was utterly shocked: 'What! After all this struggle to attain one?'" (xii). Kyger's internal tug

JOANNE KYGER
The Japan and India Journals, 1960-1964

Fig. 9. Nightboat Books 2016 *The Japan and India Journals* front cover. (Cover photograph © Allen Ginsberg; image courtesy of Nightboat Books)

of war can be attributed at least in part to relentless pressure to accept discipline and to discipline herself—not just to "lose [her] ego" as an adherent of Zen Buddhism, but to produce poetry that meets the standards of her male mentors, to expedite the adventures of male "rucksack revolutionaries," and to subordinate her creative and spiritual life to her husband's.[6] "Discipline" might suggest the control over the self integral to the practice of Zen, but it also suggests conformity, correction, and punishment, calling to mind mechanisms that bring unruly or resistant subjects into acquiescence with social and cultural norms. Kyger conceptualizes discipline as both desirable and dangerous to her self-positioning as a woman within male-centered locales, and she uses journal writing to negotiate the multiple sources of disciplinary pressure with which she contends.

Life-writing in notebook, diary, or journal form is characterized by unedited and unrefined immediacy, inconclusiveness, and discontinuity—in other words, by lack of discipline. A contingent, contextual, and episodic practice, daily writing records fragments of experience and situational moments of self-conceptualization. Thus, it seems a particularly apt vehicle for exploring a self in "clumps" and for tracking the evolution of a palimpsestic aesthetics of self-expression. Journal writing brings to light the "enigmatic" sorts of truth Judith Butler proposes appear "in moments of interruption, stoppage, open-endedness" (*Giving* 64). In its immediacy and lack of coherence, journal writing enables evasion of singular, exclusive, unified categories of identity; its "fragmentary nature," Suzanne Bunkers and Cynthia Huff assert, "calls into question conformity at all levels" (4). Free to be an incoherent life-writer, the diarist records the contradiction, ambiguity, and multiplicity often ignored or repressed in more ordered genres of autobiographical expression.

While the Kyger of 2000, writing her author's note to the second edition of *The Japan and India Journals*, "cring[es] at the often cultivated bratty willfulness carried as part of the personality equipment" (xi) of her younger self, the Kyger of the early 1960s uses her journals to give voice to "willful" perspectives and defiant desires that others, especially her husband and his admirers in the United States and Asia, do not want to hear. What is more, she is well aware that her notebooks are not fully or only a space for *private* self-expression. Writers of journals, Margo Culley asserts, address a reader, whether actual or imagined, self or other (217), and Kyger seems to have expected both. She routinely reread her notebooks for poetic "insight" ("PG" 139), and she probably expected Snyder to read them as well.[7] There is evidence she read his; she reports finding a "note" he left her "in his journal"—"when you read this Joanne Kyger, as you certainly will"—and records gaining insight from his notebook—"from G's journal see we all act wild at a certain age" (*JIJ* 9, 12). In addition to serving as "a kind of mirror before which [she] stands assuming this posture or that" (Culley 219), Kyger's notebooks function as a site of dialogic exchange and ongoing conversation—with herself and with others, including, perhaps, an anticipated reading public. Many Beat-associated writers not only employed journals as part of their composition processes but also published them.[8]

The conversations Kyger conducts in her not-so-private journals exceed disciplinary categories and preserve her willful voice and developing priorities as a poet. In her life-writing, the artistic and the commonplace sit side by side, as do dreams and dinner menus and excerpts of others' texts. Kyger positions details about housecleaning and train travel beside literary analyses and existential questions, all of which morph effortlessly into poetry. Her entry of March 22, 1963, demonstrates her tendency to blur generic, contextual, and topical boundaries:

> Old ojisan,
> Uncle farmer gets his money slowly
>   from an old used plastic bag
>   some hundreds, a thousand
>   the change goes back in
>   his fingers stiff & thick.

> Arrive 10 or so Kirishimi—short bus to Jingu. & youth hostel. Separate dormitory rooms. Gary fussing endlessly with getting arranged.

> Gary says to Japanese sometimes that he is studying:
>   Toyorekishi: history
>   Toyo tetsugaku: philosophy

> The girls after returning to the room last night insisted on covering up my feet which I had pushed out of the futon because it was so hot. She's so pitiful they said, thinking I was asleep and a long foreigner who really couldn't *fit* into Japanese accommodations. (244–45)[9]

Kyger's poetic life-writing redistributes lines of discursive hierarchy that would limit her means of responding to the world and of representing her positions within in it. Her journals consistently challenge and reconfigure pre-texts and pretexts that muffle her voice, limit her artistic potential, and draw restrictive boundaries around her identity and her possibilities for self-determination.

"Feeling Terribly Anxious and Unfree"

In *A Day at a Time*, Culley points out that "because diaries are periodic in creation and structure, incremental repetition is an important aspect of the structure of most journals, and the dynamic of reading the periodic life-record involves attending to what is repeated" (220). Details of Kyger's domestic life—laundry, garden, dinner, cats—comprise a central thread of repetition in her journals. Much of her life in Japan circulates around housewifely duties, which she records in entries such as this: "Gary off this morning to Sodo for a week's sesshin [extended meditation]. Cleaned dresser, did laundry, cleaned kitchen, finished income tax, and to Zen Institute to mail it and participate in afternoon coffee" (37). In addition to documenting her household labors, this entry reflects another repeated pattern—a gendered arrangement in which Kyger tends to domestic matters while Snyder attends to his spiritual advancement. Like Bonnie Bremser, Kyger experiences life in foreign locales through intensified caretaking responsibilities, which for her are new and not entirely welcome. At points, they feel forcibly imposed: "Asked Gary what if I was involved in doing something & didn't want to do the dishes for say a few days—I want to feel the freedom of acting that way should the possibility arise. He would not grant me that, he said. We argued and talked about it for sometime, at last in exasperation I rose from the bed and said I was going to sleep in the Genkan whereupon he grabbed me around the knees and down I fell striking my head against the edge of the table splitting it open" (33). Like the resultant bloody "furrow" (33) on her forehead, her journal entry inscribes compulsory female roles as a form of violence. This entry, like many others, establishes a painful disjuncture between Kyger's need for independence and Snyder's need for a household order that supports the life he has chosen.

Additionally, the entry demonstrates the "tug of war" dynamics characterizing Kyger's understanding of her relationship with her husband. Immediately after she records her injury, what appears to be an impossible impasse between male and female priorities gives way to a more harmonious outcome: "Thoroughly frightened we drove to the Baptist hospital & had it stitched up. . . . Gary held my hand, he has a big warm calloused comforting hand, the nails are large and well shaped, they feel and touch firmly, nothing weak or flimsy about the look or feel of his hands" (33). Kyger's shift from her bloody head to her husband's warm hands redirects her account of domestic conflict to the comforts of heterosexual love relationship; it offers a resolution that incompletely overwrites Snyder's threat to not only overpower her physically but to force her into traditional models of female identity at odds with her desire for freedom.

Numerous entries in *The Japan and India Journals* address this ambivalent and gendered tug of war. Kyger "want[s] to please" Snyder (25) and would like him "to be happy & have what he wants," but at the same time yearns for "a room all [her] own," a "light & airy" place free of his expectations (31). "I wish I had never known writing," she observes wistfully. "Then I'd be more content with what I am doing now instead of wishing I was proving myself by writing" (36). Her entry of May 10, 1960, expresses her fear of being subsumed by her husband's demands: "I don't mind Gary getting bossy within reason only it scares me when it gets out of hand, then he has no concern of another's reality or awareness of it" (8). Noting that their relationship often feels to her like "a battle to see who is going to get the upper hand," she asks: "Is his own masculinity threatened that he must fight so hard to assert himself & show no regard for my desires or identity. As far as I can recall he has always treated women this way" (30).[10] In these accounts, Kyger presents Snyder's insistence on his "reality"—one organized around his ideal of masculinity—as the only reality that matters as a tangible and significant impediment to her project of creative self-determination.

Even as Kyger's journals reveal the displacements occasioned by her husband's refusal to recognize her reality, they also reaffirm her own "desires" and "identity" (30) by denaturalizing her performance of the wife/caretaker role. On March 11, 1961, she writes: "I fix Gary marvelous dinner, martinis, lamb roast, wine, coffee and brandy, anticipate the wonderful conversations. He falls asleep, after endless tuning of guitar never played. J. Magazine from Italy inspires me to plan a Japan issue" (88–89). Having acted the role of housewife in exemplary fashion, Kyger waits in vain for her reward, never realizing the accord and "wonderful conversations" for which she had hoped. Instead, she is left with an unresponsive companion and the discordant noise of "endless tuning" that never resolves into pleasing music. Her account of unrewarded domestic labor attributes a certain futility to traditional household arrangements and offers a muted critique of Snyder's expectations, while the final line reasserts literary pursuits as her primary mode of endeavor and source of satisfaction. Another entry reveals a hidden flaw in an apparently successful domestic feat: "Made custard last night from Joy of Cooking cook book just arrived. . . . It was perfect except Gary does not know I put in too much salt. Only I" (23). Asserting her undetected deviation from the norm, Kyger issues a comparably indirect challenge to pre-scripted gender expectations.

Similar instances of irony, understatement, and subtle humor recur throughout the *Journals*. Consider Kyger's entry for a "gloomy" day in March 1962 during a much-anticipated trip to India with Snyder, Ginsberg, and Peter Orlovsky. This Beat pilgrimage was, in Lawrence Ferlinghetti's words, "known all over the US," imagined as "some kind of International sorcerer swamis' conjunction," even before it occurred; Kyger understands, however, that it was perceived as a summit between "Allen" and "Gary" (*JIJ* 190). Her journal entry records a day on which the men have gone off to explore while she stays behind to perform service work: "Reading *Kim* all day between bouts of laundry. A grey heavy wind dries the clothes on the porch. Lugging buckets from the faucets at the pumps. Soaking the clothes for 30 minutes in the room and back to rinse and bringing back a fresh bucket for new laundry soaking. Sleeping bag liners, shawl, Gary's parka, and on" (181). The word "bouts"—which suggests illness (as in bouts of malaria) and fights (as in title bouts of heavyweight boxers)—imbues her account of clothes, water, and wind with an understated sense of conflict and malaise. In its situational context—the epic India pilgrimage, which she describes in distinctly un-epic terms—the entry installs Kyger's gender-coded labor as the unrecognized other side of the male-focused Beat narrative.

She comments on other aspects of Beat gender relations through the detail she uses to record her interactions with her husband. In the following entry, Kyger constructs wry plays-on-words to undermine male Beats' tendency to "mythologiz[e]" the figure of "woman-as-muse" (Skinner par. 6):

Drawing water from the well for the bath Monday night I became aware of what I was doing in the sense of how it effects me in poetry : water—Not the water of the ocean it is of the earth.   Gary says women are always associated with water, and holes are mystic entrances.
The well is essentially a woman's thing.   And the well as KNOWLEDGE.   Well I don't know.   Well I do know. Contemplation & awareness.
Are you Well.   Well, well, how nice to see you today.
Bringing up, drawing up the water.   Drawing and painting.

Snail moves circularly in the upper damp areas of the well. I pulled
a beetle up in the wooden bucket I had seen him floating on the
surface, also before the surface was disturbed my face   I saw way
down reflected. (34–35)

Snyder's generalizations about women and water assert a clichéd woman-
as-keeper-of-mysteries-to-be-plumbed "association" that defines "a
woman's thing" from a male perspective. Kyger responds first with
humor—"Well I don't know. Well I do know. . . . Are you Well Well, well,
how nice to see you today"—piling on repetition with playful differences
that unsettle her husband's blanket linkage of "wells" with women. Then,
having evacuated Snyder's interpretation, she returns to her initial association of water with her creative process, sliding from "drawing up the
water" to "drawing and painting." The entry ends with a reassertion of her
lived knowledge of the well (rather than some transcendent KNOWL-
EDGE) and with the sight of herself "reflected" there.

In other instances, Kyger leaves moments of difference and dislocation
largely unspoken. The following is her entry for February 23, 1960, the day
she married Snyder:

Married at American Consulate's office in Kobe.
Reading about parachute jumping in America.
My name is changed. (7)

Often in journal and diary writing "what is excluded," Bunkers and Huff
note, "is as important as what is included" (1). Not only does Kyger's wedding day entry exclude her new husband, it also leaves out any mention
of love, fulfillment, or happily-ever-after promises. More a list than an
account of an important life event, notable for its lack of affect and dearth
of personal detail, this bare-bones report pointedly ignores hegemonic
assumptions about marriage as the life-defining goal of a woman's existence.[11] The juxtaposition of the boldness of parachute jumping in America
and the passivity with which Kyger stands by in Kobe as her name—that
fundamental marker of the self—"is changed" encodes her sense of displacement within traditional arrangements of male/female relationship.

Her 1963 New Year's Eve entry, which consists of two very different sets
of "resolutions"—her own and Snyder's for her—offers a more jarring
juxtaposition. Kyger's resolutions, aimed at her development as an artist,
appear first. She starts with a plan to study "the craft of poetry" by "scan-
ning poetry sheets and volumes of the past," but then arrives at the con-
clusion that "the craft should fit like a glove. Exactly: from my *own* life"

(269). Kyger's brief literary manifesto, which affirms her lived experience as an authentic source of poetic truth, is immediately followed by Snyder's resolutions, which insist exactly on the inadequacies of her lived experience. After critiquing her undisciplined literary and domestic practices, his long list of recommendations for her improvement ends:

> Fold your clothes in your drawer.
> Don't save *everything*.
> Quit reading so much trash.
> What about history and prosody?
> Genius means hard work too.

> Halfhearted scaredy-cat flower arrangement isn't
> ENOUGH.

> It *would* be nice if you could get up early and make breakfast
> while I did *soji* or worked in the garden.

> Why can't you ever have a meal ready on time??

> And wash the dishes soon after. And pay attention.

> Listening to stupid radio programs without even listening.

> Bad careless habits, like others, don't really exist.

> Learn to take criticism when it's fair without getting nasty
> in return // humility. (269–70)

Like Kyger's terse wedding day record, this New Year's Eve entry, written less than two weeks before she leaves Snyder and Japan, does not attempt to resolve the conflicts it documents. The two sets of resolutions simply sit side by side, contiguous but starkly opposed. Leaving unspoken the disjuncture between the woman she wants to be and the woman her husband wants her to be, Kyger allows her confident claim to a poetics that grows from her "own life" to answer her earlier feelings of anxiety and constriction, her fear of being forcibly co-opted into pre-scribed female roles.

"Reading about the Insanity of the Beat Generation"

A less obvious "battle" of self-fashioning in *The Japan and India Journals* involves the question of Kyger's place within the Beat movement. Her very first journal entry (January 1, 1960) registers her awareness that others see her as a Beat chick who wears "black stockings and all that eye makeup" (1). In fact, much of Kyger's explicit reference to Beatness involves appearance, especially aspects of appearance that indicate poverty or bohemian flouting of propriety. Unconvinced that Beat identity constitutes much more than costume and performance, Kyger seems to understand herself as Beat primarily in the sense of "guilt by association." But she finds that who she is often depends upon who she is with; in Snyder's company and in the context of the Beat summit in India, she cannot avoid the "Beat woman" label.

Kyger's ambivalence about Beat identification seems inevitable, given her exclusion from male-dominant Beat narratives; she critiques these narratives in both her journal entries and her poetry. Amy Friedman points to Kyger's poem "October 29, Wednesday," which describes adoring throngs following "Mr. Ginsberg and Mr. Snyder" in India while the unnoticed female poet performs the real wonder—she "completes her meditation with an effortless, unobserved levitation a foot off the ground" ("Joanne Kyger, Beat Generation Poet" 78). Another poem, "Poison Oak for Allen," similarly protests what Kyger perceives as her unnatural absence from Beat histories:

> Here I am reading about your trip to India again,
> with Gary Snyder and Peter Orlovsky. Period.
> Who took the picture of you three
>
> With the smart Himalayan backdrop?
> The bear? (*Again* 102)

Pointing to the discontinuities occasioned by female displacement, the poem, as Ronna Johnson argues, "makes use of the material that Beat literature has assigned [Kyger]; its witty coherence contradicts male Beat myths of female silence and centerlessness, foregrounding the ineradicable invisibility of the poet's status as a gendered object" ("Mapping" 19–20).[12] Kyger's art and her life-writing reflect her ongoing negotiation of erasure, her impulse to find and create space for female self-seeking and self-expression in and around intertextual nowheres.

The Japan and India Journals consistently references Kyger's "minor character" position in Gary Snyder's story, a story pursued by journalists and admirers on both sides of the Pacific. Numerous journal entries commenting on interactions with the media demonstrate her keen awareness that public interest in Snyder has prompted the circulation of skewed versions of her own story. She quotes an "article on foreigners in Japan" which holds that "Mrs. Snyder deserted her luxurious life in California to become the wife of the Zen student" (26), a characterization that erases her name, ignores her self-identification as a poet, misrepresents her life in North Beach, and miscasts her in the role of self-sacrificing helpmeet. Newspapers and journals including *Evergreen Review* dispatch photographers and publish articles about her husband and his "house in Yase and motorcycle" (27). In such representations, Snyder appears as a celebrated writer and adventurer, while Kyger seems to be along for the ride, disappearing as "Mrs. Snyder" while he is acclaimed as "the Dharma Bum" (143). Her frequent mentions of Snyder's celebrity and media profile indicate her cognizance of the lack of space in the Beat narrative to accommodate Joanne Kyger.

The much-ballyhooed India journey marginalizes Kyger even further, reducing her to a bit player in the Snyder-Ginsberg pilgrimage. She is left behind on excursions, excluded from poetry readings, and ignored at social gatherings. Feeling aimless and eclipsed amid the adulation directed at Beat icons Gary Snyder and Allen Ginsberg, she writes a letter to a friend (which is reproduced in her notebook):

> I dearly hope Time magazine pays no attention to us until I am in the foreground with my smart published novel and nifty green tore[a]dor pants and all my jewelry from the Tibetan market. I weigh 119 lbs & have crows feet at the corners of my lovely beatnik eyes. I am going to try those face recipes for rose petals you sent, very soon. Before its too late. The thing is, I am sounding rather bitter because its been *years* since I've been able to get any wild martini *attention.* All I do is stand around in this black drip dry dress in India. (195)

Even as Kyger pokes fun at all aspects of the India trip, including her own sense of aggrievement, her tongue-in-cheek commentary acknowledges her real and pressing need for recognition and respect. Additionally, her remarks on her appearance point to the different kind of "attention" aimed at Beat women and to her position as the object of a cultural gaze that judges her according to a set of criteria quite different from those applied to the often "wild and unkempt" (177) male Beats.

At the same time, however, she shows that public recognition of male Beats is rooted in intertextual fantasy rather than in a reality she can recognize. Many of Kyger's India entries seem to have been written with Beat pre-texts in mind, particularly *The Dharma Bums* and Ryder/Snyder's "vision of a great rucksack revolution" carried out by "young Americans wandering around with rucksacks, going up to mountains to pray . . . all of 'em Zen Lunatics who go about writing poems" and "giving visions of eternal freedom to everybody and to all living creatures" (78). In ironic counterpoint, *The Japan and India Journals* portrays Beat travelers less as rucksack revolutionaries and more as self-absorbed tourists. They argue with guides and "shout at" non-English-speaking officials "so [they] will understand us better" (176). Consumed with the logistical minutiae of getting from place to place, they lose their cool when faced with uncomfortable accommodations and overcrowded trains. Seeking calm and authenticity, they climb into the mountains to spend the night, but "everyone vomited . . . opium" and developed "carbon monoxide poisoning" (186). When the group meets the Dalai Lama, Ginsberg "asks him if he wants to take L.S.D." (186). No prayers, poems, or visions here.

Kyger seems especially invested in debunking Ginsberg's claims to Beat spiritual and literary authority. She punctures his status as legend—"something about Ginsberg that's stubborn unyielding & unattractive, a giant inflated ego that really believes he's god & untouchable & good" (190). At some points, she responds with humor to what she sees as his self-centeredness: "I said I wouldn't want to hear the reading of Howl twice on his record, & he looked as if the floor had dropped away" (190). At other points, she can barely contain her anger: "Overwhelming reaction against Ginsberg chokes and suffocates me and I am forced to leave the room" (197). Chafing at his standing as a primary spokesperson for the New American poets and for Beat spirituality, Kyger describes him as both self-important and selfish, noting that he seeks shortcuts to "enlightenment" and gobbles down food heedless of others' needs (191). Her anxiety about Ginsberg's "greed" (191) and propensity to consume communal resources before others get their share might reflect her resentment of his enthronement as representative Beat, a position that crowds her out of representable participation. The India pilgrimage confronts Kyger with her invisibility and lack of voice in the Beat narrative, but her life-writing recasts the Beat Generation's masculinized mythos as myopic, exclusionary, and at times a bit ridiculous.

Nevertheless, even as Kyger problematizes Beat identity, she remains an engaged participant in Beat literary communities. As noted above, her journal writing itself partakes in practices common to Beat writers. Those practices, Falk observes, include "an interest in spontaneity; a focus on mental process and on expansion of consciousness; a concern with the breath and the open line; and a commitment to quotidian or commonplace events" ("Journal" 999).[13] Kyger's journals also record distinctly Beat reading choices—for instance, "*Evergreen No. 17* . . . with stories by

[Michael] Rumaker and Lewis Welch" (93)—and engage in debate over Beat-associated writers' literary merit—"horrible discussion & quarreling over Paul Blackburn's poetry. He sounds stuffy and pretentious on tape. He just wasn't *worth* all that attention" (209). Conversely, she deems Philip Whalen "a truly great philosophic poet trying to resolve dualism" (102). Not coincidentally, Kyger herself seeks to move beyond the "dualisms" that restrict and limit even Beat literary communities professing an aesthetic of immediacy and openness.

In Japan, Kyger keeps abreast of U.S. reaction to the Beat writers, making note of newspaper and magazine articles about Snyder and other Beat figures. She takes umbrage with an "unnecessarily vicious article in 'Time' about Ginsberg, Beats, & poetry" (192) and criticizes Timothy Leary, who "says he loves the poets but . . . the way he writes about them . . . turns them into unattractive foolish asses" (181). In her December 3, 1960, entry, she comments: "Rereading Kerouac's *Subterraneans*. I keep putting him down until I start reading him then I can't" (71). When Kerouac sends Kyger and Snyder a copy of *Lonesome Traveler,* she remarks: "After reading him always left feeling so helplessly *good.*" (83). In addition to reading and discussing the work of Beat writers, she copies materials from their texts, letters, and notebooks into her journals; their philosophies form the context in which she works to form and define her own. Reading about the "beat generation," Kyger seems to attribute their "insanity" to "their attempts to bridge what goes on inside with the outer actor" (34), a concern that underpins her own self-presentation and her developing poetics.

As her life-writing examines her role in Beat networks of communication and influence, it tracks her position as both insider and outsider. Kyger's entry of March 26, 1963, documents a "letter from [Ron] Loewinsohn saying he's received poems of mine from Philip [Whalen] & likes them. Philip likes them also" (246–47). Two months later, however, Whalen writes to tell her "that [Stan] Persky says everyone very unimpressed with my poems in Change" (252). In July 1963, she reports a friend has given Ginsberg "all Philip's letters so he'd see good comments Philip made on my poetry. I'd better read your poems again says Allen the next morning" (256). Notably, Kyger is the only female poet involved in such exchanges, and it is Whalen's approval that convinces Ginsberg to reevaluate her work.[14]

A complaint she makes almost in passing about Donald Allen, editor of *The New American Poetry,* sums up her split position as Beat insider/outsider. *The New American Poetry* "introduced Beat poets and other avant-garde post–World War II poets to a wide reading audience" and remains "one of the most influential" anthologies of poetry "ever published in the United States" (Middleton-Kaplan 225). Snyder, Ginsberg, Kerouac, and Whalen are included in this groundbreaking collection; Kyger is not. She did provide poems for a planned revised edition—she reports that Allen took her "poems for his next anthology"—but nevertheless feels bypassed when he "asked *Gary* to ask [her] to send him a short biography" with "absolutely no word" to Kyger herself (195). Her journals express a conflicted sense of (dis)identification with Beat communities that provide her with precious few "words" of recognition and acceptance. The young Joanne Kyger wants "to explode . . . in print" (21), but, as the episode with Don Allen demonstrates, she knows that access to Beat-associated venues of publication come through men who view themselves as *the* New American poets.

"*Aim for* a Whole New Way of Using Language"

Kyger's October 8, 1963, entry consists of two lines: "When I have time I write. / Is this less than a poet should do" (263). The question of what a poet "should do" assumes the existence of privileged models—and Kyger has plenty of those, ranging from members of her male-dominated Beat circle to figures such as Ezra Pound and Henry James. In her journals, she enters into dialogue with texts and philosophies offered by friends and mentors, as well as by writers including Gertrude Stein and Edna St. Vincent Millay. Charles Olson's "PROJECTIVE VERSE," she remarks, "hits me like a whallop. Poetry is true stuff the way he writes of it" (60). She takes less enthusiastic notice of "old crabby daddy" Pound's pronouncement that in order to be "*great*" a poet must "write an epic . . . have the command of a world / universal view" (230, 225). In his formulation, she observes, "a woman" cannot be "great" because "her craft seems to deal with parts, particulars" (226), a characterization that diminishes and dismisses female experience and modes of expression.

In *The Japan and India Journals,* Kyger deals with parts and particulars of her experience in poetic entries rich with the personal and the everyday. Her entry/poems detail the changing seasons, explore the dislocations of travel, and sift through the give-and-take of heterosexual love relations. She offers this poetic assessment of her simultaneous resistance to and dependence on Snyder:

> indeed I *am*   bad tempered
> foul mouthed etc.

   one might even
  ask why
    he disregards me.
  o for summer when the
  bed will be warm
     all the time
  what
    independence! (13–14)

Asserting and embracing the defiant, unfeminine voice rejected by her husband, Kyger's poem looks forward to a time of "independence" when she will not feel obligated to trade self-censorship for his "regard." Other poems embedded in journal entries address conflicts between her writing life and her household responsibilities:

  Worrying as I sweep
  can I write anymore?
     poems a nag now
  to be accomplished.
    all the cats in the sun.
    Swift and the
    leaves fall, autumn ginko
     covering
  everyone of the stone steps. (216)

In addition to creating poetry out of her domestic routine and finding beauty in the small details of everyday life, this entry/poem both exposes and resolves the "tug of war" between competing aspects of Kyger's sense of self—here, the anxiety generated by her performance of the house-wife role gives way to an opportunity for the creation of art. Early in the *Journals,* she identifies "evidences of the whole self in the poem" as the "measure of the trueness of the poem" (28). The entry/poem above puts into practice her view of poetry as an expression of thought, an artifact of individual perception and truth to the experience of the moment.

  Kyger's entry/poems give voice to her developing aesthetic and enact a self-determined poetics directed toward "a whole new way of using language" (242):

           Poetry and
  art is the process of rendering ideas impotent.
  The VERGE—is the only creative
      truly creative

moment—when things have not yet condemned themselves—by coming alive—to extinction. (254)

Her journal writing, which she has described as a "kind of un-self-
conscious open utterance" ("Energy"), captures such "creative / moment[s]," the instant at which seeds of ideas erupt into fragmentary and
incomplete being, bursting with unexamined possibilities that hold at bay
the "extinction" of full, finite articulation. Further, as commentators including Jane Falk, Andrew Schelling, and Linda Russo have noted, Kyger's
poetry grows organically out of her journal-writing practices. Poems in
her first collection, *The Tapestry and the Web*, emerge from journal accounts of her experience in Japan—her garden, her travels, her contradictory position as a female poet in Beat circles. Like her journal entries,
poems in this collection express potential selves at "the verge," in prismatic moments of potential transformation. A shifting, fluid palimpsest
of myth, autobiography, and poetry, *Tapestry* fuses the epic and the everyday, pulls down boundaries between text and pre-text, and blurs hegemonic models of gendered identity calcified into binary categories of
separation and opposition.

The Tapestry and the Web answers Pound's rejection of the everyday
in his definition of the (male) poet as a maker of epics by going "inside
the story of the *Odyssey*" and "reporting on [Kyger's] life through it"
("Energy").[15] In particular, Kyger refashions the story of Penelope, that
paragon of domestic dedication, who waits twenty years for Odysseus
to return from the Trojan War. In the Homeric epic, Penelope holds off
a horde of insolent and greedy suitors by maintaining she must finish
weaving a shroud for her father-in-law before considering their propos-
als. After constructing her intricate web by day, she unravels it at night,
a self-disciplined act that demonstrates her faith in her husband's return
and serves to preserve his place in his kingdom. In *Tapestry*, however,
weaving functions as a central motif for resistant modes of female self-
expression; in Kyger's hands, weaving absorbs and transforms a pervasive
trope in Western literature that adopts weaving as a metaphor for female
art in ways that restrict women's creativity to lesser, domestic activities
dismissed as mundane and insignificant.

Coded as limited, utilitarian labor, the trope of female writing-as-
weaving posits, Nancy K. Miller observes, "a textuality hopelessly entangled with questions of its material" and thus enables readers to ignore
its "critique of phallomorphic privilege" (77, 78). Kyger's invocations of
weaving, webs, and tapestries, on the other hand, inject difference into

already-known stories that naturalize and perpetuate patriarchal norms. She points, for instance, to an odd "detail" in a tapestry that appears to depict a standard hunting scene, honing in on the figure of a "maid" whose gaze, turned "towards / the sound of the / huntsman's horn" and his "capture" of a "unicorn," only "*seems* / coquettish." To the contrary, her "puffeyes and . . . broken turned nose" indicate she is "searching / for bigger & better things" (40; italics added). The maid's non-storybook qualities might also indicate something of the violence attending the traditional heterosexual plots, roles, and representations available to women.

"Waiting again," a *Tapestry* poem, appears in *The Japan and India Journals* in an entry addressing the creative process in coded terms that install female experience as a hidden site of creative difference. Here is the material as it appears in Kyger's notebook:

> waiting again.
> what for. I am no picker from the sea of its riches
>
> I watch the weaving—the woman who sits at her loom
>
> What was her name?   the goddess I mean
> —not that mortal one   plucking the threads
>   as if they were strings of a harp.
>
>   fantastic!
>   the skill of revealing a story.
>
>   *Constructing.*
>
> Dealing with us as if we were puppets
>
> to be picked up and added to a cast. (*JIJ* 22)

And here is the poem from *Tapestry*:

>   waiting again
>   what for
>
>   I am no picker from the sea of its riches
>   I watch the weaving—the woman who sits at her loom
> What was her name?   the goddess I mean
>   —not that mortal one
>
>   plucking threads
>   as if they were strings of a harp
>   Spring, 1960 (*Tapestry* 33)

In its observation that Penelope performs the same activity as Athena ("the goddess" of wisdom and of weaving) and its equation of weaving with the production of music, "waiting again" situates the metaphorical conjunction of poetry, song, and artistic authority in a woman "at her loom." The longer entry/poem in the *Journals* more explicitly identifies the female creator-figure as a writer—her weaving constructs "a story" that fashions others' identities, "dealing with us as if we were puppets/to be picked up and added to a cast." Counting herself among the "us" dealt with like "puppets," Kyger joins the "cast" of the *Odyssey* as an "I" floating between Greece, Japan, and the United States. She layers her own experience and self-concept over and through that of Homer's characters, drawing on and redistributing their intertextual associations to "reveal a story" that finds and exploits alternative formulations of gender in a foundational Western narrative of male heroism.

Another journal entry merges the three figures of "waiting again"—the goddess who weaves, the "mortal" woman who weaves and waits, and the "I" who waits and watches: "Is the woman who waits the woman who weaves? / I wish I had some friends here to do things and go places / with. Alas" (*JIJ* 32). The entry's progression from "the woman who waits" to "the woman who weaves" to Kyger's loneliness in Japan links her position to Penelope's in a number of ways. Both women are essentially alone and isolated, waiting for husbands off accomplishing exciting and heroic feats. They share a condition of domestic entrapment and sense of exploitation; in the *Tapestry* poem "April 23. Possibilities," fourth in the "Odyssey Poems" series, Kyger's frustrations with caretaking duties and inconsiderate houseguests (and, perhaps, the ravenous Ginsberg and Orlovsky) erupt into Penelope's overrun household:

> Well, the men,
> they give a lot of insults to anyone that comes by,
> wine running
> dancing with the maids, 112 people
> eating every day
>
> She comes and rages
> quit eating the coffee cake and cottage cheese
> put the lid on the peanut butter jar
> sandwiches made of cucumber, stop eating the *food!* (56)

In addition to the strain of managing households over which they wield little practical power, both Penelope and Kyger confront potentially unresolvable uncertainties in their love relationships. "Still after 15 years or more [Penelope] doesn't know/and may go off with the likeliest and most generous suitor." As wily as her husband, Penelope "never refuses or accepts/stands against the pillar of the house/watching and planning" (*T* 56). For her part, Kyger considers leaving Snyder, has dreams about him leaving her, and describes her husband's "I want a divorce movement" as "good for [her] developing sense of independence" (*JIJ* 229). Both women come to acquire agency in and through marital displacement.

Like Athena, the goddess who weaves, Kyger and her Penelope create art through acts of weaving—Kyger with words and images and Penelope with the "Bold/DESIGN" of her tapestry (*T* 28). As Russo argues, Penelope's craft "is like that of the poet who breaks from the tightly woven web of authoritative voices and follows up new strands" (195–96). Penelope's web and Kyger's poems disrupt already-known stories and unsettle the "phallomorphic privilege" undergirding them. In *The Tapestry and the Web,* Kyger's irreverent speaker attributes transformative power to Penelope's craft, "choos[ing] to think of her . . . concocting [Odysseus's] adventures" and "bringing/the misfortunes to him" (*T* 31). Together, Kyger and her Penelope unseat male authority and control, usurping the command of both the author and the hero of the *Odyssey.*

As represented in Homer's story, Penelope's waiting and weaving make her "a byword for marital fidelity and patience" (Grant and Hazel 271), but in *Tapestry* these activities appear active and willful, dangerous to the patriarchy they only appear to serve. Kyger's Penelope is inscrutable and possibly unfaithful:

> somewhere you can find reference to the fact that PAN
>   was the
> son of PENELOPE
>   Either as the result of a *god*
> or as a result of ALL of the suitors
>   who hung around while Odysseus was
>   abroad. (29)

The assertion that Penelope is Pan's mother deepens the palimpsestic play characterizing *The Tapestry and the Web,* allowing readers to catch glimpses of other potential stories bubbling up from beneath the authoritative narrative. At no point does the *Odyssey* entertain the possibility that Pan (who is associated with Acadia and whose parentage is usually attributed to the god Hermes and a wood nymph) is the son of Odysseus's wife. As Russo notes, Kyger elaborates on "an apocryphal reference" to Penelope sporting with the suitors as a means of overturning the "canonical myth" defining her through her faithfulness (188). Proposing this improbable mother/child relationship, Kyger imbues Penelope's life in/as waiting with the potential to unleash disorder and anarchy on a world organized around clear lines of patrilineage.

A second poem, "12.29 & 30 (Pan as the son of Penelope)," returns to this subversive scenario in more insistent detail:

> Refresh my thoughts of Penelope again.
>
> Just HOW
> solitary was her wait?
>
> I notice Someone got to her that
>
> barrel chested he-goat prancing
> around w/ his reed pipes
>
> is no fantasy of small talk.
> More the result of BIG talk
> and the absence of her husband.
>
> And what a cockeyed lecherous offspring. What a birth
> THAT must have been. Did she turn away &
> sigh? (31)

The "BIG talk" here is that of Kyger's poetic persona, who draws the "small talk" of little-known apocrypha from beneath Homer's text to construct transformative possibilities for women whose husbands are absent—whether at war or a week's sesshin.

The poem's next lines—"I believe she dreamed too much. Falling into her weaving,/ creating herself as a fold in her tapestry" (31)—present weaving, like waiting, as active and creative. These lines, which immediately follow the poem's speculation about the circumstances of Pan's birth, might imply that Penelope dreams herself into being as Pan's mother, making herself the source of an undisciplined, hedonistic energy that stands in opposition to the restoration of patrilineal order concluding Homer's *Odyssey*. "12.29 & 30 (Pan as the son of Penelope)" largely dismisses the question of Pan's father to render the "cockeyed lecherous" goat-god a manifestation of Penelope's self-creative weaving. The poem ends:

And where did she hide her impudent monster?

He was acres away by then I suppose in the sunlight leching
              at some round breasted sheep

girl.

    the cock crowing at dawn never had bigger thoughts than he did
    about waking up the world. (31)

Leaving Penelope's "impudent monster" nearby but out of reach, the poem
invests her creation with the potential to upend existing orders. Out of
the cast of characters inhabiting Kyger's revised epic, Pan seems the most
elusive, the freest and least constrained by the expectations of others, and
his impudence recalls the impertinence of the poem's narrating voice. In
an interesting entry in the *Journals,* Kyger imagines herself as Pan: "Last
night [Gary] leaves me again in my dreams. I pursue him—awake fret-
fully. Who runs away pursued by Pan?" (19). Joanne-as-Pan creates her
own chaos, subverting gender/power relations and becoming in a sense
the embodiment of her Penelope's weaving. Pan's unlikely yet insistent
presence in *Tapestry* and in Kyger's dreams emblemizes her project to
"wake up" a world lulled to sleep by status quo arrangements of power,
gender, and creative authority.

    Kyger further shakes up traditional pre-texts in the *Journals* and in *Tap-
estry* by blurring gendered boundaries between herself and Odysseus—
she identifies with his voyaging as well as with his wife's domestic plotting.
Kyger is like Penelope, but she is also like Odysseus, both travelers in foreign lands, both denied control of their routes and destinations; in both
cases, authority lies outside their purview—Snyder directs Kyger's travels,
while Odysseus's efforts to return to Ithaca are subject to the whims of the
gods. Nevertheless, both Kyger and Odysseus improvise ways to pursue
their own ends, primarily through their ability to manipulate language
and their willingness to don disguises, to act as tricksters. Odysseus "is a
liar / from the bottom of his heart" (*T* 53), and Kyger is a poet who reor-
ders both Beat and mythic discourses by playing with and on expectations
for female passivity and superfluity that consign women to the sidelines
of men's epic adventures.

    Tapestry's final "Odyssey poem" describes Odysseus as a "great
fighter / having a guide, a female presence who pulls her own self into battle" (61). In the *Odyssey,* Athena, the goddess who weaves, is the patroness
of Odysseus; she engineers his homecoming, provides his disguise, and
facilitates his reclamation of his kingdom. In *Tapestry,* Kyger is the "female

presence" guiding and shadowing Odysseus. She participates in his sea
journey, "steering a course close to shore where the / sound of breakers
could be heard through the fog" (16). She hears "a song in the rope taut
against the wind" and watches water "being pushed from both sides of
the boat / as we make our passage thru it" (32). In a parallel voyage, her
Odysseus partakes in her own homecoming, is "lift[ed]"

> asleep onto the land
> he has returned to
> and doesn't know where he is.
> outside of San Francisco
> the long paths and eucalyptus
> are another country (53)

In the *Tapestry* poem "Iliad: Achilles does not die," which adds to the
general disruption of Homer's saga by restoring life to Achilles and by
considering the possibility that "perhaps" Helen "dreamed it all," Kyger
explicitly connects her voyage to Japan with Odysseus's voyage to Troy:

> How big was the distance of Troy
> & the battlefield, the shoreline
> of ships—does it stretch as far
> as the city of Kyoto (42)

Kyger's journal entries for March 27 and March 28, 1960, demonstrate
that she experiences her travel in Japan through the eyes of her Odysseus.
First the material from Kyger's journal:

Sunday March 27.60

Married one month.
> Wakanoura: fishing village. Tile
covered roofs. The large fishing boats drawn upon the shore.
Naturally a jewel. But what else. (*JIJ* 17)

Monday 3.28.60
> these are thin rows planted by hand . . .
> run parallel.   no weaving.

Ladies gathering seaweed.
> . . . at fishing village enormous craft
being constructed solely of wood.   (Ulysses) (*JIJ* 18; ellipses
Kyger's)

And in *Tapestry*:

> They are constructing a craft
>   solely of wood
> at Waka-no-ura, fishing village,
>   a jewel quite naturally
> from the blue of the farm house tile roofs.
>
>   found on the southern coast.
>
> The women pull by hand long strings
>   of seaweed across the shore
> it dries
>
>   At the other end of the town
>   the hull of a boat rises
> above the smaller houses
> A little prince of a boy in a white knit suit
>   stands with the others in a group on the beach
>
> Watching us go by, we are strange.
>
>   The women bend over
> the seaweed, wakame, changing its face to the sun. (*Tapestry* 34)

Blurring boundaries between the places she occupies and the places oc-cupied by the questing Odysseus and the waiting Penelope, Kyger makes them all "strange." Penelope at her loom, Odysseus in his disguises, Kyger newly married in Japan, and the reader engaged with *Tapestry* experience dislocations in which "the real earth / moves and falls away into pieces" (*T* 53), revealing other truths.

Another *Tapestry* poem, "vision of heaven & hell," offers an explicit re-vision of reality that resists dualistic models organizing human under-standing of the "real" world:

> This goes all around again
>
> where heaven explodes the walls.
>   against the pattern of fleur-de
>   -lis and bulls, flowers, ladies sewing
>   marigolds
>   all part of doom—that's hell, all of the fantasy men
>   and women
>   underground

the ceiling of earth where hell pushes up
they are flowers
and spider webs.   minstrels with lute stories

spun out, *connected*
and put together (36)

Rather than adhering to a linear arrangement of above and below, realms "explode" into each other. Refusing to separate and contain heaven and hell, the tapestry of Kyger's poetics spins binaristic divisions into connectedness.

This vision of connectedness, also expressed in Kyger's simultaneous identification with Odysseus's exile and Penelope's entrapment, extends into her association with another mythic figure whose story involves both conditions. Multiple poems in *The Tapestry and the Web* invoke Persephone's movement between the underworld and the world of the living. In "we are in a tighter web," the speaker takes on a Persephone-like persona, observing:

there was a meadow flower from the mountains which was
promised me
and never brought.
But I am here now
only the spoken name is different now (*T* 30)

Persephone (the queen of the underworld), Kore (the maiden, Persephone before her abduction by Hades), and Demeter (her mother, the goddess of the Earth), often appear as three aspects of the same goddess, encompassing the full round of life. The Kore/Persephone/Demeter figure was at the heart of the Eleusinian Mysteries, which bridged the ultimate division—life and death. Like the "web" of associations Kyger draws between herself, Odysseus, Penelope, and Athena, her identification with the ever-shifting Persephone demonstrates her valuing of connection over separation, her desire for an aesthetic capable of articulating fluid possibilities for unbounded being.

Persephone's story also shapes Kyger's documentation of her life in Japan in the *Journals*. Her entry/poem of January 15, 1963, draws on Kore's transformation to Persephone to describe a sudden frost that kills her flowers. This abrupt change leads her to consider the consequences of freezing human relations into set structures.

Youth. no wrinkles.

At one point when we didn't know
we could have shifted easily / more or less
I suppose—

And now set, bland, firmly made walls
on into a great brown world.

Kore: seed that won't sprout.

she's asleep—she's in hell—
nothing grows, not
a thing—not of her own doing?
Mother does it.
because the daughter is gone, not a thing grows.

Give her back her goddammed daughter.
with one fell swoop the frost came, rotted
nasturtium line to
wet flat & mush

over night frozen stiff to limp in the
noon sun, big as it was, the yellow green-
leaf of the tropical plant. (*JIJ* 224)

Such entry/poems express Kyger's ongoing resistance to rigid walls erected
in unimaginative "brown worlds," walls that prevent "shifting" among different positions and possibilities. At other moments in the *Journals*, Kyger interprets her place in Japan in relation to the "terrible" Persephone,
queen of the underworld—"I destroy when I move scatter brained and
too fast. Dreadful. Kore leaves the earth. And her mature self—Demeter,
brings her back. Song gets caught in the throat too often. Poor Gary. The
messy kitchen table is heaven" (17). Like Persephone, Kyger moves between worlds and personas, seeking alternatives to either/or, tug of war
identity conflicts. In its deployment of intertextual exchange and transformation, her poetics interjects a creative and undisciplined difference into
established narrative expectations, asking readers to consider flexibility
and porousness as just as real, perhaps more real, than traditional models
of self-positioning.

"I Want to Write the World Upside Down"

Even as Kyger and her Penelope accede in some respects to dominant expectations and already-known pre-texts for female identity, their defiant creativity constructs alternatives that recast their roles as minor characters in stories of male accomplishment. Kyger writes and questions behind the scenes of Snyder's legend, and her Penelope "watch[es] and plan[s]" (56) and "dream[s] too much . . . creating herself as a fold in her tapestry" (31). Formulating a palimpsestic poetics of mobility and multiplicity, Kyger creates difference within what only appear to be binary, closed roles (Odysseus/man/explorer/hero, Penelope/woman/wife/ weaver) and positions (questing/mythic, domestic/personal), opening up her own apparently split situations as a Beat-associated woman writer.

Like her Penelope's weaving, Kyger's poetic self-representation enacts forms of defiant femininity that resist the expectations for female silence and self-effacement that keep women in invisible, subservient places, spoken for by others. In her practice of daily writing as "un-self-conscious open utterance," Kyger redistributes the discursive resources available to her, "writ[ing] the world upside down" (*JIJ* 30). Crafting art and identity out of displacement, disjuncture, and dissonance, she assembles a sustaining self-concept in and through poetic revision of the already-said. Her life-writing illuminates the displaced yet transformative positions occupied by a woman living an intertextual life in transitional times and contexts, breaking away from the norms of a not-at-all distant past, crafting a lexicon through which to construct sustaining and sustainable alternatives.

6 CROSS-TEXTUALITY
Joyce Johnson's *Minor Characters*
and *Door Wide Open*

*Somewhere inside me, waiting to make her appearance any minute now,
was the person I really was.*
　　　　　　　　　　　　　—JOYCE JOHNSON, *MINOR CHARACTERS*

*I'd grown up believing the widely held fallacy that love could conquer all,
and it would be a long time before I could let go of it, despite evidence
to the contrary. I was Beat, but I was also a woman of the 1950s, when
marrying the man one loved was the all-important goal.*
　　　　　　　　　　　　　—JOYCE JOHNSON, *DOOR WIDE OPEN*

*Canon . . . can be mined, not necessarily for the memory of some ready-
made self, but for one half-forgotten yet half-remembered in the cultural
fabric.*
　　　　　　　　　　　　　—MARY ORR, *INTERTEXTUALITY*

Penguin's 1999 edition of *Minor Characters* (1983) attributes two different subtitles to Joyce Johnson's memoir—*A Beat Memoir,* which appears
on the front cover, morphs into *A Young Woman's Coming-of-Age in the
Beat Orbit of Jack Kerouac* on the title page (fig. 10). Other editions carry
different subtitles. In 1996 it was *Life with Kerouac and the Beat Generation,* and on the original 1983 edition it was *A memoir of a young woman
of the 1950's in the Beat orbit of Jack Kerouac* (fig. 11). These shifting and
gender-inflected subtitles, which explicitly ascribe Beatness to Kerouac
while referring to Johnson in generic and generalizing terms, preview the
complexities of an intertextual life negotiated with/in discursive contexts
in which self and story intersect in multiple and often contradictory ways
with the narratives of an already-known social and literary movement.

　　The title that remains unchanged—the playful and ironic *Minor
Characters*—clearly references Johnson's secondary (at best) status in the
Beat pantheon, her discursive position as a small shadowed satellite in
"orbit" around a big, brightly burning star. "Minor" situates Johnson in
relation to Kerouac (a "major" character) and evokes the general popular association of Beatness and maleness, an association that renders
any female figure by definition a minor character.[1] The word "characters,"

which recalls the conventions of stories and storytelling, gestures toward the familiar canon of Beat literature and lore, and registers the displacements Johnson experiences as she encounters herself—or some aspect or approximation of herself—in the narratives of others. In addition, taken literally the word "characters" signifies plurality—more than one, multiple characters. In her memoir, Johnson numbers herself with other Beat-associated women but also characterizes *herself* as multiple; Joyce Johnson née Glassman appears as multiple characters in Beat pre-texts and in her own narrative.

Johnson's already-established position as a Beat "character" is evident in the paratextual apparatus of her memoir. The photograph on the front cover of the 1999 Penguin edition of *Minor Characters* features Kerouac in the foreground, handsome and in sharp focus, while Johnson stands off to the side and behind him, hazy and shadowed (fig. 10). Photograph-Johnson looks appreciatively at photograph-Kerouac, who does not return her gaze. This well-known photo is one of a number taken by Jerome Yulsman outside the Kettle of Fish, a Greenwich Village bar frequented by the New York Beats. Another photograph from this series appears on the cover of the original 1983 Houghton Mifflin edition (fig. 11). In this picture, Kerouac-the-Beat-iconoclast looks defiantly into the camera, chin lifted in a posture of challenge; Johnson stands behind him, a blurry figure with eyes closed and head slightly bowed.[2] Kerouac's prominence on the cover of the book makes it clear who is the major and who is the minor character in the memoir the reader is about to encounter.

Also present on the 1999 Penguin cover is a note/poem written by Kerouac, in which he addresses Johnson as "my Angel in a pink slip" and announces he has "gone on the road." Penguin's inclusion of this scrap of text in its cover art seems intended to call to mind Kerouac's legendary road life and, more indirectly perhaps, his status as a primary author of the Beat Generation. The note provides a frame for his relationship with Johnson, hinting at his simultaneous presence and absence in her life— the note puts him on his Beat road, leaving her to await his return, a sexualized figure in a pink slip.[3] While the note and photo locate Johnson in Kerouac's "orbit," these paratexts seem to ascribe the value and relevance of her memoir to her standing as his "angel." Promotional blurbs on the back cover perform similar functions. One describes *Minor Characters* as "the muse's side of the story" and asserts that "the muse could write as well as anybody." Another celebrates Johnson's "portraits and evocations . . . of both the major Beat voices and the minor characters, their women." A third characterizes *Minor Characters* as "realistic rather than flamboyant."

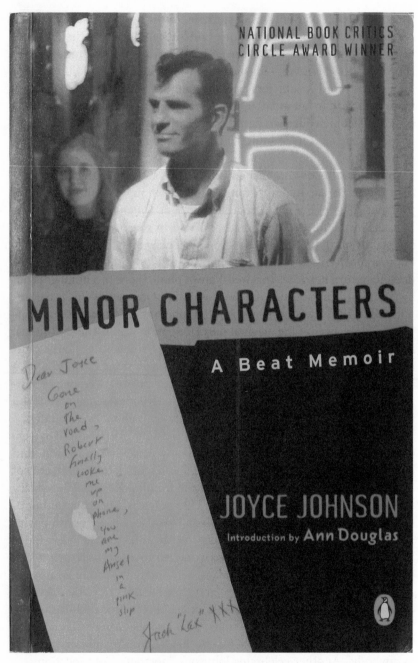

Fig. 10. Penguin 1999 *Minor Characters* front cover. (Cover photograph © Jerome Yulsman/Globe Photos)

Fig. 11. Houghton Mifflin 1983 *Minor Characters* front cover. (Cover photograph ©
Jerome Yulsman/Globe Photos)

Taken together, the blurbs induce a bit of cognitive dissonance; they present Johnson as a "real" Beat writer but simultaneously highlight her peripheral status as muse and minor character, notable primarily for her attachment to a better-known Beat man.

The paratexts around *Minor Characters* both place and displace Johnson as a Beat, and the direct and indirect references to gender in the title/subtitles, blurbs, and cover art indicate her dilemmas as a "Beat woman." In both *Minor Characters* and her later text *Door Wide Open: A Beat Love Affair in Letters, 1957–1958* (2000), Johnson searches out lexicons of defiant femininity to account for herself as simultaneously a product of her time and a girl who "dared to leave" its expectations behind (*MC* xxxiii). She is self-conscious about writing a female Beat identity post–women's movement; in fact, she credits the women's movement with prompting her "recognition that [her] story was important, that the story of the other women was important" ("AC" 113). But Johnson's attempts to articulate the importance of these stories come filtered through the often-reductive connotations of the "Beat woman" label, through Beat pre-texts (previous narratives) and pretexts (common clichés) that obscure or outright deny the importance of women's stories.

Johnson's project to recover women's lives from Beat nowheres has clear affiliations with second-wave feminism, but just as clearly necessitates conflict with the masculinist Beat mythos familiar to her readers. Her 1994 foreword to *Minor Characters*, which recounts the impetus that led to her write the memoir, implicitly acknowledges this contradiction: "I thought of the years I'd known Kerouac, the extraordinary men and women who had been part of my revolution—those who had survived and those who hadn't. But I could only tell their stories by telling my own" (xxxv). Johnson's invocation of Kerouac-the-Beat-icon encodes her own "minor" standing, and her use of the word "but" implies that she tells her story primarily as a means of getting to the more "extraordinary" lives he exemplifies. This statement, in other words, forces to the forefront the question of what makes Johnson's story both Beat and important. *Minor Characters* confronts this issue intertextually, interweaving her life and story with those other, "extraordinary" Beat figures, the texts they wrote, and the texts written about them.

Minor Characters and *Door Wide Open*, Johnson's compilation of letters, are self-consciously intertextual, in the sense that they purposefully and strategically absorb and transform Beat pre-texts and incorporate them as part of her story. Johnson's life-writing "mine[s]" the Beat canon for a self "half-forgotten yet half-remembered" in the "cultural fabric" (Orr 128) of the Beat Generation narrative. I characterize *Minor Characters* and *Door Wide Open* as *cross*-textual—they repeatedly cross paths with other narratives, constructing moments of intersection and exchange through quotation, allusion, and comparison. This strategy infuses palimpsestic complexity into already-known models of Beatness assembled around what Johnson perceives as unnecessary divisions between men and women.

In *Minor Characters,* Johnson cites and comments on the Beat "hagiography" (*MC* 126) constructed in texts ranging from articles and essays to fictional work and biographies. Her inclusion of poems, letters, material from novels, and snippets of autobiographical writing enables her to draw on the voices of Ginsberg, Kerouac, John Clellon Holmes, LeRoi Jones, Carolyn Cassady, and Elise Cowen, among others. To afford the reader more direct access to her younger self, Johnson quotes from her own journals, schoolwork, early fiction, letters, and poetry. *Minor Characters* is what Marko Juvan calls a "citational text," "one for which the reader can, in a given context of literary life," discern its author's use of pre-texts and "not only . . . recognize citational connections but . . . interpret them as an aesthetically and semantically relevant writing strategy" (146). Johnson intends the "citational connections" she builds into her narrative to unsettle her readers' confidence in the definitive standing of Beat pre-texts, to trouble what they think they know about the Beat Generation.

Johnson's *Door Wide Open: A Beat Love Affair in Letters, 1957–1958* is a mixed-genre text that reproduces letters she exchanged with Kerouac, interspersed with her commentary on the two-year relationship the letters document. The text also includes letters to and from others, including Cowen, as well as brief quotes from the correspondence of Beat figures such as Gary Snyder. References to *Minor Characters* and to Kerouac's letters to Ginsberg, Snyder, and Neal Cassady add layers of intertextual resonance to this already-known "Beat love affair," in overlapping and juxtaposed versions and interpretations of events and interactions.

Kerouac has first author credit for *Door Wide Open* and gets visual top billing on its front cover (fig. 12). A paratextual blurb from the *New York Times* appears to attribute the book's content to Johnson's "absorb[tion]" of "Kerouac's remarkable freedom." But the book focuses on the different views of "freedom" guiding Johnson's and Kerouac's Beat lives, and it was Johnson who assembled the text, piecing it together out of other texts and supplementing those pre-texts with her explanation and analysis. Moving between perspectives rooted in the 1950s and the late 1990s, she examines and interprets social, cultural, and historical contexts and explores shifting literary and artistic priorities and concerns from multiple vantage

A Beat

Love Affair

in Letters,

1957-1958

Door Wide Open

JACK KEROUAC & JOYCE JOHNSON
Introduction and Commentary by Joyce Johnson

"Wonderful . . . conveys Johnson's own
growth as a woman and writer in the
1950s, absorbing Kerouac's remarkable freedom."
—*The New York Times Book Review*

Fig. 12. Penguin 2000 *Door Wide Open* front cover. (Cover photograph © Bob
Henriques/Magnum Photos)

points. As reader of Kerouac's correspondence and composer of her own letters, commentary, and introduction, Johnson occupies a multifaceted authorial position, speaking as the young Joyce Glassman, as the older and wiser Joyce Johnson, and as a character—or characters—in texts by Kerouac and others.

Both *Minor Characters* and *Door Wide Open* quote others as a strategy of self-representation, offering cross-textual exchange as a model for understanding the evolution of individual identities. Mary Orr proposes that the meaning and authority of quotations rest not only in "who signs them" but also in "who circulates them" (33) and more, in "the why and how" of the circulation (132). While citational autobiography further opens already-overdetermined life stories to others' designations and definitions, it ultimately affords the author more agency in the absorption and transformation of pre-textual expectations. For Johnson, citation is less a matter of reference or only an attempt at appropriation, and more a means of "re-creat[ing] in the same but other words" (Orr 132). Orr views quotation as "the most condensed form of paradigm shift, transmuting the context, form and meaning of the items both inside and outside the quotation marks" (133). Quotation, she argues, constitutes "enrichment by inclusion, integration and proclamation of otherness, a dialogue not a monologue" (133). Johnson's dialogic citational practices enable her to enlist dominant notions of "the Beat Generation" and "the Beat woman" to reconfigure both concepts; her intertextual address to familiar Beat stories constructs alternatives to the already-known precisely in and through the already-known.

Cross-Textual Citation

Minor Characters opens with a cross-textual moment in which Johnson records her bemused perusal of a Beat artifact, a photograph memorialized in a book—a picture of Kerouac, Ginsberg, William Burroughs, and Hal Chase as they were before she knew them, dashingly young and vital. Leigh Gilmore describes this photo as a "pivotal intertext" (8) for Johnson, who, rather than dwelling on the photo's storied male subjects, invokes in her imagination people missing from the picture, among them "two girls, Edie Parker [Kerouac] and Joan Vollmer [Adams Burroughs]," whom she has "never seen pictures of . . . anywhere" (2). Johnson then consults the book's index, where she finds herself, or, rather, a version of a past self: "*Joyce Glassman*. And a half a dozen page references, having to do with approximately one-twentieth of my life, 1957–59, when I used to have that name" (6). Like the picture, the name in the index materializes as a cultural artifact, both familiar and unfamiliar. The photograph is familiar to Johnson not because she can place herself in the scene it captures, but because it has become iconic, part of the Beat mythos. The name in the index is similarly near and distant, the same but different, her yet not her, a trace of a past self she may or may not recognize. Situating Edie, Joan, and Joyce Glassman alongside, or rather, as in palimpsest, under the photograph, Johnson constructs a kind of intertextual metaphor for the memoir as a whole, signaling her intention to recast herself and other "minor characters," to pry Beat-associated women from their marginal positions in footnotes and indices.[4]

She goes about this project in part by constructing "simultaneities" (8) and imaginary intersections between her younger self and Kerouac, Ginsberg, Edie, and Joan. Noting that her family lived "not far" from Joan's "legendary" 115th Street apartment (4), she considers "the possibility that we passed each other hundreds of times in our everyday comings and goings. That Joan is the thin, dazed young woman wheeling her baby across Broadway; that it's Jack buying beer and cigarettes at Gristedes when my mother sends me out for tomato juice; or Allen with a notebook of early poems in his pocket ringing the doorbell of the famous professor Lionel Trilling ... who lives on the ground floor of our apartment house" (8). Creating places where their paths could have crossed as well as convergent attitudes and priorities, potential meetings-of-minds, Johnson weaves intertextual webs of association that extend Beatness beyond chronological timeline-based histories and biographies, positing an alternative, consociative Beat community.

In the process, she retells Beat stories, filling in blanks where minor characters reside and reimagining Beat legend and lore from the perspective of women who appear only as tangential figures in the dominant Beat narrative. Johnson points out that Edie and Joan provided "connective links between Jack and Burroughs and Allen and Lucien [Carr]" (2) and "set in motion" (11) relationships that brought the Beat Generation into being. Observing that Edie introduced Kerouac to Lucien Carr, she reconsiders their friendship from Edie's likely point of view, focusing on what she envisions as Edie's "unarticulated sadness" that she is "not enough" to satisfy Kerouac (9). Then, after noting that Edie was "presumably" (10) present when Carr rolled Kerouac through the New York streets in a barrel, Johnson pictures her "running after ... a little off to the side. She's telling herself she's having a swell time as she looks out for cops over her shoulder" (11). Johnson's imaginary Edie is "one of those girls who tries almost fatally hard to be a good sport," "determinedly spunky" as she "[tries] on a life that doesn't fit her" (3), a Beat life that has room for her only on the sidelines, as a spectator.

Much of Johnson's life-writing, along with many of her public statements about the Beat movement, wrestles with questions of how and why Beat life fits or does not fit women. On the one hand, she views women in large part as Beat misfits, out of place and often unwelcome in male-focused Beat contexts. On the other hand, she reformulates misfit circumstances as creative and potentially empowering, as engines of personal and cultural change. In particular, Johnson often uses comparisons between male and female experience to redefine misfit conditions as wellsprings of possible transformation. Her citational compare/contrast strategy acknowledges ways in which women do not fit the Beat norm even as it challenges the very notion that Beat can be contained within a singular, quantifiable norm or set of norms.

In *Minor Characters*, Johnson quotes from Holmes's preface to *Go*, in which he explains exactly which Beat men his male characters are meant to represent while dismissing his "girls" as "centerless," "amalgams of several people." He claims these "amalgams" are nevertheless "accurate to the young women of the time" (79). Johnson responds: "They were mere anonymous passengers on the big Greyhound bus of experience. Lacking centers, how could they burn with the fever that infected his young men? What they did, I guess, was fill up the seats" (79). Repeating this pattern of quotation and response throughout *Minor Characters*, Johnson redeploys familiar Beat pre-texts in ways that require readers to "simultaneously activate two textual worlds" (Juvan 70), to recognize alternative possibilities for Beatness in moments of intertextual coincidence and conflict.[5] In this instance, Johnson's comment about Holmes's "girls" calls to mind the chapter immediately preceding, which focuses on her reaction to his essay "This Is the Beat Generation"; she remarks that Holmes's depiction of Beat "bottled eagerness" reflects "exactly what" she and her close friend Elise Cowen feel, then asks: "Could we be somehow more a part of the Beat Generation than of the Silent one we'd been born into chronologically?" (71). Explicitly replacing chronologically based definitions of Beat identity with like-mindedness of the kind shared by Elise and Ginsberg—"that instant knowing which can exist like a mysterious current between two people" (75)—Johnson disputes "boy gang" (79) measures of Beat "fit."

Relying on her readers to recognize the disparity between Holmes's dismissal of Beat women as silent, "centerless" girls and her depiction of her own efforts to evade rigid and reductive labels, Johnson, like other life-writers included in this study, demands readers' active contributions to the formulation of an alternate Beat paradigm. Johnson's strategy of juxtaposing herself and Elise with Holmes's "girls" invites her readers to critique his easy disregard of women's experience and to question narratives and discourses that relegate women to positions of unimaginative passivity as bystanders, just along for the ride. Her reference to *Go* is just one instance of her deployment of pre-texts in ways that impel readers to cast a critical eye on the assumptions and caricatures through which the Beat movement has been represented.

Johnson's retellings of Beat stories also demonstrate that even "extraordinary" figures such as Kerouac do not quite fit the model of Beat they have been made to typify. Early in *Minor Characters,* she observes that Kerouac "seems to have" undertaken one of the journeys memorialized in *On the Road* "in mingled hope and desperation—an attempt to seek out a brand-new reality to match fantasy. He was looking, he said, for 'girls, visions, everything; somewhere along the line the pearl would be handed to me.'" She responds: "It's strange to go looking for visions. It seems more in the nature of visions to come upon you, seizing you unawares. If you look for them, they tend to recede, lead you a little farther on" (22). Invoking a well-known line from Kerouac's most famous text, Johnson draws on familiar Beat associations to defamiliarize and destabilize the male-coded Beat road ethos. In fact, she asserts that the "everything" Kerouac sought, the receding possibility of a world commensurate with his dreams, "was not to be found" (22). And she further attributes his failure to live a "successfully rootless" life to his ties to his mother, which, she asserts, "were like iron in his soul" (23–24). The Beat travel legend, she implies, is exactly that—an intertextual fantasy that makes countercultural heroes out of men with everyday flaws, foibles, and fears.

Johnson does admit to feeling the lure of Beat travel and reports making plans to join the always-moving Kerouac—first in San Francisco, then in Mexico. These plans fall through, she explains in *Door Wide Open,* in large part because Kerouac does not remain satisfied with any place for long. Interpreting his restless movement as a form of flight (*DW* 21), the young Joyce Glassman writes him: "I just wish you'd find some place in the world where there's some comfort for you and where whatever demon it is that pursues you from city to city can't find you" (*DW* 51). Johnson uses Kerouac's texts to contrast what she views as his compulsive wandering with her sense of belonging within an expansive and enriching Beat community. Countering assumptions that "real" Beats live road lives, she highlights the freedoms she enjoys in her more-rooted existence in New

York, where a "remarkable convergence . . . of young avant-garde painters, writers, actors, dancers, jazz musicians" both signals and facilitates "an enormous shift in the culture." This is not, she concludes, "the moment to be in Mexico" (*DW* 52). Given this context, her choice to stay, she indicates, is just as Beat as his decision to go.

In *Door Wide Open* and *Minor Characters,* Johnson describes her Beat bohemia as the site of a fulfilling alternative to the stifling expectations of femininity enforced by her parents, who expect her to live as if "looking out at the world from behind a sheet of glass" (*DW* xiii). Recalling Kerouac's plan to "rent a small house and settle down" with his mother, she exclaims: "He wanted to live with his *mother?* Having struggled so hard to get away from mine, I couldn't believe it" (*DW* 22). *Minor Characters* and *Door Wide Open* examine at length Kerouac's relationship with his mother, often drawing on material from his novels and letters to analyze his "primal" (*DW* 80) issues with Gabrielle Kerouac, whom her son referred to as Mémère. In *Minor Characters,* Johnson recalls finding in *The Subterraneans* evidence indicating that Kerouac's mother "possessed his soul," leaving "all other women" to "[flitter] across his consciousness like shadows" (227). Her commentary on his letters in *Door Wide Open* points out that he frequently organized his travel to accommodate his mother; she speculates that "by never staying with any woman very long . . . he'd remained faithful to Memere [*sic*] in his fashion" (xviii). Contrasting Kerouac's "suffocating life with his mother" (*DW* 146) with the open, unfettered life she creates in New York, Johnson challenges and reformulates the usual terms of comparison between male and female Beats.

She addresses readers' likely expectations about what constitutes a Beat life by linking then unlinking her own and Kerouac's experiences. Discussing her composition of *Minor Characters,* she explains: "I knew I had to tell the reader about Jack's life" in a way that "wouldn't interrupt the memoir. Then I hit upon the device of following myself and following him as two separate streams, then converge. Then, we diverge at the end" ("AC" 113). *Minor Characters* juxtaposes Kerouac's movement around the country with Johnson's movement into Greenwich Village and her explorations of bohemian sexuality, creativity, and intellectualism, simultaneously merging and separating their Beat lives. *Door Wide Open* similarly tracks Kerouac's travel alongside descriptions of Johnson's experience in New York's Beat bohemia. This structuring principle implies, as Johnson has asserted elsewhere, that while most Beat women "never got the chance to literally go on the road," their "road instead became the strange lives [they] were leading" ("BQ" 48). Nevertheless, she clearly understands that this redefinition of Beat "roads" falls outside her readers' frames of reference, and, spliced together in her life-writing, her road and Kerouac's road appear in not just different, but often opposed terms.

Johnson uses cross-textual means to address this gendered split in Beat lifestyles, constructing comparisons between herself and Kerouac, and between her self-concept and Kerouac's view of her, which she often uses his texts to articulate. Recounting the moment Kerouac asked to stay with her in her New York apartment, Johnson quotes him quoting her: "'If you wish,' I say in *Desolation Angels*, deciding fast. And I know how I said it, too. As if it was of no great moment, as if I had no wishes of my own—in keeping with my current philosophy of nothing-to-lose, try anything" (*MC* 129). This citational passage references an episode with which readers are likely familiar, but adds nuances that remain invisible in Beat legend and in *Desolation Angels*. Extricating her younger self from her object-position as a character in Kerouac's novel and a cipher in the index of Beat history, Johnson reframes and redistributes her own words—"if you wish" might seem to cede agency to Kerouac, but the "try anything" philosophy underwriting her response encapsulates Joyce Glassman's revolutionary departure from 1950s scripts for women.

In *Minor Characters*, Johnson recalls her frustration with Kerouac's inability to recognize her defiant femininity and his refusal to acknowledge elements of like-mindedness between them. She maintains that for her younger self, "too, freedom and life seemed equivalent" (137), but Kerouac doggedly insists that "what [she] really wanted were babies. That was what all women wanted and what [she] wanted too, even though [she] said [she] didn't" (136). Quoting Kerouac's description of her upon their first meeting—"An interesting young person . . . A Jewess, elegant middleclass sad and looking for something—she looked Polish as hell"—she wonders: "Where am I in all those funny categories?" (128). Pointing to "categories" imposed on her by others, Johnson asks readers of her memoir, readers who have been following her search for freedom, to register the displacements that come with being defined from the outside.

Johnson represents her younger self as an improvisational work in progress, a young woman trying on various models of identity, none of which fit her easily or completely. On workdays, for example, she assumes an "office identity" (*MC* 118) that imperfectly conceals the "unacceptable self" she "let[s] out . . . after five" (*MC* 148). Declaring that as a writer she "live[s] life to the hilt as [her] unacceptable self, just as Jack and Allen had done" (*MC* 148), she lays claim to the identity that most fully expresses the person she wants to make of herself. This defiant writer-self, however, is in competition with other versions of Joyce Glassman, manifested in others' commentary on her life choices and on her position in Kerouac's life.

When Kerouac, who calls her his "little secretary in his letters," observes that if he "had to go and apply for jobs like you, they'd have to drag me into Bellevue in two days" (*MC* 205), she seems to agree, musing: "How Beat could I actually be, holding down a steady office job and writing a novel about an ivy-league college girl on the verge of parting with her virginity?" (*MC* 205). In *Door Wide Open,* however, she remarks that although she "wouldn't have dreamed of standing up to read a chapter of my 'college novel'" at Beat literary events, "in spirit, I knew it was Beat" (68). The Beat self she understands as revolutionary is not visible to Kerouac or to those who believe "real writers would be out hopping freight trains" (*MC* 205). Johnson readily admits she has no desire to hop trains, "too innately cautious," she explains in *Door Wide Open,* "to go on the road impetuously and find myself in a situation where I lacked the resources to be self-sufficient" (27). Her characterization of her younger self as "innately cautious" leaves unspoken (for the moment, at least) the extent to which female "self-sufficiency" is itself defiantly uncautious in "the bland and sinister 1950s" (*DW* xv).

In its detailed exploration of Johnson's bohemia, her life-writing situates readers in a position to recognize the loss of possibilities for creative community that results from Beat men's failure to recognize women as fellow artists and rebels or to acknowledge the prismatic and contradictory facets of bohemian women's experience. Kerouac's "paternal and rejecting" (*MC* 253) stance, echoed in the texts and behaviors of other Beat men, reduces the complexities of Johnson's experience to caricatures of femininity, caricatures with which she struggles as both constituting and obscuring her identity. "The girl Joyce Glassman" (*MC* 261) does indeed spend her weekdays as a secretary but is also a self-fashioned writer at work on a novel for which she has received an advance from an established publishing house.[6] She has rejected traditional gender role arrangements yet avoids "old-ladyhood" as "the mainstay of someone else's self-destructive genius" (*MC* 170) primarily, it seems, because Kerouac turns her down for the job. "I was Beat," she explains, "but I was also a woman of the 1950s, when marrying the man one loved was the all-important goal" (*DW* 153). Joyce Glassman aspires to throw off the "silent generation" label applied to her peer group but is prone to self-effacement, "sitting by" in "silence" while "the voices of the men, always the men, passionately rise and fall" (*MC* 48, 262), conceptualizing new possibilities for art and culture, possibilities that could change the world.

Even as Johnson acknowledges the conflicts and discomforts occasioned by pre-scripted models of female and Beat identity, she highlights her younger self's participation in more muted Beat conversations and in unexpected moments of connection and consensus. In *Door Wide Open*, she calls on *Desolation Angels* to refute commentators' "weird paraphrases of passages from *Minor Characters*" that seem "calculated to show that what happened between [herself and Kerouac] had no more substance than the bumping together of two strangers in a subway car" (xxii):

> Although our relationship proved to be less than I had hoped,
> for Jack, it became a far more significant part of his life than the
> passing encounter he and Allen Ginsberg had initially intended.
> Between Jack's visits to me in New York, we'd write to each other.
> In putting words down on paper, we became more than lovers—
> we became friends. ("I had me a companion there," he would later
> write in *Desolation Angels*, as if the experience were a novelty for
> him.) I did not want to admit to myself that love was very threaten-
> ing to Jack; friendship was far more durable. (xviii)

Johnson and Kerouac are often geographically distant and hold divergent opinions about what women want or should want, but their discursive exchanges in their letters, she proposes, create a different sort of relationship, something "boy gang" notions of Beat cannot express or recognize. Remarking that "there were no models" for "the odd kind of relationship [they] were having" (*DW* xviii), Johnson presents their friendship as a creative and rewarding foray outside both Beat and mainstream norms.

In her life-writing, Joyce Johnson née Glassman emerges as multiple characters in her own narratives, in Beat pre-texts, and in the discourses of others. Signing her texts "Joyce Johnson," she reminds readers that the "I"s of *Minor Characters* and *Door Wide Open* mark the places of other "Joyces," different incarnations of an experimental, palimpsestic self. Gillian Thomson observes that "Johnson's quest for female independence is a transformation which is never convincingly complete" (par. 6). But human transformations are necessarily incomplete and ongoing, and transformations that engender change within reluctant socials orders are often both partial and precarious. Early in *Minor Characters*, the young Joyce Glassman awaits the "appearance" of "the person [she] really was" (85). That person never quite materializes, leaving Johnson to write an intertextual identity marked by "a permanent sense of impermanence" (*MC* 262). Notably, she does not understand impermanence as equivalent to lack or loss. Instead, her occupation of diverse pre-textual categories of identity, her construction of tentative alternatives, and her felt inconsistencies and ambiguities present a multiplicity and mutability that recast the misfit "Beat woman" as the unquantifiable outcome of creative improvisation.

Cross-Textual Dissonance

A primary source of conflict in Johnson's life-writing, as noted above, involves the tensions generated by representations of her younger self as a female iconoclast *and* as a "naively, dangerously romantic" girl (*DW* 153). She asserts that girls who left home for Beat bohemia lived bold, "brave" lives—they "flew out the door," she writes in her foreword to *Minor Characters*, with "no usable models for what [they] were doing." At the same time, she stresses the impossibility of breaking from hegemonic gender codes. "Naturally," she continues, "we fell in love with men who were rebels . . . believing they would take us along on their journeys and adventures. We did not expect to be rebels all by ourselves. . . . Once we had found our male counterparts, we had too much blind faith to challenge the old male/female rules" (xxxii, xxxiii).

Johnson's "male/female rules" locate "natural" performances of gender in the traditional heterosexual romance plot, which Rachel Blau DuPlessis has identified as a "deep, shared" structure of culture (2). Even though almost no one's "experience exactly fits the normative model of romance," as Susan Strehle and Mary Paniccia Carden note, "in the register of ideology, commonly held notions of civilization, humanity, and identity remain grounded in the structures of heterosexual union" (xi). In the United States of the 1950s, everything around girls and women—social arrangements, cultural institutions, books, art, music, media—presented the path from love to marriage to family as the only viable route to a successful, worthwhile life. According to dominant cultural scripts for female identity, Joyce Glassman's desire to be "anchored" to Kerouac (*MC* 219) is both expected and necessary; in Beat contexts, however, her longing for a commitment from him is "shameful" (*MC* 219) and her need for his love is "embarrassingly conventional" (*DW* xviii). Johnson's life-writing draws on the "iconography of love, the postures of yearning, pleasing, choosing, slipping, falling, and failing" (DuPlessis 2), to tell stories that encode both conformity and opposition to Beat and more mainstream expectations for female behavior and aspiration. For Johnson, as for many female autobiographers, heterosexual romance is "*critical* in all the multiple senses of the word"—it functions as "a central or foundational notion, an analytical and even combative stance," and "a crisis point" (Strehle and Carden xxv;

italics added). Faced with opposed models of identity for women and for Beats, Johnson seeks out alternative possibilities in the gaps and dissonances that result from simultaneous identification with traditional and Beat plots.

Although the familiar iconography of heterosexual romance in large part provides the lens through which Johnson views her experience in *Minor Characters* and *Door Wide Open,* both texts widely exceed the parameters of traditional love plots. Far from focusing exclusively on Johnson's position in "the Beat orbit of Jack Kerouac," these texts prioritize the young Joyce Glassman's search for her own voice and pursuit of a self-created life as a writer. Additionally, both memoirs highlight her determination to evade the "sheltered life" planned for her by her parents (*DW* xiii), her willingness to endure hardship and social opprobrium in order to maintain her independence.

Minor Characters traces in detail Johnson's evolution from childhood into resistant young womanhood and emphasizes her formative friendships with other bohemian women, especially Elise Cowen. Earlier, I noted Johnson's narrative "device of following [her]self and following [Kerouac]" as a structuring principle for her life-writing in *Minor Characters;* it should be recognized, however, that Johnson devotes significant portions of *Minor Characters* to following Elise, her closest friend and confidant. Both aspiring writers, the two young women enter the New York Beat scene together, opting to live sexually open, experimental lives; each endures a potentially fatal abortion and faces the dangers of being without the protection and sanction of traditional familial structures, exposed to hostile stares and condemning voices. Johnson's portrayal of their friendship presents this relationship—a relationship characterized by "conversations of . . . inexhaustible intimacy" (53), a relationship both irrelevant and invisible in the dominant Beat story—as more constitutive of her Beat identity than any other single factor, including her "love affair" with Kerouac.

Door Wide Open: A Beat Love Affair in Letters similarly portrays Johnson's refusal of pre-scripted possibilities for women as in large part a function of her friendship with Elise. A "disaffected duo" ("BQ" 44), Johnson and Elise negotiate Beat bohemia's gendered exclusions, share the strain of employment in the "straight" world, and see possibilities in each other. Together, they discover the Five Spot and "[roam] the Village and Lower East Side" (*DW* 14, 155). When Elise "abscond[s]" to San Francisco, she leaves Johnson "disoriented," writing to Kerouac that she "feel[s] as though someone took a pencil and drew a black line across [her] life"

(*DW* 162, 163). Johnson's choice of the title *Door Wide Open* for a text focused on letters documenting her relationship with Kerouac echoes a telegram she sent him assuring him of his welcome in her apartment and her life (*DW* 21; *MC* 151), but at the same time carries undertones of her defiant self-concept—her openness to new experience and "try anything" philosophy (*DW* xii; *MC* 129), a philosophy developed in company not with Jack Kerouac but with Elise Cowen.

Viewing her younger self through the partial and fractured lens of romance, Johnson critiques the coercive centrality of heterosexual union in the formation of female identities and in cultural conceptualizations of women's potential for success, pleasure, and self-actualization. Her split stance as a late twentieth-century autobiographer telling a 1950s story creates a textual "palimpsest of present attention and past deed" (Douglas xxviii). Entwining her Beat story with a misfit romance, an irregular, uncooperative story of what from a traditional "happily-ever-after" perspective can only be understood as a failed "love affair," Johnson widens possibilities for productive interactions between men and women and asserts that love relationships that do not proceed according to the dominant script nevertheless have enduring meaning and value.

Johnson presents her relationship with Kerouac as itself intertextual, framed by Beat and larger U.S. social discourses. The "love affair," she suggests in *Door Wide Open*, was precipitated not only by her "faith" in the traditional heterosexual plot but also by Kerouac's discursive presence in her world. Before actually meeting him in person, Johnson encounters him as a locus of desire in multiple contexts. In mainstream media, she comes across a *Mademoiselle* article featuring a photo of him "look[ing] as if he were passing through fire" that makes her "[want] to meet him" (*DW* xii). As she immerses herself in Greenwich Village life, Kerouac emerges as a major character in the Beat narrative being assembled by her bohemian contemporaries; he becomes "an almost palpable presence" brought to life by "everyone['s]" talk about him and the things he "was said" to have done (*DW* xi). And when she reads his first novel, *The Town and the City*, she feels that the book "was reading [her], that Kerouac could have told [her] story." At this moment, she writes, she "know[s]" she "could love him" (*DW* xvii). While what seems to be her fated meeting with her "male counterpart" (engineered, she emphasizes, by Ginsberg) echoes the happily-ever-after promises of the romance plot, it causes friction and discontinuities in her Beat plot.

Although Joyce Glassman does not seem particularly interested in the niceties of "society's perfum'd marriage," to use Ginsberg's terms (*MC* 79), she dearly wants a love relationship with Kerouac. It is clear, however, that such a relationship would hamper her independence and interfere with Kerouac's "boy gang" lifestyle (*MC* 79). Painfully aware that the male-centered Beat ethos renders romance unredeemably uncool, the young Joyce Glassman carefully revises her letters and scripts her behaviors, performing Beat cool and muffling her own needs in order to avoid revealing the depth of her feeling for Kerouac. At the same time, she assumes traditional female caretaking roles in her interactions with him, cooking for him when he is in New York and handling his correspondence and "errands" when he is on the road (*DW* 134). Like her imagined Edie Parker Kerouac, who "tries almost fatally hard to be a good sport" (*MC* 3), Johnson sacrifices her own plans to "try on" Kerouac's version of Beat life. She puts her novel on hold during his visits to New York, because she "want[s] to be with him more than [she] want[s] to be at the typewriter" (*MC* 243). Spending her nights waiting "around to get him out of places where he'd stayed too long and drunk too much" (*MC* 190), she fashions herself into a welcoming way station and source of respite, steadying and sustaining him as he faces the glare of celebrity accompanying the success of *On the Road.*

The young Joyce Glassman offers Kerouac her love, which he rejects in letters that seem intended to show her she "will never be permitted to know" him (*MC* 220). "Don't OWN me," he writes, "just be my nice little blonde friend and dont be sad because I'm a confirmed bachelor & hermit" (*DW* 161). But even as she tailors a "nice little blonde friend" sort of Joyce Glassman to meet Kerouac's expectations, "rewriting" her letters to edit "out the hurt parts, the phrases that might give [her] away" (*DW* xxv), she proposes alternative modes of interaction in friendship and like-mindedness. Her letters articulate connections between them and prod him to recognize other possibilities for male/female relationship. "I don't want to 'own' you," she responds, "but if we come together when we both want to do that and we truly swing, then that's okay, isn't it? (And I don't mean it has to be fun, fun, fun all the time—I love you equally when you're bugged.) But just one word of warning—I am *not* Allen Ginsberg! I think he's terrific in his way, but we're different. And you must learn to be more of a Frenchman and say 'Vive la difference!'" (*DW* 162). While the young Joyce Glassman seeks a "different" kind of relationship, answerable to neither the Beat boy gang nor the norms governing traditional heterosexual romance, she recognizes that no model exists that would facilitate its enactment.

In *Minor Characters,* Johnson emphasizes this lack of alternative plots for male/female interaction by weaving the unsuccessful love stories of other female "good sports" into her own. She uses her citational compare/contrast strategy to analyze women's investment of self-concept in their relationships with Beat men and to critique Beat's uneven gendered differentials of personal worth. However, her view of other women within Beat communities often comes filtered through those differentials, creating textual paradoxes—palimpsestic narrative situations in which she speaks in layered tones of solidarity and censure when telling the stories of women who have lost at love.

Recounting Carolyn Cassady's failed romance, Johnson does not overtly acknowledge that Carolyn's story contains parallels with her own—especially her younger self's desire for a commitment from Kerouac and her reluctant awareness that the heterosexual romance plot and the male-focused Beat plot are fundamentally incompatible. Johnson observes that the overburdened Carolyn vests her happiness in her husband, Beat icon Neal Cassady, even though his "frenetic wanderings" (90) make clear his dissatisfaction with all that the happily-ever-after romance promises—love, companionship, and the intimacy of a home life. Quoting Carolyn's description of her brief sexual relationship with both Kerouac and Cassady as "a season of singing days and nights" in which she "was a *part* of all they did" (89–90), Johnson speculates that this moment of inclusion is "as close as Carolyn Cassady ever gets to bliss" (90). Like Carolyn, whom men are "always disappearing on" (89), Joyce Glassman endures her lover's prolonged absences and watches from the sidelines as Beat men engage in "pursuit of the heightened moment, intensity for its own sake, something they apparently find only when they're with each other" (171). At such moments, Johnson's commentary both points to women's culturally prompted inability to fully embrace independence and indicts Beat for stranding them in secondary roles that leave them with few options beyond those offered by pre-scripted cultural plots for female fulfillment.

Minor Characters presents secondary, sideline positions as a shared condition of Beat women's lives. Describing Elise Cowen's consuming and unremitting love for Allen Ginsberg, Johnson remarks: "Elise was a moment in Allen's life. In Elise's life, Allen was an eternity" (78). When Ginsberg stops trying to adhere to the heterosexual norm, embraces his homosexuality, and goes on the road with Peter Orlovsky, he leaves Elise to "[subsist] on" his correspondence (123), a situation that echoes Johnson's on-again off-again "love affair" with the always-traveling Kerouac. Where Johnson makes willing sacrifices in her affair with Kerouac, Elise enters into love relationships with "self-abnegating devotion" (58), "[giving] herself over" completely and "asking nothing" in return (61). Johnson derives some satisfaction from her knowledge that Kerouac valued her friendship and loved her as much as he was able, but asserts that Elise finds "only confirmation of worthlessness" (76) in her love relationships.[7]

Throughout *Minor Characters,* Johnson remarks on Elise's physical appearance, noting and describing features that fall outside cultural standards of female beauty—she wears "unbecoming" clothing and scrapes her hair "ungraciously . . . back with a rubber band." Acne "flare[s] under the ragged bangs on her forehead," and her eyes confront others "sorrowfully and fiercely" from "behind her black-rimmed glasses" (51). Elise does not attempt to make herself appealing to the male gaze or to mask the honesty of her own gaze to meet behavioral standards of feminine reticence and agreeability. Johnson's narrative draws implicit comparisons between Elise and the young Joyce Glassman, described by Elise as "so girl beautiful" (258) in a poem found after her suicide.

These juxtapositions seem to suggest that had Elise been more conventionally feminine, she might not have remained mired in the fallout of failed affairs, suffered endless reenactments of her "worthlessness," and felt herself always an unwanted outsider. These juxtapositions might also suggest that Johnson's nearer performances of culturally intelligible femininity assist in her survival of her "revolution." In *Minor Characters,* the many areas of overlap between Johnson and Elise position Elise as Johnson's dark double, emblematic of the destruction wrought by powerful and pervasive ideologies that make women worthy of love and belonging only to the extent they are pleasing to men.[8] Johnson's response to this notion is multifaceted: she seems to outwardly reject it and to unconsciously accept it, to critique it but not quite detach her view of self and others from it.

Her account of Edie Parker Kerouac's failed romance conveys a set of conflicted concerns about female self-concept and about the social consequences for women involved in unsuccessful love relationships. Noting that Edie saved Kerouac from jail, Johnson remarks on her status as "a heroine in Jack's legend"; in romantic "fiction," she knows, Edie would have "won him forever." Instead, she loses Kerouac, marries "a midwestern businessman," and subsides into a mundane existence in which she no longer "feel[s] alive" (189). As presented by Johnson, Edie's options appear painfully limited—neither Beat life nor conventional life seems to "fit" her.

Johnson introduces Edie's nowhere position in the first chapter of *Minor Characters,* noting her disappearance from "literary biographies" (3) of the Beat Generation after her separation from Kerouac and quoting from a "pathetic letter" she wrote to Ginsberg, "imploring him for a list of books 'like the ones you first read,'" apparently in the hope that "by becoming an imitation Allen, intellectually, she can prove herself worthy and get Jack back" (3). Returning to the question of "what became of Edie" (3) in a later chapter, she acknowledges that Edie's "dreams of marriage" (9) are not so different than those of her younger self. Chapter 11 references another letter from Edie, this one addressed to Kerouac, in which she expresses her desire to accompany him "on the world tour she thought he was surely going to make" after the success of *On the Road* (189). The young Joyce Glassman, who shares Edie's "futile hopes of holding on to [Kerouac]" (11), perceives this second letter as "a telescope through which [she] could glimpse some point in the future in which there would be no Jack but only [her] and some different life [she] could not imagine" (189). Edie haunts *Minor Characters,* representative of a double-bind in which women's continuing investment of self-worth in "dreams of marriage" is both self-defeating and unavoidable.

Reviewing the course of her Beat experience and taking up the question of where she "fits" in Beat stories, Johnson resists aligning herself with Edie but is more willing to identify with Joan Burroughs, antiheroine of what is probably the most famously failed Beat romance. She describes Joan as a natural bohemian—a "daring witty" woman who "match[es]" William Burroughs "wit for wit" (5, 3), "startling the men by holding her own in their discussions" (4). Johnson admires the "family" of "ecstatic" outsiders (4, 5) that coalesces in Joan's 115th Street apartment, and attributes the formation of this alternative community in large part to the magnetic pull of Joan's "inner radiance" and the compelling like-mindedness she shares with Burroughs (4). But Joan's willingness to "follow" her husband "into anything" (4), Johnson asserts, ultimately extinguishes her "sharp, glittering" light (3). Mourning Joan's descent into addiction and her death at Burroughs's hand, Johnson regrets that the full complexity of her life has never been acknowledged or explored. Instead—like Edie, who "vanishes" from the Beat Generation narrative (8), and like Joyce Glassman, who appears only as a "minor character" in Kerouac's story—Joan has been subsumed into "the prehistories of the Beats," where she appears as a tragic and inscrutable figure in Burroughs's legend, "the man who played William Tell with his wife and missed" (5).

Johnson allocates considerable space in the opening chapter of *Minor Characters* to a retelling of the events that led to Joan's death, attempting to envision her life with Burroughs from what she imagines to be Joan's perspective. She speculates that Joan challenged her husband to shoot a glass from her head as a "demonstration of her faith and trust" (5) in the man she loved. In this interpretation, Joan's participation in that infamous game of William Tell constitutes an act of "blind devotion" rather than a capitulation to "despair" (5). This scenario posits a fatally narrow range of choice for a woman who, Johnson declares, is "as familiar to me as another woman very like her whom I once knew and loved, and as alien as the person who still lives on in the most dangerous depths of myself" (MC 5–6). Devoting the first chapter of Minor Characters to Joan and Edie, Johnson prefaces her own story with pointed illustrations of the enduring power of hegemonic discourses of gender and "dangerous" models of female identity that, she shows, remain intractably entrenched in women's psyches — even in alternative communities, even after enormous cultural shifts.[9]

Like Johnson, all of the women profiled in Minor Characters negotiate their individual desires and aspirations within intertextual fields composed of conflicting cultural scripts, social structures, and ideological expectations associated with Beatness and with prevailing gender norms. Although they choose to seek freedom in alternative communities, Beat women are represented, categorized, and judged (then and now) in terms of their importance to men — as Johnson's conflicted, layered retellings of their stories demonstrate. The women Johnson includes in her autobiography resist the 1950s "feminine mystique" but have internalized traditional models of female identity and invested their self-worth in Beat cultures that privilege male autonomy. The results, Johnson stresses, are often tragic — Carolyn left behind with children to support, Joan shot by her husband, Elise killed by her sense of worthlessness, Edie vanished and forgotten. However, some failed love stories, including that of Johnson and of her friend Hettie Jones, lead to more affirmative outcomes. For them, failure at love opens space for differently satisfying ever-afters.

Johnson describes the young Hettie Jones as a "woman in love" who willingly devotes herself to her husband and his literary career, cheerfully standing on "freezing street corners" to promote his poetry readings (212). "She writes poetry herself," Johnson observes, "but . . . never stood up with it at a reading of her own — makes no particular mention of it, in fact — telling herself it isn't good enough" (212–13). After her marriage to LeRoi Jones ends dramatically and painfully, with his "vitriolic abandonment" of the Beat community and "public denunciations of his wife" (216), Hettie goes on to establish her own identity as a writer, finally reclaiming "poems . . . kept mute in boxes for too many years" (262). Johnson asks: "Would Hettie have become a writer herself if her marriage hadn't broken up? How long would I have lasted as Mrs. Jack Kerouac, coping with Jack's heartbreaking alcoholism and his jealous Mémère?" She concludes that "sometimes the unhappy endings of love stories turn out to be the right ones" ("BQ" 48). Although Johnson's life-writing carries a residue of mourning for the love relationship her younger self hoped to establish with Kerouac, she is clear that she, like Hettie, lives a more fulfilled and creative life than the married woman she had wanted to be could have envisioned.

Johnson proposes that failed Beat romance plots carry possibilities for different forms of fulfillment that have remained unspoken and unaccounted for in Beat Generation histories. Carolyn Cassady, for instance, remains "lifelong friends" with Kerouac (*MC* 90), and Johnson and Hettie Jones not only develop an enduring friendship but also encourage each other to convert the wreckage of their love relationships into opportunities for creative self-expression in their poetry, fiction, and life-writing. Even Joan, Johnson believes, sparkled for a time in the "magical intensity" of "brilliance refracting against brilliance" (*MC* 4) within the community she gathered together on 115th Street.

Finally, Johnson credits Kerouac with providing her access to aspects of life ordinarily off-limits for young women (*MC* 138–39) and with fostering her self-confidence as a writer, with accepting her and treating her as a fellow artist. The voice of her younger self, she remarks, "began to stretch and change" in her letters to him (*DW* xxv). Kerouac might not have come through with the romantic commitment Joyce Glassman "had resolved never to ask for," but Joyce Johnson insists that "the reader" recognize the value of what he did "give" her in their discursive exchanges, when he wrote "to a very young woman as an equal, someone strong enough to take the truth." He "generously recognized the writer in her" and "never boxed her in" (*DW* xxv). Telling the familiar story of love won and lost, Johnson proposes that who she is and was in relation to Kerouac need not be circumscribed by the parameters of romantic plotting, the limited and limiting views of others, or even the burden of her own "embarrassingly conventional" desire.

Cross-Textual Identities

In Beat communities, Joyce Glassman, Hettie Jones, Elise Cowen, Edie Kerouac, Joan Burroughs, and other Beat-associated women are simultaneously revolutionaries and "minor characters," heroines of the avant-garde and not "good enough" to merit recognition as Beat artists and innovators. Johnson's life-writing proposes that Beat women's self-concepts develop within contexts that constitute both an uncomfortable double bind and a fruitful in-between space. Such liminal spaces, in her estimation, open possibilities for defiant femininities that demand the pursuit of something more, something different than dominant models of Beat and of American womanhood permit.

Joyce Glassman's autobiographer cherishes the "expectancy" of her younger self's position at the margins of male-dominated Beat circles, yet regrets her "silence" (*MC* 262). But Johnson's life-writing also establishes that her revolutionary identity as a Beat woman formed in the silences occasioned by her occupation of split positions, her embrace of roles and experiences for which there exist no authorizing language, no legitimizing script. Perhaps the female Beat ethos Johnson seeks to articulate in her memoirs originates in her sense that women recognized the perils of this nowhere position, yet embraced Beat bohemia nevertheless as their best option to make themselves "heroines" of their own legends.

Through comparative storytelling, imaginative reconstruction, and cross-textual citation, *Door Wide Open* and *Minor Characters* suggest that the complicated and contradictory context of Beat bohemia produces flexible and layered identities whose meanings and messages continue to evolve. Rereading the letters she exchanged with Kerouac in the late 1950s, Johnson remarks that "the Kerouac legend may be set in cement, but for [her], the reality of the past keeps fluctuating" (*DW* xxiii). And in her 2012 biography of Kerouac, she questions "whether there can be such a thing as a *definitive* biography. Even our own lives cannot be entirely defined despite our knowledge of 'the facts'" (*Voice* xix). As an autobiographer, Johnson struggles to pull "the facts" of her Beat past into line, to assert some solid truth about her experience, and about others'. Of Kerouac she writes: "He was a man whose feelings were constantly shifting. The Jack Kerouac who wrote to you last week would not be the same person who arrived on your doorstep" (*DW* xviii–xix). Johnson's serial examinations of the self and of "the extraordinary men and women who had been part of [her] revolution" demonstrate the impossibility of establishing a set of definitive facts with the authority to convey the truth of individual selfhood or to capture authentic Beatness. Instead, we fall back on categories such as "Beat woman," discursive necessities that tempt readers and writers alike to take refuge in certainties that persist in reforming and revising themselves, that, like Kerouac's pearl, continue to recede before us.

CONTEXTUALITY

Hettie Jones's *How I Became Hettie Jones* and *Drive*

> *Myself I simply expected, by force of will, to assume a new shape in
> the future. Unlike any woman in my family or anyone I'd ever actually
> known, I was going to become—something, anything, whatever that
> meant.*
>
> —HETTIE JONES, *HOW I BECAME HETTIE JONES*

> *The I is multiply coded in a range of discourses: it is the site of multiple
> solicitations, multiple markings of "identity," multiple figurations of
> agency. . . . What constitutes its representation?*
>
> —LEIGH GILMORE, *AUTOBIOGRAPHICS*

The front cover of *How I Became Hettie Jones* (1990) is crowded, virtually
overflowing with representations of its subject (fig. 13).[1] It presents three
images of Hettie Jones—in the first, she appears at the rear of a group
photograph of Beat writers and their spouses; the second shows her playing with her two daughters; she is alone in the third, wearing sunglasses
and looking away from the camera. The cover also contains two iterations
of the name "Hettie Jones"—in the title and autograph. As Leigh Gilmore
observes about another text, "in a conventional understanding of autobiography, only the title is needed to indicate the 'subject': title plus author
plus photograph would pile repetition upon redundancy" (215).[2] But the
proliferation of Hettie Joneses on the cover of her autobiography seems fitting, given the multiplicity of the "subject" delineated within. Summoned
by shifting discourses of cultural difference rooted in changeable models
of femininity, whiteness, Beatness, literariness, and Americanness, Jones
relies on a principle of *contextuality* to stake out a place for herself within
multiple and often contested locales of identity.

Her contextual strategy of self-representation has affinities with the
cross-textual autobiographical stance of her longtime friend Joyce Johnson; like Johnson, Jones directly addresses pre-textual descriptions of Beat
women and responds to narratives that depict her in relationship with a
better-known Beat man—in her case, the African American writer LeRoi
Jones/Amiri Baraka. While all of the autobiographers included in this
study construct supplementary counterhistories to already-known narratives, Jones is unique in her detailed and specific attention to a variety

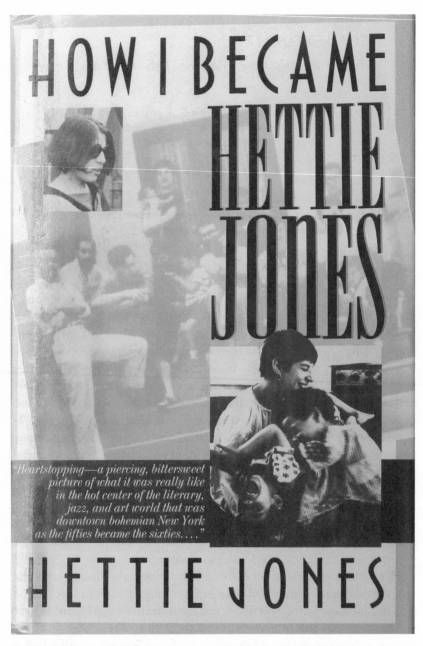

Fig. 13. Dutton 1990 *How I Became Hettie Jones* front cover. (Cover photograph of Hettie Jones © Fred McDarrah/Getty Images; group photograph by Laurence Hellenberg; family photograph by Lawrence B. Fink)

of wider historical trends and events, manifested in her self-conscious incorporation of contextual references ranging from philosophies underpinning the New American poetry to national concerns such as race relations and Cold War politics. Indeed, the sheer volume of historical and social commentary at points threatens to overwhelm self-representation, to render *How I Became Hettie Jones* less an autobiography and more "a memoir of the times" and a "social document," as it is characterized in a *New York Times Book Review* blurb on the back cover of the Penguin 1991 edition. Like di Prima's lies, Johnson's comparisons, and weiss's "women of the beat," Jones's relentless contextualizing forces readers back on their expectations, impelling them to revise what they think they know about the Beat movement and about the women affiliated with it. Jones's discussions of her social, political, and artistic contexts also raise questions about the limits of individual agency in constructing and communicating off-script identities within "dialogically agitated and tension-filled environments" (Bakhtin 276) of discourse.

The epigraph to *How I Became Hettie Jones*—a quote from Jane Bowles's *Two Serious Ladies*—addresses precisely this issue: "The idea . . . is to change first of our own volition and according to our own inner promptings before they impose completely arbitrary changes on us" (n.p.; ellipsis Jones's).[3] This paratext echoes the theme of self-determination announced in the memoir's title and in Jones's stated desire "to *become*—something, anything" (10), but at the same time acknowledges the complexities and contingencies involved in individual efforts to "become." The epigraph valorizes the "inner promptings" of the individual even as it warns of the imposing power of outside forces; at the same time, its collective pronouns convey a sense of identity as communal and contextual. *How I Became Hettie Jones* concerns itself with women's desire for "becoming" in contexts where self-direction, like Beat, has been defined as a male property and prerogative.[4] For Jones, so aware that her story has been prominently featured in the narratives of others, establishing self-direction for "Hettie Jones" is both paramount and problematic—she seems intent on wresting her story away from others and aligning her story with others', on locating herself within recognizably Beat and national contexts and dislocating herself from them as a woman for whom there is "no precedent" (*H* 44) and thus no authorizing script.

An author of poetry, short fiction, and children's books, Jones decided to write her autobiography because she "realize[d] that nobody knew" about Beat-associated women's contributions ("D" 159). She came to see telling her story as "a way to teach" (*LH* 3). Jones's life-writing was further motivated by the 1984 publication of her ex-husband's autobiography ("D" 159), which paints a trivializing portrait of her and dismisses their relationship as lacking "passion" (Baraka 217). In *The Autobiography of LeRoi Jones*, her ex-husband refers to her as "Nellie Kohn"—a barely altered version of her maiden name, Hettie Cohen. Since it is no secret to whom "Nellie Kohn" refers, this name change might strike a reader, particularly if that reader is Hettie Jones, as a vivid and perhaps unwelcome reminder of other versions of "Hettie Jones" occupying other Beat pre-texts, as an illustration and consequence of her intertextual life.[5]

Jones's focus on self-motivated "becoming" amid, in Gilmore's terms, "multiple solicitations, multiple markings of 'identity,' multiple figurations of agency" (42) aligns her autobiography with a Beat ethos invested in autonomous individualism but also compels her to confront the constitutive force of others' texts, discourses, and expectations in forming self-concept and directing self-expression. Elements of her autobiography suggest that (as in Kyger's experience) who "Hettie Jones" is depends on her contextual and intertextual surround, on when and where she is, with whom and according to whom. As an autobiographer, Jones attempts to contain and control her various contexts and intertexts by positioning herself as their historian, a stance that enables her self-presentation as both an engaged participant in the Beat movement and a self-directed woman beyond the reach of its defining narratives.

Becoming (More Than) Beat

How I Became Hettie Jones is composed of twenty-three (roughly) chronological chapters arranged into four sections; chapters contain occasional flashbacks and shifts between present and past tense, a device that blurs distinctions between past and present selves. Jones names each of her autobiography's four sections for a place she lived during the period covered in the narrative—Morton Street, Twentieth Street, Fourteenth Street, and Cooper Square—and presents storied Beat locales as sites of personal as well as group creativity. Readers familiar with Beat history would likely recognize the Twentieth Street apartment as a site where Jones and her husband, LeRoi Jones, produced *Yugen* and managed Totem Press, and thus as a center of Beat literary innovation. Jones describes 402 West Twentieth Street as the salon-like locale of a party that "never ended," a communal space teeming with energy and connection (*H* 71).[6] She remembers "Twentieth Street" as "a young time, a wild, wide-open, hot time, full of love and rage and heart and soul and jism. Like everyone else, I tried to get my share" (71). Transforming "Twentieth Street" into a "time," she stakes her claim to the Beat movement by making her home an expression of the Beat zeitgeist. In this Beat home, she demonstrates, she functioned as an engaged cocomposer of "the big-life-poem" (76) of a beloved community.

As a cocomposer of Beat, Jones contests the relegation of women to "minor character" status by challenging pre-texts and pretexts that render them irrelevant "background features or ornamentation" (Gilmore 9) and by illustrating her own pursuit of a life out of the ordinary. Like Johnson, weiss, and di Prima, Jones clearly and pointedly establishes that she chose independence and self-direction long before coming into contact with "major" Beat characters, stressing her long-standing determination to "[leave] home" (5) and her defiant choice to live a bohemian life in Greenwich Village. Her brief preface—which begins a text by and about Hettie Jones by inviting the reader to "meet Hettie Cohen" (1)—introduces a younger self who "started leaving home when [she] was six and weighed thirty-eight pounds" (5). The preface also describes her first encounter with LeRoi Jones in the office of the *Record Changer,* where she worked as subscription manager. She particularly remembers his delight at finding her reading Kafka and his surprise that she "had so much to say" (2).[7] This prefatory material seems intended to establish her standing as a young woman in no need of others' intervention or instruction, a Hettie Cohen who speaks and seeks for herself.

Later, she and LeRoi, whom she calls "Roi," fall in with "a small but provocative literary group" known as "the 'Beats,'" a name, she notes, "ambiguous enough to include anyone" (45). And she does feel included, almost instantly, in Beat "bohemia's slippery, discontinuous social fabric" (93). Although she considers herself and Roi "almost too sane in a group where shrink-time seemed mandatory" (45), they share with this group, which includes Kerouac, Holmes, Ginsberg, di Prima, and Gregory Corso, a common project "to burst wide open—like the abstract expressionist painters had—the image of what could be (rightly) said" (46). When she moves to the *Partisan Review,* she brings this new mode of expression to its pages, pulling "we of the 'misalliance,' we of the new world" (45), into wider recognition. Placing herself firmly in what mainstream America viewed as "the enemy camp" (47), Jones presents her younger self as a full participant in and cocomposer of "something new downtown" which "hadn't existed before we'd staked it, and wasn't yet called counterculture" (126). In a related claim to Beat insider status, her assertion "we were *the place* to pass through" situates herself, her husband, and their Fourteenth

Street apartment at the center of the "new consciousness" that would come to be identified as "Beat" (126; italics added).

As she establishes her credentials as an insider-historian, Jones gathers the authority to supplement and redistribute dominant ideas about the Beat Generation. She disputes representations of Beats as "apolitical" (127) by recounting her circle's investment in the Cuban revolution and concern with world events.[8] As she does at many other such junctures in her narrative, she uses cross-textual citation to bolster her position; in this instance, she inserts material from Ginsberg's journals into her discussion of the Beats' developing political consciousness: "This is Allen Ginsberg's journal entry of November 1, 1960: 'Now that the Congo is independent how come Nelson Rockefeller campaigning for president owns 22½ percent controlling interest in Universal Mines in Katanga?'" (127). Using this intertextual methodology, Jones unsettles un-nuanced, totalizing definitions of a Beat community she experienced as diverse and complex.

As an alternate Beat historian, Jones adds complicating facets and dimensions to the Beat story readers may think they know. Like Johnson, Jones pries open the "boy gang" image of the Beat movement by drawing on other women's stories to piece together mosaic portraits of bohemian life. In *How I Became Hettie Jones,* her New York Beat milieu is imbued with the energy and creativity of Martha King, Dorothy White, Helene Dorn, Sara Blackburn, Aishah Rahman, Rochelle Owens, Vertamae Smart-Grosvenor, Garth Shepp, and Joyce (Glassman) Johnson. Additionally, Jones insists on the presence of families and children in the New Bohemia and uses familial terms to describe Beat communities. Her commentary on a group photograph that appears on the cover of the 1990, 1991, and 1996 editions of her memoir (fig. 13) explicitly describes her Beat circle as an alternate family: "In front, leaning on the banister, is a slim, ironic, cheerfully arrogant Roi. I'm standing at the back with the baby, plainly pleased. . . . Seated between the two of us, the Twentieth Street poets, posed with their wives and children, appear to be a large extended family of which Roi and I are the proud and satisfied parents" (92). Jones's representations of Beat as an extended family, together with her detailed accounts of everyday life and her attention to the families of Beat friends, contest and revise definitions of the Beat Generation as a purely male cohort.

Additionally, Jones's references to the East Village "black avant-garde" (172) and to her many African American artist, musician, and writer friends, including Ted Joans, A. B. Spellman, Archie Shepp, and Bob Thompson, serve to emphasize that Roi is far from the only black member of New York bohemian communities. She mentions other biracial couples and describes the mixed-race group that coalesces at the famed Five Spot as a life-affirming alternative to the postwar United States of the 1950s: "I remember a whole lot of laughter at the Five Spot. You can hear it on all the recordings made there. I think of us trying to laugh off the fifties, the pall of the Cold War, the nuclear fallout—right then, the papers were full of it—raining death on test sites in Nevada. I think we were trying to shake the time. Shake it off, shake it up, shake it down" (34). Jones tells her Beat story as a fully invested part of a multifaceted "we" that resists and reshapes Cold War America and, in a subtle intertextual gesture, invites readers to reencounter this "we" on the jazz recordings of the day.

Jones employs more specific forms of cross-textual citation to establish her meaningful participation in Beat literary endeavors. For example, she combines her words with Roi's to describe her role in the inception of *Yugen*: "Our magazine—*Yugen, a new consciousness in arts and letters*—was Roi's idea, but, as he's written, I 'went for it.' I think I threw myself at it, actually" (53). Quoting Roi, editor of *Yugen* and of Totem Press, Jones emphasizes the importance of her contributions, work often ignored as nonliterary, grunt-type labor disconnected from artistic aims. Asserting that her "late-night cutting, pasting, aligning, and retyping" tasks teach her "what comes from reading things over and over, taking apart and putting together, the heart of the matter, the way it feels" (75), she redefines her overlooked labor as its own form of artistic production. Jones further presents this work as the basis for her stance as an expert on Beat literary practice; pointing to the skills and insights she develops working on *Yugen* and Totem, as well as for *Partisan Review* and Grove Press, she defends Kerouac's "spontaneous bop prosody" (47) and rebuts dismissive responses to Beat writers.

As a "proud parent" of the "new consciousness," Jones occupies positions typically gendered male in the Beat mythos. She reports feeling akin to Ginsberg, who "like Roi and me ... made his own rules" (78), and quotes male Beats, including Kerouac, who marvel at her ability to "understand" them and their art (71, 103).[9] Jones further demonstrates her affinity with the Beat ethos by incorporating Beat poetry into discussions of her experience, declaring that the poets she publishes write of and for her. Admitting she "hadn't yet managed to speak for [her]self," she observes "at least there were these others" (55) whose voices convey her defiant sense of self and desire for social change.

Jones draws on the first issues of *Yugen* to construct a conarrated Beat philosophy of art and life in the postwar United States. "The first poem you come across, opening *Yugen 1,*" she writes, "is 'Further Notice,' by Philip Whalen," and she quotes it in its entirety as a means of expressing her sense of identity and place in the world. This use of the poem enables Jones to connect herself to Beat sensibilities of self-reliance and creative play, and to share the displacements that come with perceiving oneself as simultaneously an outsider in America and an exemplar of national principles of independence and individuality. After announcing *"I can't live in this world / And I refuse to kill myself / Or let you kill me,"* the poem resolves *"I shall be myself— / Free, a genius, an embarrassment"* (55). Quoting Whalen's poem, Jones simultaneously describes and provides endorsement for her feeling of cultural difference and impulse toward self-direction, both of which she articulates in her recurrent claim to "always be my *own* self" (38). In a parallel gesture of inclusiveness and consociation, her reference to "the first poem *you* come across" in *Yugen 1* draws the reader into her Beat contexts, situating us in her position, seeing through her eyes.

Throughout her autobiography, Jones weaves lines of poetry by Roi, Whalen, Ron Loewinsohn, Charles Olson, Michael McClure, and others into her accounts of the literary work she performs and the Beat principles by which she lives. To illustrate poetry's role in her "becoming," she references and responds to a poem by Loewinsohn:

It begins

> *The thing made real by*
> *a sudden twist of the mind:*

and ends

> *. . . thunders into*
> *the consciousness*
> *in all its pure & beautiful*
> *absurdity,*
> *like a White Rhinoceros.*

I read those words at all hours, in all strained lights, always to see that rhinoceros snorting toward me. The poems *were* our lives. (72; ellipsis Jones's)

Her inclusion of Loewinsohn's words encourages her reader to experience a similar "twist of the mind" that allows a more direct and immediate encounter with worldviews formative of her sense of self. Jones's use of others' poetic renderings of Beat philosophies of art and identity establishes Beat intertexts as her younger self's lens on the world.

As Nancy Grace observes, the bits and snippets of others' texts Jones "embeds" in her autobiography "present the literary and political culture of Beat history" and "enact [her] sense of self as relational" ("Snapshots" 157). Jones crafts this relational, intertextual self in both coincidence with and opposition to others' lexicons of identity. She quotes Diana Trilling's "complaint" about "the 'girls'" associated with the Beat Generation: "'So many blackest black stockings,' she wrote with distaste" (129). Earlier in her narrative, Jones had recounted finding those iconic black stockings at a dance supply store, "dirt-defying, indestructible tights," which freed her and her friends "from fragile nylon stockings and the cold, unreliable, metal clips of a garter belt" (46). Where Trilling makes the tights a synecdoche for Beat girls' lack of appropriate girlishness—"she didn't find us pretty," Jones explains (129)—for Jones they signify liberation from restrictive markers of femininity. Following her discussion of Trilling's comment, she recalls finding the black tights on a mannequin in a store window: "It felt odd to have so prompted the culture, to have many other women want to seem to *be* you, whatever they thought you were" (130). At such moments, Jones contends with symbols and signifiers that seem both part of her desired self-concept and overwritten with reductive cultural connotations. Acknowledging that those "blackest black stockings" have been co-opted and frozen into stereotype, she moves to reclaim them as something more authentic—as emblem and expression of her project to "ease the possible past the expected" and "make [her]self happen" (27) by slipping free of dominant models of female identity.

She is clear, however, that even in Beat bohemia women remain encumbered by "the expected." For her, she understands, "everything is different than for [Roi]" (123). Where Roi exercises his male prerogative to concentrate his life on his art, to have affairs, to be guided by and answerable only to his own "inner promptings," Jones is increasingly overwhelmed by caretaking duties. At first, she views her choice of wife- and motherhood as transgressive of "the expected," reporting that her parents essentially disowned her for disputing their "claim [to her]" by marrying a black man (64). Recounting her decision to marry Roi and have his child, she remarks: "Sometimes you have to go on the road" (62). With this echo of the text that most famously defined Beat, Jones seeks to assert a female version of Beat iconoclasm; she "go[es] on the road"—breaks with her family and her past, smashes through societal constraints, and defies expectations for normative American femininities—by choosing an interracial marriage in the segregated 1950s and living a bohemian life at a time when "no *decent* woman opened her legs to a man who couldn't support her" (178). However, her iconoclasm has no noticeable effect on the uneven distributions of labor, value, and authority structuring male-centered Beat communities. Jones points to a Beat double standard that shuts down possibilities for women's self-directed "becoming" by demanding their subordination to men's social and artistic priorities. As Roi's wife and typist, she is "an energetic young person . . . serving others" (148), a woman who, despite her work on *Yugen* and Totem, will be written off as "charming but noncontributing" (199).[10]

At least in part due to conflict between Beat individualism and the Beat double standard, "Hettie Joneses" proliferate on the pages of her autobiography in even greater numbers than they do on its front covers; her text teems with both self-definitions and outside classifications. Hettie Jones appears as a "weird chick" (128) who rejects the norms of 1950s America and as an "artist's wife" relegated to "the sidelines" with the other wives, a group expected, after all, to "grow up and get into [their] girdles" (101). She functions as both a female trailblazer making herself happen and a wife who "subvert[s]" her own "ambitions" (173) to support her husband. The memoir encourages readers to ask if Hettie Jones is an "independent" woman living an "uncommon" life, as she characterizes herself in company with Joyce (Glassman) Johnson (81), or "nothing," as Roi asserts, without him (98). Is she a creative force in her own right or Roi's "secretary" (208)? Is she "Hettie," or "faithful loyal stalwart Mrs. Jones," or LeRoi Jones's "white wife" (224, 217)? These multiple identifications highlight the tension between Jones's claim to "always be my *own* self" (38) and her depictions of that self as mutable and contextual, a shifting palimpsest imbued with others' views and voices. She chooses and claims "Hettie Jones" to signify the person she becomes, but the name remains attached to other, intertextual incarnations and variations that shape her public identity and press against her self-concept.

Becoming (More Than) "His White Wife"

Of course, the name Hettie Jones also preserves her link to LeRoi Jones and the story of their failed marriage, and thus to a public persona she both accepts and rejects. Readers with even a basic familiarity with the Beat and Black Arts movements know that in the early to mid-1960s Roi's growing antipathy toward white America shifted his artistic, social, and personal focus away from the Beat scene and toward Black Nationalism. They know that in order to become Amiri Baraka, leader of the Black Arts movement, Roi disavowed "his white wife" and his Beat compatriots; he moved to Harlem, founded the Black Arts Repertory Theatre/School, and espoused a philosophy of militant separatism.

A good deal of what readers think they know about Hettie Jones comes from Roi's texts—his poems, plays, and autobiography—and she incorporates significant material produced by her ex-husband into her reconstruction of her life with him. In the following example, she uses Roi's work to illuminate a point of tension in their relationship: "His poems, like those of any honest person . . . held moments of personal failure between us. Mainly he'd wanted the world to hear from me and it hadn't, at least not in terms of the going (male) intellectual positions. He liked my inventive clothes but where was my tongue? This had been part of his expectations. This was important to him. I should speak my mind. Why didn't I write criticism? 'I/love you/ & you hide yourself/in the shadows,' he wrote" (85). This cross-textual passage weaves together Roi's poetic lament of her failure to assert a public voice, her paraphrase of his position on her silence, and her analytical response. While Jones acknowledges her lack of voice, her emphasis on Roi's "expectations" suggests his concern with her "tongue" has more to do with his priorities and what is "important to him" than with her literary growth. Perhaps more significantly, she implies that he dismisses the contributions she does make because he views them, and her, through the lens of "going (male) intellectual positions." This gesture toward the masculinist Beat aesthetic allows Jones to admit her literary silence but at the same time to critique Beat's muting effect on women situated outside the "positions" staked out and validated by male writers. Absorbing and transforming Roi's words, she attempts to undo his command of her story and public persona but also registers "Hettie Jones" as a palimpsestic construction entangled in already-known narratives and gendered discourses of worth, creativity, and authority.

She refutes Jones/Baraka's denial of her and his erasure of their significance in each other's "becoming" using his own words; she draws on poems from his Beat period to document their love relationship, while material from his dramatic works serves to illustrate the dissolution of their "quiet, original certainty" in each other (140). She references his well-known plays *Dutchman* and *The Slave*, written and produced as he became a spokesperson for black anger and proponent of the "any means necessary" (223) philosophy of social change, to analyze the discourses that reconstitute "Hettie Jones" as "his white wife." A central motivating factor of Jones's autobiographical project involves critiquing those discourses and resisting the lexicons of gender and racial identification that Roi and others use to define the "Hettie Jones" with whom her reader is likely familiar.

How I Became Hettie Jones argues both implicitly and explicitly that what she and Roi had in common was more authentic than the racial considerations that prompted Roi to leave her and their Beat community. She attempts to establish that they are more alike than different by illustrating their like-mindedness. When she meets Roi, she reports, she "recognize[s]" in his "hurry-up, headfirst way" her own drive and work ethic (22). They share the assumption they have been "liberated . . . from all that has gone before [them]" (29), and her portrayal of their "easy collusion" (55) shows it is "natural for [them] to be together" (39). Pointing to his "pleasure" in her "usual antic self" (41), a self corrected and rejected by her parents, she demonstrates that Roi recognizes and embraces her as a kindred spirit.

Jones consistently describes herself and Roi as alike, aligned, akin— "two clocks" that had "been wound up the same amount" (32). Using cross-textual citation to support this characterization, she points to others' perceptions of them as "tight as ticks" (38) and quotes from Roi's poems, including those that refer to her as his "wife" before they marry (37). A poem that begins "*My wife is left-handed. / Which implies a fierce de- / termination*" shows Jones that her husband recognizes and accepts the person she feels herself to be, that "what [she] prized in [her]self he loved most" (89). She describes Roi as her "perfect mate," a man for whom she "wasn't a fantasy . . . but a woman who'd just begun to make her own self up. A man who knew I was weird, whose own hopes I respected, and in whose arms I wanted to be" (32). Early in their relationship, she dismisses the possibility of racial "complications" as "a crock," sure that she and Roi "could handle them" (32). And for a time, it appears they do.

Jones remembers their relationship as a creative partnership. "Accomplishment," she comments, "is the virtue of our life together" (76). As a group of friends and collaborators put together *Yugen 4,* Jones watches her husband: "With a wide, satisfied grin, his chin tucked in and his arms folded tight across his chest, he's leaning against the wall. . . . It's as if he's trying to contain his pride, to keep it from bursting out of his body the way it has on his face. I know how he feels" (76). Their shared pride in their magazine echoes and corresponds to their pride in each other and in their literary community, and demonstrates their success in melding artistic, social, and familial forms of creativity. Jones compares the "imminent birth" of *Yugen 4* with the impeding birth of their first child, observing "something like the baby, its cover will be black with a white abstraction" (73). Illustrating their ability to cross borders and to combine contexts— especially literary and domestic—so often held separate, Jones seeks to establish the productive, mutually enriching nature of their partnership.

She recognizes tension in their relationship but, until Roi begins to view their marriage through a black/white lens, does not attribute it to race. For the most part, *How I Became Hettie Jones* presents their conflicts as outcomes of unequal distributions of rights and freedoms along gender lines—the privileges he claims as an artist and her breaches of what is "expected" and "permitted" for "artists' wives" (101). Describing a fight about her affair with a painter, she appeals to the reader: "Look at us there, if you will. . . . Two twenty-five-year-old kids with a kid, in the middle of a lot of commotion. Do you see race in this?" (104).

However, while "race disappears in the house—in the bathroom, under the covers, in the bedbugs in your common mattress, in the morning sleep in your eyes," the context of 1950s America forces Jones to make distinctions between their indoor life and the "outdoor life" of a nation in which "thirty states still had miscegenation laws" (36). In the eyes of others, she knows, she could easily (dis)appear as "one-half of the blackman/whitewoman couple, that stereotype of lady and stud," or as a white hipster "attracted to the black world's sexy, existential violence" (35). Jones acknowledges a wider historical basis for such expectations: "In the United States white people have historically made their way to places like the Five Spot in times like the late fifties." But she also insists on the "particular history" of her time and place, observing in "what would later be called the New Bohemia . . . going to the Five Spot was not like taking the A train to Harlem. Downtown was everyone's new place" (34); in her descriptions of the downtown scene, jazz and literary expression flourish in forms of creative exchange that echo her partnership with Roi. In this set of considerations about interactions between black and white Americans, Jones forces larger historical trends to yield to the specificities of the local; for her, New York's bohemian contexts frame interpersonal dynamics in unique ways that exceed national vocabularies of race.

She employs a similar tactic to situate her personal story within larger narratives of American history; her contextual references to national conflicts over race acknowledge the social and historical situatedness of her interracial family, even as they demonstrate that her family overflows the boundaries those references seem to erect. Jones spends many pages of her autobiography reviewing events related to the civil rights movement, including the Montgomery bus boycott and student-led lunch-counter sit-ins. Situating these events alongside her own experience, she attempts to establish distance between national and local, to show that for her at least, national contexts do not determine relationships between *individuals*.

As individuals, Jones insists, she and Roi enjoy a "natural" affiliation. They exceed racial expectations and stereotypes for blacks and Jews: she is "the one who kept watermelon," while "it was Roi who loved a good sour pickle" (41). As individuals, she and Roi's mother share "the stance . . . of a woman who stood her ground, a woman who'd take a stand" (40). Jones describes an easy and immediate kinship between herself and Anna Lois Jones that extends to other black women in the Jones family orbit. She portrays her enduring bonds with black men and women in her New York bohemian community, enumerating, for instance, the "many aspects of *like*ness" she shares with her close friend Dorothy White: "We saw ourselves in each other and approved," she writes (173). Noting that it is only outside of their community that her relationship with Roi draws hostile attention and that Roi endures insult and provocation (176), she describes a "downtown avant-garde" (172) that appears already-integrated—a local, "inside" exception to the national climate of racial strife.[11]

However, Jones's indoor/outdoor distinction does not consistently hold, as demonstrated by strained, sometimes contradictory juxtapositions of national and local events. For example, she mentions the violence attending integration in Little Rock, Arkansas, then asserts "nothing touches *us;* people stop and stare and we sail on." But her next sentence reveals that others' reactions do touch her. The stares, she admits, provoke her anger and frustration—she wants to "toss [her] head or stick out [her] tongue or shriek *We are not illegal.*" Ultimately, she takes none of these actions because she has "learned" (42) that culturally determined racial identifications do matter. Subject to others' interpretive narratives, her family becomes a "sign . . . of the times" (211), made to symbolize things she believes have nothing to do with them. On a train with her daughter Kellie, Jones feels "the eyes of the world" on them as "if we were wearing a skin of public opinion, that stuck and clung and pressed and forced a change in the way you could breathe" (106). Her characterization of public opinion as a clinging, tangible "skin" acknowledges the capacity of hegemonic discourses to overspread individual self-definition and to force individuals into predetermined patterns of performance and response.

Insisting binary "black/white" opposition is "a slippery division" (34), Jones posits differently raced possibilities for identity. She asserts that as a Jew, she had long considered herself separate from "the *goyim*" (11), the white Christian majority composing mainstream America. Among her

lily-white classmates at her genteel southern college, she perceives herself, as Deborah Thompson observes, as "other to white non-Jews" (91).
Jones characterizes herself as a "mutation" (13) situated between dominant
models of raced and gendered identities, a position she finds liberating:
"As an outsider Jew I could have tried for white, aspired to the liberal
intellectual, potentially conservative Western tradition. But I never was
drawn to that history, and with so little specific to call my own I felt free
to choose" (14). Having chosen a life with Roi, she continues, in Thompson's words, "to feel other to whiteness," but her "feeling of otherness no
longer stems . . . from her Jewishness, but from being in a different relation to people of color, and having a different sensitivity to racism" (92).
Interacting with "whites-only groups," Jones feels "misrepresented, minus
a crucial dimension, and seeing race prejudice everywhere." A friend in
a similar position describes this condition as "feeling 'disguised in your
own skin'" (202). *How I Became Hettie Jones* proposes that one's "race" is
primarily a matter of context and of relationship with others; Jones represents her own "skin" as a palimpsest, a site of ambiguity and negotiation,
an abstract rather than a concrete ground of identity.

Although Jones does not group herself with whites or perceive herself
as white in ways that national discourses of race can register or recognize,
she cannot avoid being *made* white by others, including Roi. She references larger national contexts to articulate the friction she experiences
between her sense of identity and her husband's politics of skin color:

> The South was seething with demonstrators and "outside agitators";
> there had been actions in eight hundred American cities. Tear gas
> and cattle prods had been used, as well as dogs and water hoses
> strong enough to strip the bark from trees. The whole world had
> reporters in Birmingham, sometimes called Bombingham, Ala-
> bama, where Police Commissioner Bull Conner said, "Damn the
> law. Down here I am the law." It was no longer impossible to ignore
> the war that for a century had been called "our Negro problem."
> Roi's position was, "It's *your* Negro problem." But if the problem
> is yours, who are you? And what about me? (202)

In this passage, Jones's narration of events in Birmingham as representative of America's racial history is interrupted by Roi's position statement,
which threatens to render her other to him by extending the national into
the local. His attribution of the U.S. "Negro problem" to an all-inclusive
white "you" seems to assert an absolute black/white division that contests
his wife's choice to be differently raced.

How I Became Hettie Jones chronicles her escalating loss of control over identifications of "Hettie Jones" as *Dutchman* and *The Slave*, which are all about black/white opposition, impose an unwelcome intertextual valence over her "indoor" world. As Roi's plays garner acclaim, she finds herself the object of wide public scrutiny that redefines her as "a white woman," LeRoi Jones's "white wife, the former Hettie Cohen" (217). As "his white wife," she is "used against him" by the white media to "[blur] his indictments" (217), while black commentators protest "he talked black but married white" (218). Roi comes to accede to what Jones considers "outdoor" definitions, refusing to take her to a performance of *Dutchman* at Howard University "because," he says, "you're white" (218). Although she tells a drama critic that Roi's plays are "not [her] life" (221), she cannot prevent others from superimposing his stories over hers in reidentifications that create unrecognizable, "reshaped" (226) "Hettie Joneses." Feeling as if she lacks "substance, as if everything I am, all of *I* . . . has been emptied" (221), Jones experiences an intertextual overwriting of identity that threatens to render her other to herself.

Dutchman and *The Slave*, which depict relationships between white women and black men characterized by intractable racial antipathy, invite this emptying and reshaping.[12] Jones reads in the "glances of strangers" the question "who [is] that at the playwright's side—[his character] Lula the murderer, his white wife, or the former Hettie Cohen?" (218). Painfully aware that another white character, Grace, the racist ex-wife of a black writer-turned-revolutionary, is "taken for [her]" (202) by others, Jones notes one of Grace's lines "came from an argument we'd had: 'I am not in your head,' says Grace, right out of my mouth. 'So close to our real lives, so close to that living image,' he wrote later" (220). *How I Became Hettie Jones* reverses Roi's appropriation of her voice, using his words to take back her "living image" and to contest his view of their "real lives."

As Jones presents LeRoi Jones's "white wife" as a construction of others, she implies Roi's Black Nationalist identity is constructed in much the same way. She characterizes his public persona as a performance (137), describes his relationship with a black woman as "the image he thought he needed" (219), and asserts he comes to "think of himself the way his audiences thought of him" (214). Comparing Roi to one of his characters—"Walker Vessels with the right script in his hand"—Jones draws into question his "his grand new view" (222) as well as the authenticity he claims through rejection of white America, the Beat community, and her. Jones stresses that she does not question the need for real equality for African Americans or for "the collective release of black anger" (223) reflected in the Black Arts movement; she argues only that ideologies of black/white opposition are not capable of accounting for individual identities and interactions.

Jones's sense of her un-whiteness and her capacity for choice in her position between black/white categorization cannot be articulated using the binary vocabulary of the national narratives she weaves into her story. As a result, her life-writing at points oscillates between national and local, leaving historical references to sit beside discussions of her experience without causal or symbolic relationship.

> The white South showed its face on Kellie's second birthday, May 16, 1961. The Congress of Racial Equality (CORE) had organized a "Freedom Ride"—for the right to the bus, the restroom, and the restaurant in the terminal. There were shocking, blatant brutalities, burning houses, and blood. A new, angry, viable politics, a coalescing vision called the civil rights movement.
>
> My own life was reduced to economics. Without Roi, I'd have to . . . get a "real," uptown job. But he had never changed his address. He came daily to pick up his mail, invited me to his nearby apartment for lunch. Got embarrassed when I wouldn't go to bed. (138–39)

While this passage begins with an implied link between the vision energizing the civil rights movement and her daughter's emerging life possibilities, Jones leaves this comparison unexplored, shifting away from the dramatic events in the South to recount the everyday concerns of her life in New York. The reader seeks in vain for a contextual relationship between the civil rights "vision" and her economic situation or her interactions with Roi, who has left her for the first but not the last time. Jones cannot incorporate national history smoothly into her story because she does not perceive it as truly reflective of *her* story.

Jones's life-writing conveys the message that history is only just beginning to allow for an intelligible account of identity not dependent on the false certainties of binary opposition. "Whether Roi was wrong to leave me then," she concludes, "is less important than that such a move, for those reasons, would be useless now. Too many of us unnamed—light and dark—inhabit these woods. African-American is one specific history; there's more, and no easy answer" (238). Her autobiography offers a supplemental counternarrative of the "more" that cannot be contained within the parameters of "one specific history"—African American, U.S., or Beat. Giving name to at least one of the unnamed, or mis-named, *How*

I Became Hettie Jones endeavors to scrape these cultural and historical "skins" from the Hettie Jones emptied, othered, and reshaped by pre-texts and pretexts of gender and race. Asserting that many more "of us" remain hidden in "these woods," Jones asks her readers to recognize the potential for multiple alternatives to mono-histories and to either/or categories of identity.

Becoming (More Than) "Hettie Jones"

How I Became Hettie Jones tracks Jones's attempts to formulate methods of expressing and valuing alternative cultural positions, focusing primarily (but not exclusively) on her faltering and intermittent development as a poet. Surrounded by celebrated authors and negotiating ever-expanding service demands, she composes infrequent "occasional poems" (180) that she is "ashamed to show" Roi and her friends—because, she believes, "Roi [is] so much better; everyone else [is] so much better" (48). In contrast, Jones feels like "a swollen silence, struggling for words" (87), unable to find a voice of her own. However, *How I Became Hettie Jones* demonstrates that even when she is quiet in the context of male "intellectual positions," she is loud enough in other ways.

Pregnant with her first child, Jones comes to sewing and garment design out of necessity, but "stitchery" (83) quickly becomes an absorbing craft and liberating means of self-expression:

> It was a quick seduction: the fabric, the eye-hand thrill, the color and shape and texture that are also the terms of music. The only drawback was the pattern, which I promptly discarded, as if throwing away the score, because to make it all up, to improvise, became a way—as Ron Loewinsohn's poem over my sink instructed—to "relate the darkness to a face / rather than / impose a face on the darkness." Or, as Roi wrote, "There cannot be anything I must *fit* the poem into. Everything must be made to fit the poem." Or maybe, after all, sewing was just another excuse to put off writing, to find something that plagued me less, and, as Djuna Barnes reminded: "One hides behind the hat with which one bows to the world." (84)

This citational passage presents Jones's patternless sewing as a form of creative improvisation akin to the composition of music and poetry. Aligning her practice of her craft with the artistic principles articulated by Roi and Loewinsohn, Jones suggests her art, too, resists "imposed" patterns;

it provides a means of making herself up and "weav[ing]" her "ambitions" (171) into the fabric of Beat life. Roi complains that Jones hides herself in the literary shadows, and perhaps she does, as her nod to Barnes implies. At the same time, however, she stands out in the "lovely bravado" of the "anti-clothing" (84) she designs, wears, and shares with others.

As with those "blackest black stockings," Jones's anti-clothing frees her from constricting norms of femininity; "once you release the shoulder, and allow the breast its natural room," she observes, "you make way for the next step, that of taking off the hard, restrictive bra (soon, soon)" (84). Like music, which she identifies as her "first language" (36), and like Beat poetry, which speaks her worldview, Jones's anti-clothing communicates her sense of cultural difference and her desire to "become." Additionally, her sewing helps to maintain and strengthen female community, liberating her friends from uncomfortable standards regulating female appearance and behavior. Giving Dorothy White a dress she made, Jones feels Dorothy's "freedom to move as if it were my own, as if my intention had also been passed along" (173). She shares her love of stitchery and her desire to make art with other women, including her close friend Helene Dorn, who "painted when she could" (129).

Jones remarks that she and Helene—both wives of Beat poets, both haunted by their "incomplete" art—hide "the same shame at having abandoned" their creative ambitions (130). But, in its focus on the energy and effort the young Hettie Jones devotes to the in-depth letters she writes to Helene, *How I Became Hettie Jones* demonstrates that while she might not be composing and publishing poetry, she remains an engaged and evolving writer. As she compiles "long, detailed, continued accounts" of her life, she spends countless hours "absorbed . . . with trying to *tell*," finding ways to tap into "something in language" that goes "where nothing else could go" (130, 131). Rather than the tutelage of men or the expectations of her husband, Jones credits the unsung art of letter-writing with empowering her to "[leave] the Singer and [take] up the pen" (131), enabling her to locate her voice and to develop the confidence to expose it to the wider world.

Her letter-writing allows Jones to experiment with the form and content of life-writing. In her letters, she intersperses analyses of cultural and literary issues—including "politics," "social history," and "comparative economics"—within her narration of daily experience (182, 183, 184). The narrative structure of *How I Became Hettie Jones* closely mimics the mosaic-like structure of Jones's letters, with their melding of life-writing, historical commentary, and social observation.[13] Letters to Helene, which

Jones inserts into her narrative, function as pre-texts and intertexts for the memoir. Chapter 14 opens with a full letter from 1961 (142–45) describing Jones's busy life after the birth of her second child. It recounts Roi's arrest on charges of "sending obscenity through the mails in *The Floating Bear*" (143), an episode described in many Beat pre-texts but not through Hettie Jones's perspective and never as one more "unnecessary thing to deal with" among other family "crises and changes" (144). In these moments of intimate access to her younger self in conversation with the similarly situated Helene, two creative women engaged "in . . . gradual redefinition" of themselves (*LH* 1), Jones supplements the already-known, constructing alternative forms and foci of Beat community and of Beat literary practice.

Jones's insertion of materials from her letters into her memoir creates community with her own reshaped and reclaimed self. Substantial segments of *How I Became Hettie Jones* move back and forth between the words of her past self and the words of her past self's autobiographer, creating the effect of a story narrated in tandem by past and current "I"s. Most of chapter 16 consists of a trading of autobiographical telling—a sharing of the I-the-author position—between a March 31, 1962, letter and Jones's narrative reconstruction of the events it addresses:

> Roi's new book—newly titled *Blues People*—was going to be very good. His latest affair, with the ex-wife of the California poet
>
>> . . . didn't last long. Then he was sorry again. Poor Roi, he should never be a cocksman because he's directly out of the Baptist tradition and suffers more guilt and shame than anyone I know. As he did last spring and as I suppose he'll do again . . . So I figure, being myself near to twenty-eight years old, and getting wiser every year
>>
>> let him.
>
> The person who wrote this? Who gave those last two words their own paragraph? I recognize her, a little. To be always chasing him meant less time for her, and of the two, she was the more elusive. (167–68; ellipses Jones's)

As Jones's conarrator, her younger self becomes vividly and immediately present, and the two Hetties conduct an intrapersonal intertextual exchange that extracts "Hettie Jones" from LeRoi Jones–focused pre-texts and dislodges his story as the primary context for understanding hers. On its surface, the passage above is about Roi, but its main point of interest in Jones's memoir resides in her response to his affair(s), especially her resolution to detach her self-concept from his fidelity. Summoning her own voice from 1962, Jones validates and values her twenty-eight-year-old self, and encourages her readers to do the same.

In a similar autobiographical strategy based in conarration, Jones often uses the words of other female artists—such as the painter Paula Modersohn-Becker, writer Kay Boyle, and poet Marina Tsvetayeva—to chase her elusive younger self. To illustrate her feeling that she possesses multiple "set[s] of limbs and senses" to accommodate her multiple service responsibilities, she quotes Paula Modersohn-Becker—"I am writing this . . . in my kitchen, cooking a roast of veal" (121; ellipsis Jones's). She frequently draws on Marina Tsvetayeva to articulate both her artistic frustration and her recourse to alternate modes of expression, noting, for instance, that "like Tsvetayeva's notebook, which kept her 'above the surface of the waters,' the letters I sent to Helene kept me from sinking" (184). Jones's invocations of other female artists' ambivalence and anxiety connect her experience to that of creative women across boundaries of time and space. As she shows that her desires and conflicts are shared by other women, she invites readers of her autobiography, which she intended to be "a woman's book" ("D" 162), to read their experiences through hers and to consider themselves part of the like-minded intertextual community she pieces together in her narrative.

Chapter 14 ends with an interpersonal intertextual meditation on artistic frustration that combines cross-textual reference, autobiographical recall, and her own poetry:

My feelings—with never anything literary to them and all I ever wanted to write about—were left tangled for lack of time. . . . There are different reasons for silences, but . . . Tsvetayeva, describing her own, came closest to mine: "It's precisely for feeling that one needs time, and not for thought." Anyway, now I think I'm lucky to have, from Fourteenth Street, the one poem that mattered, which offered at last . . . a future I'd invented and therefore couldn't disappoint— the rest of my life from prophetic twenty-seven:

I've been alive since thirty-four
and I've sung every song
since before the War

Will the press of this music
warp my soul

till I'm wrinkled and gnarled
and old and small—

A crone in the marshes
singing and singing

A crone in the marshes singing
and singing

and singing
and singing
and singing
and singing
and singing (149–50)

Redeeming silence with song, Jones's Fourteenth Street poem suggests that the process of creating art actually creates the artist—altering the contours of her "soul," "warping" her into a figure of difference. But the poem also anticipates Jones's older "crone" self not being substantially altered from her "weird chick" younger self. Bearers of alternative knowledge, crones and weird women inhabit the outskirts of culture and are often viewed with suspicion and disdain. In her poem, Jones (a woman who does not fit within normative models of female identity or "going" literary modes, and who was indeed born in 1934) posits a place of belonging in a marginal locale that seems attuned to and welcoming of alternative modes of being—"marshes" are in-between spaces, encompassing and combining earth and water, and by necessity must be understood in both/ and rather than either/or terms. This "prophetic" poem foretells Jones's invisibility in Beat and national histories, but its insistence that her singing goes on and on promises that concealment does not equate to silence.

How I Became Hettie Jones contains a number of Jones's poems, including the last she wrote while she and Roi "were together," a poem in which the autobiographer discerns "a voice that now seems entirely [hers]" (208). The poem implores her *"dearest darling"* to *"take out / the garbage, the fish heads / the cats / wouldn't eat"* (209), making art out of Jones's everyday life of children and dinners and strained interactions with an increasingly distant husband. Another poem in the autobiography portrays another everyday experience, recalling a weary return trip from a visit to Jones's in-laws in Newark. After following her younger self as she wipes up baby vomit, boards the subway, and tends to her sleeping children, the poem describes her as *"twenty-seven / and very tired."* It ends:

> *Let me always*
> support her
>
> *Having been her*
> befriend her (186)

How I Became Hettie Jones answers and fulfills this request, "support-ing" and "befriending" the younger self so publicly devalued by her ex-husband and overwritten by the already-known Beat story.[14]

This poem, "Having Been Her," and the Fourteenth Street poem, now titled "Aftertune," appear in Jones's first collection of poetry, *Drive* (1998), recipient of the Poetry Society of America's 1999 Norma Farber First Book Award. *Drive* extends Jones's focus on a number of concerns addressed in *How I Became Hettie Jones,* especially female silence and routes of female "becoming," and continues her practice of making art out of everyday life. The collection seeks cultural spaces capable of accommodating female difference and befriends others struggling to throw off constrictive struc-tures imposed by social expectations.[15]

Poems in *Drive*'s "The Woman in the Green Car" series present driv-ing as a metaphor for self-exploration and self-determination. In Jones's work, cars are loved "friends" conducting her "onto life's inviting byways" ("Ode to My Car" 17) and enabling women to speed "right past / the nar-row walls of [their] destiny" ("Ruby My Dear" 22). While her car poems extend the metaphor of driving as self-directed self-discovery to women in general, the woman in the green car is clearly Jones herself. Events in the "Woman in the Green Car" series recapitulate events in her life and reflect her desire to "become."

The woman driving the green car "does / not know where she is go-ing / so she goes doggedly." Her movement remains unseen as she "race[s] past" an unmoving listener:

> · Providence
> gives you nothing
> save her passage
> what disturbance
> what mute
>
> air (12)

Making muteness a "disturbance," Jones suggests that the woman's "pas-sage" constitutes a disruption because it is unquantifiable. The woman in the green car does not need or want the recognition of others, and her silence in no way diminishes her. A figure of female difference and desire, no words account for her and "nothing" fixes her within the structures of a larger order.

Moving "too fast" and facing danger in the passing lane, the woman in the green car remembers the words of an old boyfriend who, echoing an episode in *How I Became Hettie Jones*, predicts "when you grow up you'll go to live in Mamaroneck/with Marjorie Morningstar." In the memoir, Jones remarks that this comment left her "shaken" at the thought of giving "up her life before she'd tried it" in order to embrace the feminine mystique as a "suburban matron" (26). In "The Woman in the Green Car," written decades after this encounter, she savors the satisfaction of having "invented her own life." She tells an "interviewer":

> I remember this guy,
> he said Mamaroneck and I couldn't see it, you know?
> My mind was empty, like . . .
>
> Like death? says the interviewer.
>
> Well yes, she says, I guess . . . death, she
>
> pulls ahead of the too-wide truck, avoids
> the light holds the wheel tight
>
> fear is death
> cheat it twice
>
> leave it
>
> in Mamaroneck (13; ellipses Jones's)

Conarrating this moment from her past with her ex-boyfriend and the overeager interviewer, Jones stakes her claim to self-determination even as interlocutors interrupt and interpret her life story. Confronting risks—a "too-wide truck" and the figurative "death" of being spoken for by others—she acknowledges her fear and powers on, evading others' discursive attempts to reshape her in their terms.

In "The Woman in the Green Car," the female silence characterizing the first part of the poem gives way to female self-assertion in the second half. Other *Drive* poems are more ambivalent, identifying language, especially when wielded by others, as a kind of necessary evil, a mutable and undependable intertext for self-conceptualization. "Words," Jones observes in her poem of the same name, "are keys/or stanchions/or stones"

(25); depending on conditions and contexts, words may function as barriers, weapons, or building blocks, opening or shutting down possibilities for self-expression and for connection to others. And words can easily be hijacked and usurped. The speaker "give[s] [her] word" to an unidentified "you," who takes and alters it—"pocket[s] it / and keep[s] the change" (25). Finally, she chooses to keep her most important word to herself:

> Here is a word on
> the tip of my tongue: love
>
> I hold it close
> though it dreams of leaving (25)

Ending her poem with her word's unrealized hope for escape, Jones leaves unaddressed a crucial yet unanswerable question about the nature of female silence: if her word remains unspoken, has she preserved its possibilities or hindered its fulfillment?

"The Third Poem" describes words as dangerous, even deadly. Having been burdened with "stone words / when / all [she] wanted was feathers," the poet observes that rather than "grow[ing] on" her, the heavy and violent discourse of an unidentified male figure "fill[s]" her "with word shot." She had hoped for a different kind of transformation—the growth spurred by collaboration. Instead, the man addressed in the poem inflicts lasting damage in words that compel her to return to the original injury, her "heart full of / blood" and "red / wounds / remembered" (31). Exposing her wounded heart in her poetry and autobiography, Jones absorbs and transforms multiple pre-texts and pretexts, reckoning with the "word shot" peppering the "Hettie Jones" occupying Beat histories.

Her poem "In Answer to Your Question" appears to ponder the limitations and possibilities of intertextual self-representation:

> I write a hall
> of mirrors, risky distortions
>   to shatter
>   repose.
>
>   I write
> from fear, from what I
>   can't know
>
>   but I write
> on the high horse of my life

and I write with time in my one
good hand (67)

Like Bonnie Bremser looking in her mirror, frustrated in her attempt to produce a self-portrait, Jones must confront the selves reflected in the "mirrors" of others' defining words and endure the strain and pain of processing, repurposing, and incorporating often uncomfortable layers of intertextual association. At points in her poetry and her autobiography, these "risky distortions" that "shatter / repose" lead her to assert she has been "[her]self all along" (*H* 216), to imagine Hettie Jones as solid and certain, a rock against which break streams of defining discourse formulated by others. For the most part, however, as she writes "on the high horse of [her] life," she welcomes the uncertainties of risky self-definition as a woman with "no precedent."

As *How I Became Hettie Jones* draws to a close, Jones recalls encountering an acquaintance from her Beat days and watching as he struggles to "search out a name" for her:

Is she Cohen? No, she was Jones. Is she yet that, or is the name removed like the man from whom she got it?
I smiled. I'd help if I could.
But then he came out with it, what he'd decided to ask—and it was a smash!
"Are you still . . . Hettie?" he said.
"By all means," I said laughing. By all means. (239; ellipsis Jones's)

Embracing the single and singular name "Hettie," Jones ends her autobiography with an exuberant affirmation of a female self free of the familial and marital associations that encumbered her with others' claims to the authority to define her. While the title *How I Became Hettie Jones* might seem to fix and define its subject as a finished product, in Jones's self-representation she never definitively "becomes" "Hettie Jones" so much as never stops becoming.

CODA
Rerouting Beat Nowheres

all my selves are returning
to tell me the story of travels

—RUTH WEISS, "LIGHT"

The self constructed in women's autobiographical writing is often based in, but not limited to . . . an awareness of the meaning of the cultural category WOMAN for the patterns of women's individual destiny. Alienation is not the result of creating a self in language. . . . Instead, alienation from the historically imposed image of the self is what motivates the writing, the creation of an alternate self in the autobiographical act. Writing the self shatters the cultural hall of mirrors and breaks the silence imposed by male speech.

—SUSAN STANFORD FRIEDMAN, "WOMEN'S
AUTOBIOGRAPHICAL SELVES"

I began *Women Writers of the Beat Era: Autobiography and Intertextuality* with a promise to avoid constructing a one-size-fits-all model to account for Beat-associated women's strategies of self-representation. Over the course of this study, I have, however, pointed to a number of shared priorities, among them impulses to absorb and transform the "Beat woman" label, with its "historically imposed image of the self," and to challenge and supplement pervasive expectations that entrench a single, specifically male-centered Beat paradigm as a stable, certain foundation for communities, cultures, generations, and movements. I further argued that while women writing Beat lives seem intent on critiquing their invisibility within the dominant Beat narrative, they also reconstitute Beat nowheres as creative sites in which defiant femininities might be improvised and "cultural hall[s] of mirrors" shattered. With these general areas of intersection in mind, I will bring this study to what incomplete conclusions its diverse subject matter permits by briefly examining an additional common characteristic of these women's life-writing: frequent references to roads and journeys. All of the writers included in *Women Writers of the Beat Era* rely on unusual, sometimes discordant, and often palimpsestic metaphors of travel to illustrate the complexities of their intertextual lives. I end my investigation of those lives with a selective review of some of these travel-related tropes because it seems to me they encapsulate Beat-associated women writers' attempts to convey a sense of their transformative Beat difference.

Since "autobiographical truth," as Paul John Eakin asserts, "is not a fixed but an evolving content in an intricate process of self-discovery and self-creation" (*Fictions* 3), it is in no way new or startling to find metaphors and images of travel in autobiographical writing. Roads and paths are common symbols for the trajectories of human lives, and readers are accustomed to finding processes of self-definition represented as quests or journeys, complete with arrivals and departures, abrupt turns and perilous detours, assorted bumps, forks, and dead-ends. Selves-in-progress have much in common with travelers seeking their way, encountering the unexpected, accommodating changing circumstances, and amending what they think they know about themselves and about their social and cultural contexts.

For girls who dared to leave home for Beat bohemias of the 1950s and 1960s, travel-related images and tropes reflect their search for a vocabulary capable of conveying dramatically different yet already-known lives, of describing the discoveries and dislocations that come with "construct[ing] relations to the new and unknown, even when already thoroughly imaginatively colonized" with others' defining discourses (Bartkowski xv). In their autobiographical work, women writers affiliated with the Beat movement step out onto congested, thickly plotted roads. They find their routes and byways already occupied by storied Beat travelers and marked by masculinized performances of freedom, creativity, and nonconformity. Exploring their means of departure from both Beat and mainstream paths, the writers included in this study use and abuse travel-related lexicons in ways that create "textual turbulence" (Siegel 5)— moments of narrative confusion, awkwardness, dissonance, and/or incongruity. These instances of textual turbulence reflect the difficulties and dilemmas occasioned by women's attempts to stretch and recenter language to account for the off-script worldviews, behaviors, desires, relations, and modes of creative expression I have termed "defiant femininity."

Journeying is a trope familiar to both writer and reader—defiant femininity, not so much. Writers' meldings of these two concepts produce textually turbulent intersections in which possibilities for the conceptualization of alternate female selves and for the formulation of alternate Beat cultures materialize, even if just briefly and even if partially overwritten by the dominant Beat narrative. Odd, idiosyncratic, or discordant linkages of travel and female self-concept serve as textual levers that dislodge the already-known and move Beat in new directions. They serve, in other words, as metaphors in miniature for Beat-associated women writers' intertextual self-representation.

Living Roads: Beat Lives as Travel

Journeying appears most obviously as a trope for differently Beat lives in the work of Bonnie Bremser and Joanne Kyger, whose texts track the evolutions and transformations of self-seeking during the course of actual journeys. Both women align the uncertainties of travel and accompanying feelings of alienness with strained and uncomfortable performances of scripts for female identity. Bremser describes her sojourn in Mexico as a source of both self-alienation and "self-determination" (T 54); a woman whose identification "papers" are perpetually suspect, she is "fugitive" and unfree, subject to cultural judgment and punishment but nevertheless open to potential "metamorphosis" (39). Having returned to the United States "naked and lost" (208) but determined to tell her story, Bremser, as noted in chapter 3, describes her struggle to "distill" her experience into her own kind of "poetry" as "an enormous drive," then exclaims, "look at this book!" (116). Readers trying to understand how her "book" constitutes "an enormous drive" might recall the exertions and exigencies of her journeying in Mexico and might also consider that the word "drive" connotes effort and determination as well as referencing a mechanism of movement and travel. In this sense, Bremser's odd linkage of "drive" and "book" conveys something of the energies she expends crossing and recrossing categories of identity. Her "drive" of a "book" similarly traverses deep and daunting distances—geographical, cultural, interpersonal, and literary—to tentatively piece together a diversified self, a self that exceeds expected and accepted parameters of female identity.

When Kyger puts herself at the helm of Odysseus's ship and describes her travels through his story, she rejects traditional plots available to women and parlays displacement into a fluid poetics of possibility. In her *Journals*, Kyger questions whether she has "ever had a home" (25), and as a woman writer she struggles for purchase in a world that views freedom and creativity as male dispositions. In her poetry, however, she creates a "world" she describes as "slippery to hold on to" (T 35), where everything "goes all around again" (T 36). And this unstable, insecure movement of the world, she declares, is "all we can hope for" (T 44). In her journals and her poetry, Kyger's layering of the positions of the voyaging Odysseus and the home-bound Penelope over her own position as a female poet makes

"strange" (*T* 34) the dominant gender expectations that separate possibilities for male and female opportunity and experience, thus offering a
muted critique and reformulation of the Beat already-known.

Travel-related imagery fashioned by Diane di Prima, ruth weiss, Joyce
Johnson, and Hettie Jones performs similar functions. weiss writes autobiographical prose poetry infused with motion and elasticity, identifying herself as a "dragon" traversing spaces in which "there is no road"
(*DJ* 70). In *DESERT JOURNAL*, she describes "wandering" as her "home"
(102), writing her identity in terms that consistently force together concepts commonly understood as opposites. Describing a self in continuous process—"the soul keeps moving," she observes, "as soles of feet / on
burning sand" (108)—weiss blurs boundaries of gender, race, and sexuality to offer, as the first epigraph to this coda suggests, multiple and open
possibilities for identity. Her Beat-claiming poetry gives the same treatment to the Beat movement, seeking to restore "movement" to a social
and literary phenomenon reified and frozen into caricature.

Di Prima also deploys movement as a trope for alternative identities
in her autobiographical work. Whether moving in and out of scenes in
Memoirs of a Beatnik or tromping through the streets of New York in
Recollections of My Life as a Woman, di Prima presents her younger self
as an explorer and cultural outsider—unstoppable, uncontainable, and
unquantifiable. A "self-defined" woman who "carve[s]" out and "follow[s]"
her own path at any cost" (*R* 224, 269), whether in unrestrained sexuality
or uncompromising artistry, she tromps and tramples over barriers of
all kinds to achieve sometimes playful, sometimes defiant forms of self-
determination. It is largely because she is a moving target, a voyager on
paths of her own making, di Prima asserts, that she is able to evade social regulation and construct alternatively gendered and differently Beat
"life forms."

Johnson's life-writing, in contrast, insists on the impossibility of extracting female self-concept from pervasive and ingrained cultural structures that gender independence male and obscure alternative paths for
women. Acknowledging that she would have married Kerouac even as he
sank into alcoholism and depression, she muses: "If you were a woman,
wasn't your 'road' the man you gave yourself to?" (*DW* 154). Johnson's discordant use of the loaded term "road" as a metaphor for the expectations
of heterosexual romance points to the complex performances of gender
negotiated within Beat bohemias, where women's modes of adventuring
both overlap and clash with mainstream gender norms and with male-
centered models of Beat identity. Her "road" draws attention to the con-

trasting connotations of "Beat" and "woman," and evokes the question of what makes women Beat, a question confronted by all of the writers addressed in *Women Writers of the Beat Era*, all of whom write their lives through limited and gender-inflected vocabularies that cannot fully or comfortably account for them.

In *How I Became Hettie Jones*, Jones appropriates and misuses the male-coded "road" to convey her ambiguous position as a female Beat. As she discusses the implications of her choice to marry LeRoi Jones and bear his child, she remarks, as noted in chapter 7, "sometimes you have to go on the road" (62). This phrasing links her commitment to Roi to countercultural rejection of mainstream American values; it makes her reception of traditional plots for women—love, marriage, family—daring and rebellious. Jones's "road" life might not appear particularly independent or iconoclastic to readers who draw their impressions of Beat from texts like *Go* and *On the Road*, but *How I Became Hettie Jones* asks readers to recognize previously unacknowledged modes and expressions of female boldness that produce defiant femininities—lives in which women's improvisations on dominant gender role expectations produce something unprecedented and unquantifiable.

Eight years after the publication of *How I Became Hettie Jones*, Jones titled her first collection of poems *Drive*, fully claiming the road as a metaphor for defiant female self-fashioning. This text portrays women drivers smashing through barriers—"knocking them flat with one blow / and driving over them clear into / paradise" ("Ruby My Dear" 22). Women in motion, Jones suggests, evade containment by the gender norms regulated and enforced by patriarchal institutions and by male-centered social arrangements. *Drive* announces its intent to denaturalize those norms in its first poem, "Hard Drive," which introduces a gendered "dilemma" Jones describes as its own "solution." After being confronted with a sight "at once so exquisitely light and dark" that the poet "cri[es]" as she drives "north along the Saw Mill" River Parkway, she observes:

I have always been at the same time
woman enough to be moved to tears
and man enough
to drive my car in any direction (11)

The poem explicitly directs this "dilemma" to the attention of "young women" (11), anticipating and encouraging, perhaps, another generation preparing to leave home. Claiming the freedom to move one's life "in any direction" imaginable, Jones asserts, means "driving past" either/or models of gendered identity to find or create alternatives, a project she shares with other Beat-associated women.

Intertextual Journeys

I hope this detour through the travel-related imagery of Beat-associated women's life-writing serves to sum up *Women Writers of the Beat Era*'s argument about the challenges and the rewards of intertextual self-representation. Mapping the uncharted terrain of *female*-centered Beat in and around and through the texts and discourses of others, the women writers represented in this study liken themselves to travelers exploring new territories, actively choosing risky routes, seeking new, freer forms of individual and communal creativity. As they renegotiate the relation of Beatness to gender, they travel roads they find exhilarating and terrifying, illuminating and alienating, rewarding and disappointing—sometimes all at once. These roads demand and inspire alternate modes of self-expression, imaginative and improvisational strategies for absorbing and transforming the Beat mythos. Infusing a different kind of mobility into the "Beat movement," they unmoor their identities from the certainty of the already-known to narrate Beat lives formed in the openness of possibility.

NOTES

Preface

1. For discussion, see Ronna Johnson's "'And then she went': Beat Departures and Feminine Transgressions in Joyce Johnson's *Come and Join the Dance.*"

2. The German-born weiss, a refugee from the Nazi regime, explains that she decided to use all lowercase letters for her name as a way of expressing her rejection of totalitarian systems. "In German," she notes, "all nouns are capitalized" ("S" 69).

3. Throughout this study, italics are original unless otherwise indicated.

4. *Minor Characters* is the title of Joyce Johnson's 1983 memoir. I use the phrase to stress the pervasiveness of the "minor character" designation in commentary on the Beat movement's literary production. *The Oxford Companion to American Literature*, for instance, lists Allen Ginsberg, Gregory Corso, Lawrence Ferlinghetti, and Jack Kerouac as Beat's "leading literary figures"; no female authors appear in its description of the "Beat movement" ("Beat Movement" 61). For the most part and until fairly recently, women have been similarly scarce in other texts—literary anthologies, critical evaluations, and pop-culture articles alike—describing and defining Beat literary practice.

Introduction

1. See Manuel Martinez's *Countering the Counterculture* for discussion of Beats and "reactionary, nativist, racist ideologies" (25).

2. For an overview, see Friedman's "'Being Here as Hard as I Could': The Beat Generation Women Writers." She points out, for example, that Joanne Kyger, an invested participant in the San Francisco Renaissance (sometimes referred to as the West Coast arm of the Beat movement), "had begun to compose and publish poetry in her childhood" (233). Beat-associated women writers have publicly resisted the idea that without their links to male Beats they would not have taken up writing lives. In an interview with Nancy Grace, weiss notes that she "wrote [her] first poem at age five . . . and always knew [she] was a poet" ("S" 61). Joyce Johnson stresses that she identified herself as a writer and organized her life in support of her calling before she encountered Allen Ginsberg and Jack Kerouac, or heard of something called the Beat Generation. In her autobiogra-

phy *Recollections of My Life as a Woman,* di Prima reports that at fourteen years of age she vowed to "take up the challenge" of a writing life (78).

3. This brief overview of Beat-associated women's literary productivity is not meant to be exhaustive. The publication detail in this paragraph and in the preceding two paragraphs is drawn from the Knight and Peabody anthologies, as well as from James Egles's *Beats and Friends. Reality Studio's* "Bibliographic Bunker" contains downloadable versions of a number of Beat and Beat-related magazines, including *Floating Bear, Yugen,* and *Fuck You.* See also entries in Beat reference works edited by Kurt Hemmer (*Encyclopedia*) and Ann Charters (*Dictonary*) for more specific and comprehensive information on individual authors.

4. This text is the first in Wave Books' new interview series.

5. See *Elise Cowen: Poems and Fragments,* edited by Tony Trigilio.

6. As George Dardess explains, spontaneous prose aims to "render the details of consciousness simultaneously with their occurrence within the mind" and thereby to unite "art and life" (294; see Dardess for discussion). Despite its association with Kerouac, spontaneous writing is not a specifically male form unique to him and his immediate circle. For instance, weiss has practiced her own mode of spontaneous composition throughout her long career; she explains that she does not rewrite, preferring to "let the heart, the eyes, the hands just move with it. It comes out . . . and trails off sometimes into unfinished sentences, and I leave it that way. That's the way I do spontaneous writing" ("S" 60). Further, not all Beat writers subscribe to the spontaneous writing philosophy; Johnson and Grace point out that the better-known male writers follow more traditional literary conventions and processes when it suits ("Visions" 16).

7. Drawing on the work of Gérard Genette, Whitlock recognizes two categories of paratext: "The first, 'peritext,' includes everything between and on the covers. . . . The second, 'epitext,' are the elements outside the bound volume: interviews, correspondence, reviews, commentary, and so on." She argues that attending to "these thresholds" is "a vital component of any enquiry into the cross-cultural routes of contemporary life narrative" (14).

1. Intertextual Lives

1. The "beat" concept appears to have originated with Herbert Huncke, "Times Square existentialist-thief" (Lee 4) and one of Ginsberg's "angelheaded hipsters" (*Howl* 3). For Huncke, beat signified a state of being in which one was "without money, without a place to stay, without drugs for withdrawal symptoms" (Charters, "Introduction: What" xxii). The word referenced the "'beaten' condition of worn-out travelers for whom home was the road. Huncke used it to explain his 'exalted exhaustion' of a life lived beyond the edge" (Knight 2). Huncke introduced the term to the New York circle of Kerouac, Ginsberg, and Burroughs, where it took on additional meanings and interpretations. For Ginsberg, to be B/beat meant being "exhausted, at the bottom of the world looking up or out, sleepless, wide-eyed, perceptive, rejected by society" (qtd. in Charters, "Introduction: What" xxii). For further information, see the multiple articles and essays defining and discussing Beat in Ann Charters's *Beat Down to Your Soul.*

2. The male-centered Beat ethos expressed in Beat literature, in popular and scholarly responses to the Beats, and in general cultural discourses portrays Beat, in Ronna Johnson and Nancy Grace's terms, as "iconoclastic, freewheeling, *masculinist* community and dissent from both literary convention and conformist 'lifestyle'" ("Visions" 1; italics

added). This gendering of Beat identity persists even among commentators who criticize rather than admire or romanticize it. For instance, "The Only Rebellion Around," a scathing article published in 1959, characterizes "Beatdom" as "largely a male society" and asserts that what "Beats really seem to want from femininity . . . is financial support." And, it hastens to add, "the 'chicks' who are willing to support a whiskey male are often middle-aged and fat" (O'Neil 437–38). In this version of Beat society, women are either absent or repellent, at best secondary, quasi-Beats, and "Beat" because they could not do any better. In its disparaging description of women as "financial support" for men, the article also denigrates and dismisses Beat men by exposing their economic dependence on women during a time in which masculinity was defined largely through the provider role. Beat-associated women writers express mixed feelings about economic arrangements that assign them breadwinning responsibilities. Joyce Johnson reports that buying dinner for the broke Kerouac made her "feel very competent and womanly" (*MC* 127). While often impatient with her nine-to-five jobs in the publishing industry, she gloried in the self-sufficiency those jobs enabled and recognized the advantages they provided in advancing her writing career. Hettie Jones asserts that she chose to work full-time to preserve her husband's burgeoning literary opportunities but also points to her own lack of opportunities to develop her poetic voice. Of course, not all Beat women financially supported Beat men, but many understood breadwinning as a necessary outcome of their escape from traditional gender role arrangements that kept women financially reliant on men. For discussion of this issue, see Johnson and Grace, *Girls Who Wore Black;* and Grace and Johnson, *Breaking the Rule of Cool.*

3. While some of the women writers included in *Women Writers of the Beat Era* have resisted being characterized as Beat, all of them consented to be interviewed for *Breaking the Rule of Cool*, Grace and Johnson's volume of interviews and discussion of the lives of Beat women writers, and all accepted inclusion in Knight's and/or Peabody's anthologies of Beat women's writing.

4. The term "pre-text" is used fairly commonly to indicate prior texts and the "intertextual encyclopedic code" that Marko Juvan describes as "a fluctuating field of representations that arises from recurring textual structures and coinciding sign constellations that continue to pervade social discourse, but also through selection, accumulation, storing, and normative-descriptive categorizations of such patterns in research, education, the media, publishing, and so on. The intertextual encyclopedia encompasses primarily the repertoire of representative, republished, reviewed, discussed, and cited works, utterances, themes, motifs, images, stereotypes, and clichés, as well as a collection of more or less fixed intertextual techniques, figures, and genres" (146).

5. This statement appears in a 1954 letter from Ginsberg to John Clellon Holmes, which Johnson quotes in *Minor Characters.*

6. The historian Ruth Rosen describes a postwar America that enforced women's acquiescence to this ideal: "During the 1950s, the president of Harvard University saw no reason to increase the number of female undergraduates because the university's mission was to 'train leaders,' and Harvard's Lamont Library was off-limits to women for fear they would distract male students. Newspaper ads separated jobs by sex; employers paid women less than men for the same work. Bars often refused to serve women; banks routinely denied women credit or loans. Some states even excluded women from jury duty. Radio producers considered women's voices too abrasive to be on air; television executives believed they didn't have enough credibility to anchor the news. No women

ran big corporations or universities, worked as firefighters or police officers, sat on the Supreme Court, installed electric equipment, climbed telephone poles, or owned construction companies. . . . Few people knew more than a few women professors, doctors, or lawyers. . . . [I]f a woman wanted an abortion, legal nowhere in America, she risked her life, searching among quacks in back alleys for a competent and compassionate doctor. The public believed that rape victims had probably 'asked for it,' most women felt too ashamed to report it, and no language existed to make sense of marital rape, date rape, domestic violence, or sexual harassment" (xi–xii).

7. Anne Waldman notes: "A woman might be whisked away to mental institutions, lobotomized through shock treatment because of an affair with a person of color, or a lesbian relationship, or for supporting Adlai Stevenson and hating Joe McCarthy" ("Fast" 261). Indeed, research conducted by Stephanie Coontz establishes that "institutionalization and sometimes electric shock treatments were used to force women to accept their domestic roles" (32). See Wini Breines, who identifies urban Beat bohemias as one of the few places that "disaffected" girls might find alternatives: "A subterranean life, acted out or dreamed about, was generated by a culture that penalized girls and young women who were unable or unwilling to fit the model of the perky, popular teenager eagerly anticipating marriage and motherhood. The rigidity of what was acceptable in that culture made some young women feel discontented and unreal, as if their lives had not yet begun" (390, 402). For historical accounts of female "pockets of resistance" to postwar U.S. conservatism, see Breines and other essays in *Not June Cleaver: Women and Gender in Postwar America, 1945–1960.*

8. Tony Trigilio, editor of *Elise Cowen: Poems and Fragments,* observes that Cowen "has appeared only as a cameo figure in most histories and biographies of the Beat period in U.S. literature, often portrayed merely as the mad girlfriend-typist who flashed briefly into Ginsberg's life, with little or no mention of her work as a poet" (xiv).

9. As I have noted elsewhere, as Beat men defined themselves in large part through disregard of models of male identity based in capitalist conformity and preservation of nuclear family, they transferred social obligation and breadwinning drudgery to female keeping and constructed a gendered Beat economy in which male independence was often a function of female labor and caretaking ("Adventures"). See Ronna Johnson's "Mapping Women Writers of the Beat Generation" for analysis of women's transformations of Beat antidomestic discourses.

10. Aware of public hunger for intimate detail about bohemian lives, Jones long resisted being interviewed about her Beat experience. People "wanted to get between the sheets," she states, "and I had no desire to put my personal life on the line like that" ("D" 159). Early in her essay "Babes in Boyland," she writes: "Sex of course—let's start with this and get it out of the way" (51). Readers are no doubt interested in the open sexuality characterizing Beat communities and aware of the autobiographical nature of much of the Beat literary canon; many of the texts produced by the movement's best-known figures are based more or less directly on their lives. The bulk of Kerouac's work, including *On the Road, The Dharma Bums, The Subterraneans, Tristessa,* and *Desolation Angels,* is plainly autobiographical. His texts, Joyce Johnson suggests, are more "true-life novels" than "fiction" ("AC" 111). Critics point to strongly autobiographical elements in Burroughs's novels *Junky* and *Queer,* and, to a lesser extent, *Naked Lunch.* Commentators routinely describe Holmes's *Go* as a semiautobiographical novel and read Ginsberg's "Kaddish" and "Howl" through his biography. Jane Falk notes that Beat writers' "empha-

sis on the personal and autobiographical as central to the literary work stood in opposition to the New Critical idea of the objective and autonomous work of art," and thus contributed to their position of defiant literary outsiderness ("Journal" 1000). Johnson remarks that when Kerouac and Ginsberg "were first writing their rather confessional literature, it was a strange thing to be doing—shocking" ("AC" 111).

11. I do not limit possibilities for the emergence of "intertextual lives" to the Beat movement. It seems to me that such lives tend to develop in the seams and fault lines that attend moments of historical flux and cultural change. In the United States of the 1950s and early 1960s, Beats were among the groups that became focal points for national conversations on matters such as the value of art, the proper enactment of self-determination, and the nature of deviance and conformity. Prominent Beat figures such as Kerouac and Ginsberg actively encouraged such conversations. As Mel van Elteren points out, male Beats turned "moral panics about their behavior . . . at the local level into national events," attracting disaffected youth and provoking culture mavens to discuss and dissect their texts (73). The "shocking messages" they promoted in the media "were even more disturbing or dismaying to middle America," van Elteren suggests, "because of the almost programmatic ruthlessness that was linked to their impudence in public performances" (74). These defiant public performances helped to produce an alternate category of American identity but also led to oversimplification and caricature that overshadowed their calls for meaningful change.

12. Jay Clayton and Eric Rothstein observe that Kristeva's "social text" "may be thought of as the network of anonymous ideas, commonplaces, folk wisdom, and clichés that make up the background of one's life" ("Figures" 22).

13. Beyond literary fields, theories of intertextuality also figure prominently in areas including art, cinema, and music. For discussions of intertextual "cross-fertilization between literary and visual works of art" (Landwehr 1), see the 2002 special issue of *College Literature,* edited and with an introduction by Margarete Landwehr.

14. For detailed analyses of the evolution of theories of intertextuality, see Graham Allen; and Marko Juvan.

15. Like literary texts, theories of intertextuality constitute ongoing interactive conversations characterized, in Susan Stanford Friedman's terms, by a "multiplicity of 'intertextual' revisions, grafts, and adaptations" ("Weavings" 159). Most discussions of intertextuality take pains to acknowledge this multiplicity. Graham Allen explains that "intertextuality seems such a useful term because it foregrounds notions of relationality, interconnectedness, and interdependence in modern cultural life" (5). As "the culminating critical term for processes of cultural interconnectivity centered on the printed text," intertextuality, Mary Orr argues, cannot be codified in "a single definition or delimited application" (170, 60). Juvan notes that "intertextuality is situated at the crossroads of quite old techniques, like citation and pastiche, and modern theories of text" (73), and "was born of the interaction between many streams of thought, from Russian Formalism to deconstructivism and psychoanalysis" (74). Clayton and Rothstein describe "the face of 'intertextuality'" as "less a simple, single, and precise image, a bronze head by Rodin, than something shattered, a portrait bust by an avid exponent of analytic cubism too poor to afford a good chisel" ("Figures" 11).

16. Graham Allen points out that some feminist writers argue that women are "'split' subject[s] whose utterances are always 'double-voiced,' their own and yet replete with an 'otherness'" associated with "a socially oriented notion of intertextuality" (165). In

other words, because they occupy positions of otherness, women write in and from intertexts.

17. As is probably obvious, I am of the school of thought that existential difficulties with the nature of language and subjectivity do not necessarily vacate writerly agency or necessitate the "death of the author" and substitution of "language itself for the person who . . . had been supposed to be its owner" (Barthes 143). Readers (and most theorists) recognize that *somebody*—a person situated in a particular time, place, and cultural environment—initiates and shapes the production of a text meant to account for a particular life experience. In other words, "a 'subject' already exists before he or she is reconstituted (again) in a text" (S. Friedman, "Weavings" 147). "It is people-as-actors (authors, writers)," Susan Stanford Friedman observes, who devise methods to convey their stories, "even if they don't originate them" (146). See also Nancy K. Miller, who argues that acknowledging the culturally inflected "body" of the *somebody* who selects words and arranges them upon the page reveals "the sometimes brutal traces of the culture of gender" and "the inscriptions of its political structures" (84).

18. In *Touching the World: Reference in Autobiography,* Eakin examines the function of memory to "[revise] and [edit] the remembered past to square with the needs and requirements of the selves we have become in any present." In this sense, he argues, all life-writing is palimpsestic because it "evoke[s] both the conscious and the unconscious dimensions of the relation between present and past that occur in the autobiographical act" (67).

19. "Palimpsestuous" is an adjective coined by Philippe Lejeune in "Le Roland Barthes sans peine" (1984).

2. Truthiness

1. The text we know as *The Autobiography of Thomas Jefferson* was originally entitled *Memoir* (for discussion, see Cox 123–24).

2. This definition holds for the period in which di Prima was writing *Memoirs of a Beatnik.* In later years of the twentieth century, as G. Thomas Couser notes, memoir exploded as a popular genre, leading to the publication of "so-called nobody memoirs— memoirs by hitherto anonymous individuals. Ironically, the publication of such narratives helps to explain the ascendance of the genre; it appears open to anybody" (5).

3. The term "beatnik" was first used by the San Francisco journalist Herb Caen in 1958, and he did not intend it as a compliment. Some commentators view the word "beatnik" as a kind of shorthand for the "trend followers" who came after the actual Beats (van Elteren 76), but John Clellon Holmes, in his 1965 article "The Game of the Name," characterizes "beatnik" as "a handy caricature for everyone associated with Beatness." The word, he notes, "quickly entered the smear-vocabularies" of people "who like to call intellectuals 'eggheads.' And for the same perceptive reason: if you can't understand them, brand them" (636). More recently, the Beat scholar Rob Johnson notes that by 1960 the term had "come to stand in for every anti-establishment juvenile delinquent, commie, and rock-and-roll hoodlum type in America" (82). Nancy Grace argues that "beatnik" is "a pejorative that through the suffix '-nik' transformed Beat into the evil Soviet 'commie' of the cold war decades. Simultaneously, these three small letters diminish and trivialize the demon Beat, converting evil into the childish and comic, effectively nullifying the potential cultural threat posed by those known as Beat. Thus di Prima's story of being a

'Beat/nik' reflects the ways in which mainstream American culture, particularly popular media representations, constructed Beat avant-gardism as paradoxically degenerate/
dangerous and infantile/inconsequential" ("Snapshots" 162). For further discussion, see
Holmes; and Tim Hunt.

4. It is probably unnecessary to point out that Colbert brought the term "truthiness"
into common usage on Comedy Central's *The Colbert Report*. In the sense intended by
Colbert, I suggest that the memoir's "truthiness" comes from its reference to things we
believe "without regard to evidence, logic, intellectual examination, or facts" (Meyer;
see also "Truthiness").

5. The original 1969 Olympia Press edition front cover contains an abstract female
figure, positioned in a window-like oval, which matches the art of other texts published
in the series.

6. The "Maurice" of di Prima's afterword is Maurice Girodias, founder and editor
of Olympia Press. Olympia was famous (or infamous) for its publication of William
Burroughs's *Naked Lunch,* and di Prima composed her memoir amid reverberations
from its obscenity trial. Olympia Press published controversial books including *Lolita,*
Tropic of Cancer, and texts by the Marquis de Sade; it also published straightforward,
unabashed pornography. Like Olympia itself, *Memoirs of a Beatnik* is in-between and
self-contradictory—serious and silly, dirty and literary, patently fabricated and representative of di Prima's experience. Given the complexities evident even on the surface of di
Prima's text, it is not surprising that Last Gasp, attempting, perhaps, to cover all literary
bases, designated it "Ficto-Biography; Erotica."

7. Di Prima married Alan Marlowe in California in 1962. In *Recollections of My Life
as a Woman,* she has difficulty accounting for the marriage and has little positive to say
about Marlowe. In her 2014 collection *The Poetry Deal,* she explains that she moved to
San Francisco in order "to *actualize* what in New York [she'd] only been able to write
about." She came to the West Coast in order "to work in new ways for change" (2).

8. Of course, not all readers are necessarily turned on, as demonstrated by notable
critical differences over the nature of the sex presented in *Memoirs of a Beatnik,* variously
characterized as coldly pornographic and pleasantly erotic, playful and harsh, passionate
and detached. Where one reader finds the sex exuberant, another finds it depressing. The
larger implications of the sex are also a matter of debate. While a male critic asserts that
"the lesbian scenes are . . . a little unusual because shaped by female desire, rather than
fetishized for a male spectator" (Libby 55), a female critic argues that the same scenes
"function much as they do in male-focused pornography, as a salacious trigger of male
sexuality" (Grace, "Snapshots" 164).

9. "Cool" seems a central yet slippery concept for di Prima. Interestingly, *Recollections of My Life as a Woman* dates the "code of cool" to her affiliation with a group of
Swarthmore women, especially Tomi and Susan O'Reilley, noting that "after a year and
a half" of removal from their home and high school lives, "the ethos of cool [had] been
built into [their] bones" (97). Later in *Recollections,* she discusses having an abortion
even though everything in her tells her not to. She could not discuss her feelings with
her lover because "the sense of cool, of what was expected of [her] as a 'chick,'" would not
allow it (229). But she also aligns the code of cool with "the code of the Italian woman:
to do what *he* wanted and take the consequences" (231). In *Dinners and Nightmares,* she
recounts her resentment when a male lover expects her to perform household tasks "just

because [she] happen[s] to be a chick." She is angry that he ignores her priorities as a writer, but she does the work and does not complain "out loud" because "it's so fucking uncool to talk about it" (73–74).

10. At points, *Recollections of My Life as a Woman* directly contradicts claims made in *Memoirs of a Beatnik*. For instance, of di Prima's relationship with her friend Tomi, which *Memoirs* describes as sexual, she writes: "We were friends, but never lovers, though once we tried. She impatient as I groped blindly, seeking her pleasure. Totally inexperienced and voiceless. I finally burst into tears and hid in the bathroom" (106). In this notably different story, di Prima claims none of the apparently inherent sexual confidence she attributes to her younger self in *Memoirs*.

11. Early chapters of *Recollections* detail her father's violence. She remembers that he "turned into a battering madman at the sight of a low-cut blouse. A dress he didn't like. A neatly mended tear in a skirt. There would be nights I returned after whatever arbitrary curfew had been set, and would go to bed bleeding from something [he] threw at me. Or days when [her mother] would burst into tears at some book I was reading." Where di Prima's father represents a constant threat of violence, her mother poses the danger of another sort of abuse; at any moment, she might become "wild and hysterical, threatening a fit" (85).

12. *Recollections* also responds to autobiographies written by other Beat-associated figures. For example, di Prima's discussions of her affair with LeRoi Jones at points seem to address Hettie Jones's *How I Became Hettie Jones* and Amiri Baraka/LeRoi Jones's *Autobiography*.

13. Di Prima suspects she is excluded from the anthology because of her affair with LeRoi Jones; she notes that he, however, is included (238). The following statement made by Allen Ginsberg encapsulates male Beats' assumptions about gender and literary merit: "It's all right to blame the men for exploiting the women—or, I think the point is, the men didn't push the women literally or celebrate them." He then qualifies, asserting "among the group of people we knew at the time," there were no women "writers of such power as Kerouac and Burroughs." Male Beats, he argues, cannot be held "responsible for the lack of outstanding genius in the women we knew." Finally, he allows that "where there was a strong writer who could hold her own, like Diane di Prima, we would certainly work with her and recognize her" (qtd. in Peabody 1). As di Prima suggests in *Recollections*, such grudging recognition reserves true literary merit to men.

14. "As woman," di Prima asserts, "I felt myself so much the *channel* of new life, the door into the world," and as an artist, "I felt so deeply that whatever happens has its reasons, and that if you 'go with it' everything will be taken care of" (230–31). When she gives into her lover's demands and "what was expected of [her] as 'a chick'" (229) to abort what would have been her second child, she experiences a breach in her existence; time "splintered along the flaw line of the abortion," and her life becomes "shot through with darkness" (236). *Recollections* contrasts di Prima's openness to the full range of human experience with male Beats' tendency to regard women's potential maternity as an entrapping obligation to be avoided at all costs. Mocking "their fear of being 'caught,' as if anyone would *want* to live with them" (158), di Prima replaces, Erik Mortenson observes, "the inward thrust of the penis so celebrated by the male Beats ... with the outward movement of the child" (117) leaving the female body. She considers childbirth, "being opened *from the inside out*," the means through which women "truly lost [their] virginity. Torn open so the world could come through." Over the "semipleasant invasion

from a man," she prefers "the joy, the power of being OPEN. Something unconquerable and deep about it" (*R* 190). Motherhood is a consistently strong and pervasive theme in di Prima's poetry (for discussion, see Libby; and Quinn).

15. In fact, in his review of *Recollections,* Jack Foley remarks on a "woman friend's" reaction to di Prima's brief discussion of this peripheral woman, which "implicitly asks us to identify ourselves with di Prima and her friends" and to view Joan "as an outcast." Foley's friend, however, came to identify with Joan and to "see di Prima's curt dismissal . . . as cruel, perhaps even unfair" (348).

3. Diversification

1. Since *Troia* is signed "Bonnie Bremser," I use this name in my discussion of the memoir; I refer to her as "Brenda Frazer" in the last segment of this chapter, which deals with her more recent life-writing. Readers, critics, and peers use varying names when referencing her texts and presence on the Beat scene. Ann Charters calls her "Bonnie" in her introduction to *Troia,* and refers to her as both "Bonnie Bremser (Brenda Frazer)" and "Brenda Frazer" in *Beat Down to Your Soul.* In the Peabody and Knight anthologies, she appears as "Brenda Frazer." For M. Christine Anderson, she is "Bonnie Bremser Frazer." In Grace and Johnson's *Breaking the Rule of Cool* she is Brenda (Bonnie) Frazer; in their *Girls Who Wore Black,* she appears variously as "Brenda Frazer (Bonnie Bremser)," "Brenda (Bonnie) Bremser Frazer," and "Brenda Frazer." Anne Waldman calls her "Bonnie Frazer," and ruth weiss calls her "Brenda Frazer." Locating her in others' texts—memoirs, anthologies, interviews, and critical appraisals—requires detours and substitutions within and across indices, works cited pages, and tables of contents. There is also variation in Bremser's self-naming. In her autobiographical sketches "Breaking out of D.C." and "The Village Scene" she calls herself "Bonnie." In *Troia: Mexican Memoirs,* she twice quotes others calling her "Brenda" (168, 204) without comment or explanation; she, however, calls herself "Bonnie." According to Ronna Johnson, she sometimes signs e-mail and written correspondence "Brenda (Bonnie) Frazer" and sometimes "Bonnie Frazer" ("Beat Transnationalism" 66).

2. "Troia" can translate as either "Troy" or "slut." Many readers assume "troia" is a Spanish word, but it does not appear in Spanish dictionaries. Others believe it is French. In a letter to Kurt Hemmer, Bremser/Frazer writes "the name *Troia* means 'whore' in French," and notes "it could very well have come from a Fellini film but I don't know" (qtd. in "The Prostitute" 102). However, "troia" does not appear in French dictionaries, either. It does appear in Italian dictionaries, and Italian-speaking friends describe the term, which can also mean "sow," or female pig, as crudely insulting.

3. For discussion of the somewhat muddled timeline of Bremser's composition of the letters, see Ronna Johnson, "Beat Transnationalism."

4. Nancy Grace notes that despite Perkins's attempt to create the "linearity" of an "adventure story," *Troia* "relies most fully upon the free movement of mind through memory and feeling, the original form of [Bremser's] letters. The result is fragmentation and surrealism. Chapters and paragraphs, for example, begin in medias res. Time shifts suddenly within paragraphs and sentences . . . and the narrative voice frequently repositions itself, breaking the illusion of narrative consistency and character development" ("Snapshots" 173).

5. While Ray is Bremser's primary addressee in the letters, Bremser envisions a larger audience of "people reading this" (141). She answers readers' likely questions, such as

"Did Ray ever meet any of my Mexcity johns?" (182), and anticipates the concerns of "girls who might get envious and discontented" (213).

6. I share Ronna Johnson's attention to Bremser's performance of multiple roles, but my concern is less with the ways in which she "modif[ies] the road tale with domestic determinants" and brings to light the implications of "female seizure of prerogatives of the male road hero" (Johnson, "Beat Transnationalism" 60), and more with the ways in which her multiplicity plays out in intertextual self-identification and exposes the palimpsestic nature of women's self-representation as Beats.

7. For further interpretation of this scene, see Ronna Johnson ("Beat Transnationalism"), Helen McNeil, and M. Christine Anderson, who notes that Bremser "escaped the U.S. with and for Ray, but he is part of what binds her, as does her responsibility to keep her baby healthy and happy" (256).

8. For Beat men, having sex, especially sex unencumbered by family or faithfulness constraints, signifies autonomy and dominance; it demonstrates a self-determined individualism that defies social conformity and expectation. Beat icon Neal Cassady's letters to Kerouac center on his efforts to "make" women, offer advice on making women, and request that Kerouac make women for him: "If you love me, you'll do all in your power to find a girl" (189, 197). In a discursive system in which "making" women signifies making masculinity, *On the Road*'s Dean Moriarty is admired for his prowess with women, his ability to "just [race] in society, eager for bread and love; he didn't care one way or the other, 'so long's I can get that lil ole gal with that lil sumpin down there tween her legs'" (10). In Kerouac's "confessional narrative" (Nicosia i) *The Subterraneans*, his character Leo Percepied views Mardou Fox as his "prize" but also believes that "any other chick will do" (111). He insists on his love for her while measuring her worth against his work and his friends, as well as against other women who might be less trouble (61, 142). Percepied responds to his loss of Mardou's love by "go[ing] home" to "write this book" (152), parlaying his experience with her into profitable self-expression.

9. Some commentators interpret this letter as instructions specific to Bremser's New York letter-writing, but its position in *Troia* shows it predates this period. Nevertheless, it seems to have a clear bearing on her motivation for writing and her sense of her audience. At the end of book 1, Bremser describes this letter as an announcement from Ray that he is "*in Webb County jail, Laredo, Texas, under arrest for unlawful flight.*" In the letter, Ray demands that Bremser write to him: "*I need you just like I needed you yesterday and always*" (72). This letter trails off in an ellipsis with the statement "*Think of me; they let me keep your picture and I look at you . . .*" (73). The letter then resumes at the opening of book 2: ". . . From a letter written to me in Nuevo Laredo, Mexico sent by Ray from the Webb Country Jail in Laredo, Texas. / '. . . tell me some sexual items . . . draw up a plan, a plot, a sequence! Start alone, self-sex, then me, then he, then he or she and so on!'" (77; ellipses in original).

10. Some of Bremser's "sexual items" are more sensually detailed than others, and, as with di Prima's sexual scenes, critical interpretation varies. Kurt Hemmer, for example, remarks that "it is difficult not to find the more licentious passages titillating" ("The Prostitute" 105).

11. This potential for epistolary disappointment recalls Ray's haunting of post offices across Mexico, waiting and hoping for letters containing money, letters that for the most part do not arrive to ameliorate their poverty and homelessness. And Bremser's letters did go astray when they were handed over to Perkins, formed into a "memoir," and ex-

posed to the reading public. Bremser has noted that in addition to losing control over her story, she also lost its potential financial rewards. In a 1999 letter to Hemmer, she remarks that even though *Troia* "slipped into obscurity . . . somehow all the books got sold anyway and are now enriching dealerships etc, all independent of me" (qtd. in "The Prostitute" 102).

12. Bremser has explained that Perkins constructed the introduction, and she does not recall "where those sections were in the original manuscript" ("A" 120). It is unclear why Perkins decided to situate these statements at the opening of the memoir. Perhaps this textual arrangement was intended to introduce Bremser as a woman who accepts, even welcomes, positions of lack, a move that might serve to preempt criticism of Ray.

13. The memoir ends with a parallel gesture: Bremser asks Ray for money, then returns it to him to signify that she has "decided to stay" with him in New York (213).

14. Ironically, as Hemmer points out, her "selling of her body becomes a ritualized sacrifice that reinscribes her desire to stay together with Ray even as it tears them apart" (106).

15. After she and Ray sign away their rights as parents, she does not see her daughter again.

16. Bremser's characterizations of her relationship with Ray also "get indiscriminate." She claims that her husband has not harmed her (17), but is clear that he "forced" her into a life of prostitution she finds miserable and reductive (32). Bremser insists she loves Ray "desperately" (79) and "long[s] for him to be with [her] at every moment" (135), but is relieved when they separate and she is "free from one half of [her] problems" (188) and able to explore "this personal sense that has to be satisfied" (175). She presents Ray as a stern taskmaster, sending her out to walk the streets despite her "pleading," but she also mocks his "distinguished services" as her pimp (34). She "get[s] very scared at [his] violence" (148) but asserts she does not "love him any less" (154). Her references to their sexual compatibility contend with her comparisons of Ray to homosexuals; after writing disparagingly about "fags," she finds their characteristics in Ray. She also claims that she comes to "dig" anal sex, "pretending that [she] was getting back at Ray for his homosexual jail experiences" (160).

4. Consociation

1. This choice was intended to express "her antipathy for Nazi totalitarianism by rejecting the conventions of her native language" (Grace, "ruth weiss" 340). In German, as noted in the preface to this study, nouns are capitalized. As evidenced by the titles of her texts, weiss also disregards English standards of capitalization in her use of all capital letters in selected words and phrases. In her article on *DESERT JOURNAL* (at this writing, the only academic essay devoted to weiss's work), Nancy Grace suggests that weiss's frequent use of capital letters conveys "exuberant boldness" (61). In general, weiss tends to use uppercase for titles, names of important places, and names of people, as well as for emphasis. Because she is an oral poet—her focus is on jazz performance—the capitals might also have something to do with tone and breath. In a personal communication, weiss told me that she prefers to write in English because it affords her optimal opportunities to "play with language." Her capitalization practices seem part of this project.

2. In a personal communication, weiss used the phrase "autobiographical prose poetry" to characterize her work.

3. In his introduction to *CAN'T STOP THE BEAT*, Horst Spandler explains that

"Goddess of the Beats" was a label applied to weiss "by Herb Caen, the journalist who first used the expression 'beatnik'" in the 1950s (xix).

4. Warren French cites an article by Wilber Wood for the first designation and a letter from Jory Sherman for the second (25).

5. As the appearance of this title indicates, the English/German editions of weiss's work alter her practice of using capital letters for titles.

6. Holmes uses this language to describe "Howl" and *On the Road*.

7. Circles constitute a recurring motif in weiss's work: "that's the point/become the line/become the circle/that's the point" ("SOMETHING CURRENT" 132). Her poetic lines facilitate a free flow of thought and improvisation, thus conveying connection and continuity.

8. *DESERT JOURNAL* is not a record of an actual sojourn in the desert; however, weiss did travel to a desert when she "was about three-quarters through the book" and found that the experience "confirmed [her] reference to it" ("S" 68).

9. Inclusivity and interconnection are hallmarks of weiss's work. When she performs selections from *DESERT JOURNAL*, she invites listeners to call out numbers between one and forty; she then reads the corresponding day-poem, a practice Grace suggests "empower[s] audience members, now artistic collaborators . . . to call the poem into being" ("ruth weiss's *DESERT JOURNAL*" 62). weiss describes her poetry readings as communal events and reports that after her *DESERT JOURNAL* performances, listeners "always ask 'how do you know this about me?'" (*DJ* 207). Her frequent use of the inclusive pronouns "one" and "you" links her internal landscape to that of the reader or listener, and she maintains the present tense in her poems in order to "write it like I am there, so then the person who reads it, or hears it from me, is there with me" ("S" 61). Ensuring poems are "all in the present tense," weiss explains, is virtually the only form of revision she undertakes ("S" 61).

10. In other poems, weiss uses water to exemplify "life-blood" ("LIGHT" 46), a substance that is simultaneously the most intimate ground of self and the basis of connection to all others: "i reflect as in a mirror/a lake/but no/more as ocean/wave upon wave/not placid but rhythmically/i place myself/as all the creatures/and thus create" ("TURNABOUT" 146).

11. In her author's note at the end of *DESERT JOURNAL*, for instance, weiss declares that her poetry "has a life of its own" and she is "only the instrument" (*DJ* 207).

12. In a personal communication, weiss told me that the poems had been "commissioned," and in her foreword to the collection she explains that "John Hunt of AUDIO LITERATURE, who had bought the rights for a sound issue, asked me to write & record the following poems" (n.p.).

13. The importance of this theme is further illustrated by a number of drawings included in *DESERT JOURNAL* (created by the artist Paul Blake, weiss's partner), many of which portray phoenix/bird figures and bird/human hybrids.

14. weiss performed her first jazz poetry reading in 1949 in Chicago and has "always considered [her]self a jazz poet" ("S" 60). She explains: "My phrasings and rhythms depend upon what I hear. It's a dialogue with the musicians. I never use music as a background. I give the musicians room to come up with riffs of their own. I lower my voice, raise my voice. I may repeat phrases. I may make up sounds. . . . It just comes to me. I don't know what I'm going to do. And that's what is exciting" (66). In her account of the development of the San Francisco poetry and jazz scene, she asserts that she first

"did poetry and jazz" at the Cellar on Wednesday nights, then invited other poets. "It was only after that that some of the other well-known poets, whose names I'm not going to mention because everyone knows them, ended up doing the same thing. Only they were very smart. They recorded them and got records out of it" (71).

15. About being excluded by male Beats, weiss has been frank: "Somewhere there was an ego thing that was to keep the women out. My luck with some of the names like Kerouac was that I was never anybody's girlfriend, so they treated me a little better than the other women they were involved with. I had very good friends, but they didn't treat their women well. When it came right down to it, we were not invited into the center of things, just the periphery. I mean, there was the Auerhahn Press; Philip Lamantia did his best to try to get me published by it. No, we don't publish any women. Ferlinghetti said the same thing to me" ("S" 73).

5. Displacements

1. *The Japan and India Journals: 1960–1964* was originally published in 1981 by Tombouctou Books. The text was reissued in 2000 by North Atlantic Books as *Strange Big Moon: The Japan and India Journals* and in 2016 by Nightboat Books as *The Japan and India Journals*. Citations in this study reference the 2000 edition.

2. In 2000, Andrew Schelling characterized Kyger as the "preeminent living poet of the journal or notebook" (par. 4). Amy Friedman points out that Kyger's poems are "often titled by date as if entries in a journal" ("Joanne Kyger, Beat Generation Poet" 76).

3. Kyger reports being asked: "'Everybody's published their India journals. What about yours?!'" ("PG" 145). She had previously published *Desecheo Notebook* (1971), an account of her experience on the Caribbean island of Desecheo. The *Notebook* also merges travelogue, journal, and poetry, and reconsiders issues that occupy her in *The Japan and India Journals*. Here is an example: "Thursday. // the quality of mind / like I am keeping track of / 3 or 4 people at one time / bathing naked / A letter to Bobbie Creeley / no place to sit / all these men / I just want a place / for myself" (n.p.). *Desecheo Notebook* is reproduced in Kyger's 2002 collection *As Ever*. For discussion of Kyger's shorter travel notebooks, see Carden, "Joanne Kyger's Travel Chapbooks: A Poetics of Motion."

4. This image, among the first found in an Internet search for "Joanne Kyger," appears inside the 2000 edition of the *Journals* and is also used in Brenda Knight's *Women of the Beat Generation* anthology, though without Ginsberg's signature and caption. This photograph of Kyger is not included among the pictures in Ginsberg's updated *Indian Journals*, in which he does not mention meeting up with Kyger and Snyder in India, though a caption on the first photograph that appears in his journal does reference "travelling in northern India with Gary Snyder and Peter Orlovsky" (n.p.).

5. Kyger, on the other hand, tends to "indulge" herself by skipping zazen or by departing from proper practice and allowing her mind to follow "associative thought" (*JIJ* 70, 19). Snyder studies with a Zen master and collects accomplishments, including passing koans (39) and being initiated as a "Yamabushi, one of the conch horned, mountain climbing, magical Buddhists" (103); Kyger has trouble with the fundamentals of Zen and makes little effort to learn Japanese, a condition (as Falk notes) for individual study with a Zen master. Her journals do not overtly address the gender distinctions built into the practice of Zen Buddhism, which was for the most part restricted to men. Falk points out that the First Zen Institute did allow women to study, but Kyger "could not sit in the

main meditation hall" because it "was reserved for men only" ("Two" 103). As a man, Snyder is able to organize his life around Zen; as a woman, Kyger is permitted only a part-measure, a distinction that might be behind her reluctance to engage in an endeavor in which she intended to participate from the start. She "*refuse*[s] to be forced into sitting until [she] freely chooses to do so" (10), and when she does sit she has frequent lapses and setbacks.

6. In her author's note to *The Japan and India Journals*, Kyger credits her four years in Asia with making her "a bit more disciplined" (xii); however, her note to the second edition mentions her "frustration at failing to live the 'perfect' disciplined life of Japan" (xi). Also, it seems telling that her response to Snyder's urging to "lose [her] ego" anticipates feminist critiques of postmodern challenges to the nature of individual subjectivity. As Nancy K. Miller observes, "because women have not had the same historical relation of identity to origin, institution, production that men have had, they have not . . . (collectively) felt burdened by *too much* Self, Ego, Cogito, etc." (106). In other words, it is the privileged subject already and unquestioningly invested with authority, solidity, and self-possession that "has the luxury of flirting with . . . escape from identity" (83).

7. Lynn Bloom argues that "for a professional writer there are no private writings" (24). She defines "truly private diaries" as "bare-bones works." "Written with neither art nor artifice, they are so terse they seem coded; no reader outside the author's immediate society or household could understand them without extra-textual information" (25).

8. Kerouac, for instance, carried pocket notebooks "in which he was constantly recording daily events and memories"; he published his dream diary as *Book of Dreams* in 1961 (Falk, "Journal" 992).

9. Kyger uses a symbol to indicate the word "and" that I am unable to replicate. Following the example of other commentators, I use "&" to represent her shorthand. Also, note that I have reproduced minor spelling and punctuation irregularities, as well as her italics.

10. The implications of marital "battle," with its gain/loss connotations, might have something to do with Kyger's tendency in the *Journals* to include long lists of birthday and anniversary presents given and received, as well as with her careful accounting of purchases and notations of things lost. Her discussions of frequent injuries and illnesses offer another measure of her embattled sense of nonbelonging in Japan. "Sunday night a mukate fell in my hair and mildly bit me on the ear. Monday the iron fell off the table burning & blistering my hand and leg. Tuesday my leg seems to be swollen up, that is my ankle, from the bite of a smallish dragon" (34). Many entries detail the physical discomforts she endures—blisters, illnesses, pinched nerves, "familiar stomach troubles" (239), "adhesions" caused by "bumpy motorcycle rides" (53).

11. Kyger's journal leaves out entirely her second wedding, this one "a Buddhist ceremony at Daitoku-ji monastery in Kyoto" (Berkson 326), some five days later.

12. For more, see Amy Friedman, "Joanne Kyger, Beat Generation Poet"; and Bill Berkson, "Joanne Kyger." Kyger has remarked that she "resisted the Beat label during the time I was associated with the Beat writers because they never considered me a Beat writer," and suggests "it was the media that made it the movement it was" ("PG" 140, 141). In an interview with Linda Russo, Kyger challenges the notion of "a 'beat writer'" and protests the designation of women such as herself, Anne Waldman, and Lenore Kandel as "Beats." The identification, she asserts, is "not useful to me" ("Particularizing"). While acknowledging Kyger's distinctions between herself and the Beat Generation writers she

sees as a male brotherhood, I suggest that her representations of Beat in the *Journals* seem more ambivalent. As Friedman argues, "although it is problematic to identify Kyger wholly and completely as a Beat poet, she reflects Beat influences." Friedman points out that while there were conflicts between East Coast and San Francisco poets (including Kyger's mentors Duncan and Spicer), "Kyger shares with other Beat writers her contemplation of Eastern religions, the elevation of quotidian reflections in her art, the repeated mention of other Beat writers that creates a sense of familiar artistic community, and a suggested patina of spontaneity in the generation of her writing. Like a number of West Coast Beat writers—Lew Welch, Gary Snyder, and Philip Whalen (with whom Kyger shares some particular similarities)—Kyger's poetry employs the Beat focus on the simultaneous journey of outward travel and inward states" ("Joanne Kyger, Beat Generation Poet" 86, 75).

13. Commentators including Falk, Schelling, and Jonathan Skinner point out that Kyger's journal writing practices also have affinities with Japanese traditions of literary diary keeping.

14. In interviews, Kyger has stressed that "the writers [Ginsberg] loved and was close to, he'd work very hard to get them published" ("Particularizing"). For him, she has asserted, "the Beat generation" constitutes a "brotherhood of poets" ("PG" 140).

15. Kyger projects her everyday experience "upon a mythic frame," Russo argues, constructing "poems as a structure in which to observe her situation as an American poet/wife abroad." Russo further observes that "Kyger's desire to write through the *Odyssey*, coupled with her refusal to occupy the place designated feminine in the process, overturned an epic mode of production that imagines text to be communicated to the male poet by the disembodied female muse" ("To Deal" 187, 192). See Russo for in-depth analysis of Kyger's revision of *The Odyssey*.

6. Cross-Textuality

1. The title seems both straightforward—in the sense that it reflects the less-than position of Beat women in larger cultural discourses—and ironic—in the sense that the memoir contests this position. As Amy Friedman notes, in overlooking the irony of Johnson's title, commentators also "over[look] the fact that she asserts strenuously the ignored presence, rather than the absence, of women among the Beat writers" ("Being" 233).

2. This photograph appeared in an advertisement for the clothing chain The Gap, with Johnson airbrushed out.

3. Johnson reproduces this note in *Door Wide Open*, observing that it signaled "the beginning of the end" of her relationship with Kerouac: "We'd just had the best days of our entire relationship. Once Jack installed [his mother] on Long Island, he would never be as tender with me again" (116). At the point he wrote the note, he wasn't hitting the road of Beat adventure so much as going to Florida to stay with his mother.

4. In "Snapshots, Sand Paintings, and Celluloid: Formal Considerations in the Life Writing of Women Writers from the Beat Generation," Nancy Grace observes that at points in Johnson's narrative "a self emerges through the juxtaposing of her own memory with someone else's scripting of memory," an intersection that suggests "'reality,' the historical construction of Beat no less than other moments in time, lies somewhere within the transactional meeting of subjects and objects, an amorphous and serendipitous meeting and shifting of possibilities" (148). Grace remarks that "reading the book is

not unlike flipping through an album of photographs arranged somewhat haphazardly but nevertheless telling a coherent story, a compilation of linguistic images presenting the self as a fragmented entity existing in fluid time and struggling to inscribe individual identity" (146).

5. This citational practice partakes in the "subvert/install tactic" Ronna Johnson has identified as a hallmark of Johnson's novel *Come and Join the Dance;* she argues that "the novel appropriates and then sabotages" central elements of the dominant Beat narrative, a "double move" that "rejects the patriarchal, canonical tradition which masculinist Beat follows even in its iconoclasm" and "alter[s] the male-defined, male-centered discourse field of Beat" ("And then" 73).

6. In her essay "Beat Queens," Johnson remarks that Kerouac supported her as a writer and was "critical only of the way I was arranging my life. Instead of wasting so much of my time on the dreary secretarial jobs that supported me, why didn't I go for broke the way he had—see the world, put all my energy into writing, try to become great. I couldn't respond to his question; the answer was too humiliating: Because I was a woman. Because I didn't see how I could survive without a safety net. Yet oddly enough, I never expected that a man would provide me with one" (45).

7. Both *Minor Characters* and *Door Wide Open* record Kerouac's parting words to Joyce Glassman: "Unrequited love's a bore" (*DW* 172). But both texts challenge the idea that her love for Kerouac was unrequited using evidence from his texts and letters. *Door Wide Open* quotes from a letter to Ginsberg in which he confides: "Broke up with Joyce because I wanted to try big sexy brunettes then suddenly saw evil of world and realized Joyce was my angel sister and came back to her" (115) and notes his declaration in *Desolation Angels* "I still love her tonight" (xxiii). As the text draws to a close with a series of quotes from Kerouac describing their relationship, Johnson writes: "He surprised and touched me by saying it was 'perhaps the best love affair I ever had'" (174).

8. As noted in chapter 1 of this study, in *Minor Characters* Johnson examines in detail Elise's sense of alienation and quite deliberately retells Elise's story, writing her into Beat history as more than simply or only Allen Ginsberg's crazy ex-girlfriend. As her narrative draws to a close, Johnson highlights Elise's muted, unacknowledged identity as a poet, quoting from poems found after Elise's suicide, including what is likely the last she wrote. It ends with the plea: "Let me out now please— / —Please let me in" (258).

9. The memoir's multiple moments of similarity and connection—factual or imagined—also serve to bind Beat-associated women together in consociative community. Grace observes that "forging a kind of solidarity in both lived and imagined experience, [Johnson] suggests that the self can be known only by knowing/creating others. The individual is the compilation of concentric circles, centers fluctuating, boundaries expanding and contracting with the telling of each new story" ("Snapshots" 149). Writing the stories of other women into her own, Johnson offers "a different kind of truth," using "metaphorical narrative" to convey "what she and other women associated with the Beat movement felt" (150).

7. Contextuality

1. Indeed, the Penguin 1991 edition shifts to the back cover one of the three photographs that appear on the front of the 1990 Dutton first edition. The Penguin 1996 edition returns this photo to the front, but a subsequent 1997 Grove edition cover contains only two small photos. Citations in this study reference the 1991 edition.

2. Gilmore makes this observation in the course of an analysis of Gertrude Stein's *The Autobiography of Alice B. Toklas.*

3. While Brenda Knight characterizes Jane Bowles as a "precursor" to the Beats, Ronna Johnson and Nancy Grace describe her as an early Beat "who had affiliations with Ginsberg and Burroughs" and "epitomized Beat's embryonic connections to and departures from experimental modernisms" ("Visions" 12). Bowles's household in Tangiers was a center of Beat expatriate life, and Knight notes that "both Hettie Jones and William Burroughs cite her unique voice and worldview as an inspiration" (18).

4. In other gestures toward communality, the front matter of *How I Became Hettie Jones* also includes a dedication to Jones's daughters and an acknowledgment that she "owe[s]" her book to women who enabled and encouraged her writing (n.p.). For other analyses of Jones's focus on "becoming," see Grace ("Snapshots"); Chelsea Schlievert; and Deborah Thompson.

5. *Love, H* includes letters documenting Jones's reaction to her ex-husband's "Nellie Kohn" characterization, including her remark that the unflattering portrait "beats his trying to kill me for *real*" (51). Nevertheless, she felt "not only disappeared from [her] past but effectively shunned in the present, silenced, restricted." While this feeling stalled for a time her progress on the memoir, "the support of women" kept her from "giv[ing] up" (53). Instead, she wrote the poem "A Nebula of Noteworthy Nellies," which bears the dedication *"for Nellie Engle and for the Nellie/ character in a recent literary work."* She wanted the poem to "do away with having been 'Nellie'd'" (*LH* 123) by absorbing and transforming the weak and insecure "Nellie" of *The Autobiography of LeRoi Jones*:

for strength I give you
    Nellie Taylor Ross, the first woman
    governor. Elected by Wyoming, 1925

and for inspiration
    Nellie Monk, wife to Thelonious

and though I'll admit there are nervous Nellies
    and fussy Nellies

Nellie, f.y.i., is a form of Helen, that beauty
    who caused such havoc

and sometimes Helen is confused with *heleane*
    a word describing a planetary aura
    named by sailors for their patron saint:
    St. Elmo's fire

and when two electrical conductors meet
    the air is ionized, changed
    in a coronal discharge
    called St. Elmo's fire

So burn on burn on burn on Nellie (*All Told* 88)

6. The novelist and poet Gilbert Sorrentino describes apartments occupied by Jones and Roi as home to "readings, discussions, talk, and drinking, and often these gatherings would turn into all-night parties. A not at all atypical party at Jones' would include Selby,

Rumaker, Kerouac, Ginsberg, Bremser, Corso, Rosenthal, Oppenheimer, Finstein, and, when they were in New York, Wieners, George Stanley, Dorn, and Burroughs. There was often music played by Ornette Coleman, Archie Shepp, Wilbur Ware, and Don Cherry. About 1960 or so, Frank O'Hara, Koch, Bill Berkson and other people of the New York School also began to frequent Jones' place. It assumed the character of a freewheeling and noisy salon" (qtd. in J. Miller 7).

7. This episode is one of many in which Jones's recollection of events conflicts with Amiri Baraka's. In *The Autobiography of LeRoi Jones,* he asserts he interviewed with the editor of what he calls the *Record Trader* and Nellie/Hettie arrived after he had been given the job; in his account, she is the "secretary" and they barely speak (202–4). Baraka consistently presents his ex-wife, as Barrett Watten observes, as "a figure for nonidentity and lack" (102). Jones's account fills in that lack, asserting, for instance, that she was alone at the *Record Changer* when LeRoi arrived and they talked for an hour before the editor appeared and mentioned the job; they had forgotten about it, having been caught up in their literary conversation.

8. Cuba figures highly in Jones's narrative; she reports attending demonstrations in support of Castro and discusses Roi's visit to Cuba and his essay "Cuba Libre." For exploration of Cuba and Beat consciousness, see Todd Tietchen's *The Cubalogues.*

9. On one memorable evening after a Kerouac reading, "Jack kept running to [her] with different people," telling them, "she was listening so hard at the reading, she was really listening to me—she *understood* what I said!" (*H* 71).

10. Jones implies her behind-the-scenes work goes a long way in the production of the Beat literary canon. She is behind the publication of Roi's rebuttal of Norman Podhoretz's "The Know-Nothing Bohemians" (*H* 56–57), and she enables Roi's ascendancy as a literary figure when she goes to work full time. She runs the "business" end of Totem Press, and one of their primary backers "joked to Roi that he was giving him money only because he trusted his wife" (*H* 148).

11. See Watten for further discussion of Jones's "imagination of a culture not divided by race" and the "progressive politics" (111) of her autobiography.

12. In Jones's synopsis of *Dutchman,* she explains a white bohemian woman named Lula kills "the young, middle-class black man she's been tormenting" (*H* 207), then awaits her next black victim. *The Slave* centers around the confrontation between Walker Vessels, leader of black forces in a futuristic race war, and Grace, his white ex-wife; Grace had left Vessels, "taking their two daughters to the white side," and married "his former literary buddy" (*H* 219).

13. Grace describes Jones's book as a whole as mosaic-like, noting "many of the chapters are composed of subsections of varied length, some just a short paragraph, skipping back and forth in time, creating the illusion of the human self in perpetual generative movement" ("Snapshots" 153).

14. *How I Became Hettie Jones* claims and displays Jones's poetic voice but also values other, nonpoetic modes of written expression. The concluding chapters depict her development as an award-winning writer of children's books, in a return to a project she began years before but did not have the time to pursue, the manuscript lost, "probably in the pile on [her] desk, most of which weren't [hers]" (149). Additionally, Jones describes extending her "ties to the neighborhood settlement where [her] children had been in day care" by formulating and directing "a large after-school program there." She produces a curriculum and then goes on to generate "evaluations for Head Start programs and

after-school programs modeled on the one we'd started." In these pursuits, she notes, "I wrote all the time and never thought of myself as a writer" (234); in the autobiography, however, she demonstrates that this "nonliterary" writing makes meaningful contributions to multiple communities. She shows that the world does indeed hear from her in ways that matter.

15. A number of poems in *Drive,* including "Adultery—Kandahar, Afghanistan 1996," "A History of War in Five Acts," "Look at How We Live, Look at How We Die," and "Dresses: Four of Mine for Naima Belahi," address people disenfranchised and ignored, and those oppressed by autocratic political and religious institutions. They assert community with occupants of other cultural nowheres and offer "identification and solidarity with women in other patriarchal contexts" (Watten 114). Many of the poems in *Drive* are autobiographical, or, as Chelsea Schlievert characterizes them, forms of "self-narrative." Schlievert defines "self-narratives" as "works that give their creator insight into her understanding of self-identity—of constructing her story out of the relationships between memory and experience. In this way, the process of writing is as significant as the finished product." She further notes "self-narrative writers must be aware of the multiple discourses that have shaped their experiences, or as Jones stated in a January 2006 interview, one must acknowledge oneself 'as a person in a context'" (1098).

WORKS CITED

Adams, Timothy Dow. *Telling Lies in Modern American Autobiography.* Chapel Hill: U of North Carolina P, 1990.

Allen, Graham. *Intertextuality.* New York: Routledge, 2008.

Anderson, M. Christine. "Women's Place in the Beat Movement: Bonnie Bremser Frazer's *Troia: Mexican Memoirs.*" *Women's Studies International Forum* 26.3 (2003): 253–63.

Bakhtin, Mikhail. *The Dialogic Imagination.* Ed. Michael Holquist. Trans. Caryl Emerson and Michael Holquist. Austin: U of Texas P, 1981.

Baraka, Amiri. *The Autobiography of LeRoi Jones.* 1984. 2nd rev. ed. Chicago: Lawrence Hill Books, 1997.

Barthes, Roland. *Image/Text/Music.* Trans. Stephen Heath. New York: Hill and Wang, 1977.

Bartkowski, Frances. *Travelers, Immigrants, Inmates: Essays in Estrangement.* Minneapolis: U of Minnesota P, 1995.

"Beat Movement." *The Oxford Companion to American Literature.* 5th ed. New York: Oxford UP, 1983.

Berkson, Bill. "Joanne Kyger." Charters, *The Beats* 324–28.

"Bibliographic Bunker." *Reality Studio.* Subvert, 2017. realitystudio.org /bibliographic-bunker/.

Bloom, Lynn Z. "'I Write for Myself and Strangers': Private Diaries as Public Documents." *Inscribing the Diary: Critical Essays on Women's Diaries.* Ed. Suzanne L. Bunkers and Cynthia A. Huff. Amherst: U of Massachusetts P, 1996. 23–37.

Breines, Wini. "The Other Fifties: Beats and Bad Girls." *Not June Cleaver: Women and Gender in Postwar America, 1945–1960.* Ed. Joanne Meyerowitz. Philadelphia: Temple UP, 1994. 382–408.

Bremser, Bonnie [Brenda Frazer]. "Breaking out of D.C." Peabody 60–64.

———. Interview by Nancy Grace. "Artista." Grace and Johnson, *Breaking* 109–30.

———. "Poets and Odd Fellows." Charters, *Beat Down to Your Soul* 18–25.

———. *Troia: Mexican Memoirs.* 1969. Champaign: Dalkey Archive Press, 2007.

———. "The Village Scene." Charters, *Beat Down to Your Soul* 26–35.

Bunkers, Suzanne L., and Cynthia A. Huff. "Issues in Studying Women's Diaries: A Theoretical and Critical Introduction." *Inscribing the Daily: Critical Essays on Women's Diaries.* Ed. Bunkers and Huff. Amherst: U of Massachusetts P, 1996. 1–20.

Butler, Judith. *Gender Trouble: Feminism and the Subversion of Identity.* New York: Routledge, 1990.

———. *Giving an Account of Oneself.* New York: Fordham UP, 2005.

Carden, Mary Paniccia. "'Adventures in Auto-Eroticism': Traveling Masculinity in Autobiographical Writing by Jack Kerouac and Neal Cassady." *Journeys* 7.1 (2006): 1–25.

———. "Joanne Kyger's Travel Chapbooks: A Poetics of Motion." *Journal of Beat Studies* 6 (2018).

Cassady Neal. *The First Third & Other Writings.* San Francisco: City Lights, 1971.

Charters, Ann, ed. *Beat Down to Your Soul: What Was the Beat Generation?* New York: Penguin, 2001.

———, ed. *Dictionary of Literary Biography, Vol. 16: The Beats: Literary Bohemians in Postwar America.* Detroit: Gale, 1983.

———. Foreword. Johnson and Grace, *Girls Who Wore Black* ix–xii.

———. Introduction. Bremser, *Troia: Mexican Memoirs* i–vii.

———. "Introduction: What Was the Beat Generation?" Charters, *Beat Down to Your Soul* xv–xxxvii.

———. "Panel Discussion with Women Writers of the Beat Generation (1996)." Charters, *Beat Down to Your Soul* 611–32.

Clayton, Jay, and Eric Rothstein. "Figures in the Corpus: Theories of Influence and Intertextuality." Clayton and Rothstein 3–36.

———, eds. *Influence and Intertextuality in Literary History.* Madison: U of Wisconsin P, 1991.

Coontz, Stephanie. 1992. *The Way We Never Were: American Families and the Nostalgia Trap.* New York: Basic, 2000.

Couser, G. Thomas. *Memoir: An Introduction.* Oxford: Oxford UP, 2012.

Cowen, Elise. *Elise Cowen: Poems and Fragments.* Ed. Tony Trigilio. Boise, ID: Ahsahta, 2014.

Cox, James M. "Recovering Literature's Lost Ground through Autobiography." *Autobiography: Essays Theoretical and Critical.* Ed. James Olney. Princeton: Princeton UP, 1980. 123–45.

Culley, Margo. From *A Day at a Time: Diary Literature of American Women, from 1764–1985.* 1985. Smith and Watson, *Women, Autobiography, Theory* 217–21.

Dardess, George. "Jack Kerouac." Charters, *The Beats* 278–303.

di Prima, Diane. *Dinners and Nightmares.* 1961. San Francisco: Last Gasp, 1998.

———. "Keep the Beat." 2010. di Prima, *The Poetry Deal* 81–83.

———. *Memoirs of a Beatnik*. 1969. San Francisco: Last Gasp, 1988.

———. *The Poetry Deal/Diane di Prima/Poet Laureate Series Number 5*. San Francisco: City Lights, 2014.

———. *Recollections of My Life as a Woman: The New York Years*. New York: Viking Penguin, 2001.

Douglas, Ann. Introduction. "Strange Lives, Chosen Lives: The Beat Art of Joyce Johnson." 1999. Joyce Johnson, *Minor Characters* xiii–xxix.

DuPlessis, Rachel Blau. *Writing beyond the Ending: Narrative Strategies of Twentieth-Century Women Writers*. Bloomington: Indiana UP, 1985.

Eakin, Paul John. *Fictions in Autobiography: Studies in the Art of Self-Invention*. Princeton: Princeton UP, 1985.

———. *How Our Lives Become Stories: Making Selves*. Ithaca: Cornell UP, 1999.

———. *Touching the World: Reference in Autobiography*. Princeton: Princeton UP, 1992.

Egles, James D. *Beats and Friends: A Bibliography of British Library Holdings*. The British Library (n.dat.): 1–745. britishlibrary.typepad.co.uk/files/bl-beats -bibliography-printed-collections-1.pdf.

Ehrenreich, Barbara. *The Hearts of Men: American Dreams and the Flight from Commitment*. New York: Anchor, 1983.

Falk, Jane E. "Journal as Genre and Published Text: Beat Avant-Garde Writing Practices." *University of Toronto Quarterly* 73.4 (2004): 991–1002.

———. "Two Takes on Japan: Joanne Kyger's *The Japan and India Journals* and Philip Whalen's *Scenes of Life at the Capital*." Grace and Skerl, *Transnational Beat Generation* 101–14.

Foley, Jack. "On Diane di Prima's *Recollections of My Life as a Woman: The New York Years*." *Paterson Literary Review* 39 (2011): 346–54.

French, Warren. "A Visit with 'The Matriarch of the Beats.'" *Kerouac Connection* 24 (1992): 25–28.

Friedan, Betty. *The Feminine Mystique*. 1963. New York: Norton, 2013.

Friedman, Amy L. "'Being Here as Hard as I Could': The Beat Generation Women Writers." *Discourse* 20.1–2 (1998): 228–44.

———. "Joanne Kyger." Hemmer, *Encyclopedia* 183–85.

———. "Joanne Kyger, Beat Generation Poet: 'A Porcupine Traveling at the Speed of Light.'" Skerl, *Reconstructing* 73–88.

Friedman, Susan Stanford. "Weavings: Intertextuality and the (Re)Birth of the Author." Clayton and Rothstein 146–80.

———. "Women's Autobiographical Selves: Theory and Practice." *The Private Self: Theory and Practice of Women's Autobiographical Writings*. Ed. Shari Benstock. Chapel Hill: U of North Carolina P, 1988. 34–62.

Genette, Gérard. *Palimpsests: Literature in the Second Degree*. 1982. Trans. Channa Newman and Claude Doubinsky. Lincoln: U of Nebraska P, 1997.

George-Warren, Holly, ed. *The Rolling Stone Book of the Beats: The Beat Generation and American Culture*. New York: Hyperion, 1999.

Gillan, Maria Mazziotti. "On *Recollections of My Life as a Woman: The New York Years* by Diane di Prima: An Appreciation." *Paterson Literary Review* 39 (2011): 297–99.

Gilmore, Leigh. *Autobiographics: A Feminist Theory of Women's Self-Representation.* Ithaca: Cornell UP, 1994.

Ginsberg, Allen. *Howl and Other Poems.* San Francisco: City Lights, 1961.

——. *Indian Journals: March 1962–May 1963.* 1970. New York: Grove, 1996.

Grace, Nancy M. "ruth weiss." Hemmer, *Encyclopedia* 340–41.

——. "ruth weiss's *DESERT JOURNAL*: A Modern-Beat-Pomo Performance." Skerl, *Reconstructing* 57–71.

——. "Snapshots, Sand Paintings, and Celluloid: Formal Considerations in the Life Writing of Women Writers from the Beat Generation." Johnson and Grace, *Girls* 141–77.

Grace, Nancy M., and Ronna C. Johnson, eds. *Breaking the Rule of Cool: Interviewing and Reading Beat Women Writers.* Jackson: UP of Mississippi, 2004.

Grace, Nancy M., and Jennie Skerl, eds. *The Transnational Beat Generation.* New York: Palgrave, 2012.

Grant, Michael, and John Hazel. *Who's Who in Classical Mythology.* New York: Teach Yourself, 1979.

Hemmer, Kurt, ed. *Encyclopedia of Beat Literature.* New York: Facts on File, 2007.

——. "Frazer, Brenda (Bonnie Bremser)." Hemmer, *Encyclopedia* 104–5.

——. "The Prostitute Speaks: Brenda Frazer's *Troia: Mexican Memoirs.*" *Paradoxa* 18 (2003): 99–117.

Hibbard, Allen. "William S. Burroughs and U.S. Empire." Grace and Skerl 15–30.

Holmes, John Clellon. "The Game of the Name." 1965. Charters, *The Beats* 636–42.

——. "This Is the Beat Generation." 1952. Charters, *The Beats* 629–31.

——. "The Philosophy of the Beat Generation." 1958. Charters, *The Beats* 631–36.

Holton, Robert. "'The Sordid Hipsters of America': Beat Culture and the Folds of Heterogeneity." Skerl, *Reconstructing* 11–26.

Hunt, Tim. "Many Drummers, a Single Dance?" Johnson and Grace, *Girls* 251–60.

Jay, Paul. "Posing: Autobiography and the Subject of Photography." *Autobiography and Postmodernism.* Ed. Kathleen Ashley, Leigh Gilmore, and Gerald Peters. Amherst: U of Massachusetts P, 1994. 191–211.

Johnson, Joyce. "Beat Queens: Women in Flux." George-Warren 40–49.

——. Interview by Nancy M. Grace. "A Conversation with Joyce Johnson." *Artful Dodge* 36–37 (2000): 108–19.

——. *Minor Characters: A Beat Memoir.* 1983. New York: Penguin, 1999.

——. *The Voice Is All: The Lonely Victory of Jack Kerouac.* New York: Viking, 2012.

Johnson, Rob. "Did the Beatniks Kill John F. Kennedy?" *Journal of Beat Studies* 2 (2013): 81–100.

Johnson, Ronna C. "'And then she went': Beat Departures and Feminine Transgressions in Joyce Johnson's *Come and Join the Dance.*" Johnson and Grace, *Girls* 69–95.

———. "Beat Transnationalism under Gender: Brenda Frazer's *Troia: Mexican Memoirs.*" Grace and Skerl, *Transnational Beat Generation* 51–66.

———. "Mapping Women Writers of the Beat Generation." Grace and Johnson, *Breaking* 3–41.

Johnson, Ronna C., and Maria Damon. "Recapturing the Skipped Beats." *Chronicle of Higher Education* 1 Oct. 1999, B4+.

Johnson, Ronna C., and Nancy M. Grace, eds. *Girls Who Wore Black: Women Writing the Beat Generation.* New Brunswick: Rutgers UP, 2002.

———. "Visions and Revisions of the Beat Generation." Johnson and Grace, *Girls* 1–24.

Jones, Hettie. *All Told.* New York: Hanging Loose, 2003.

———. "Babes in Boyland." George-Warren 51–54.

———. *Drive.* New York: Hanging Loose, 1998.

———. *How I Became Hettie Jones.* 1990. New York: Penguin, 1991.

———. Interview by Nancy M. Grace. "Drive." Grace and Johnson, *Breaking* 155–78.

———. *Love, H: The Letters of Helene Dorn and Hettie Jones.* Durham: Duke UP, 2016.

———. "A Nebula of Noteworthy Nellies." Jones, *All Told* 88.

Juvan, Marko. *History and Poetics of Intertextuality.* 2000. Trans. Timothy Pogačar. West Lafayette: Purdue UP, 2008.

Kerouac, Jack. *The Dharma Bums.* 1958. New York: Signet, 1959.

———. *On the Road.* 1957. New York: Penguin, 1976.

———. *The Subterraneans.* 1958. New York: Grove, 1981.

Kerouac, Jack, and Joyce Johnson. *Door Wide Open: A Beat Love Affair in Letters, 1957–1958.* Introduction and commentary by Johnson. New York: Penguin, 2000.

Knight, Brenda, ed. *Women of the Beat Generation: The Writers, Artists, and Muses at the Heart of a Revolution.* Berkeley: Conari, 1996.

Kristeva, Julia. *Desire in Language: A Semiotic Approach to Literature and Art.* Ed. Leon Roudiez. Trans. Thomas Gora, Alice Jardine, and Leon Roudiez. New York: Columbia UP, 1980.

Kyger, Joanne. *Desecheo Notebook.* Berkeley: Arif, 1971.

———. Interview. "Energy on the Page: Joanne Kyger in Conversation with Dale Smith." *Jacket* 11 (April 2000). jacketmagazine.com/11/kyger-iv-dale-smith.html.

———. Interview. "Particularizing People's Lives: Joanne Kyger in Conversation with Linda Russo." *Jacket* 11 (April 2000). jacketmagazine.com/11/kyger-iv-by-russo.html.

———. Interview by Nancy M. Grace. "Places to Go." Grace and Johnson, *Breaking* 133–53.

———. "Poison Oak for Allen." 1996. *Again: Poems 1989–2000*. Albuquerque: La Alameda, 2001. 102.

———. *Strange Big Moon: The Japan and India Journals: 1960–1964*. 1981. Berkeley: North Atlantic, 2000.

———. *The Tapestry and the Web*. San Francisco: Four Seasons Foundation, 1965.

Landwehr, Margarete. "Introduction: Literature and the Visual Arts; Questions of Influence and Intertextuality." *College Literature* 29.3 (2002): 1–16.

Lee, A. Robert, ed. *The Beat Generation Writers*. London: Pluto, 1996.

Libby, Anthony. "Diane di Prima: 'Nothing Is Lost; It Shines in Our Eyes.'" Johnson and Grace, *Girls* 45–68.

Martinez, Manuel Luis. *Countering the Counterculture: Rereading Postwar American Dissent from Jack Kerouac to Tomás Rivera*. Madison: U of Wisconsin P, 2003.

McClure, Michael. "Painting Beat by Numbers." George-Warren 32–39.

McNeil, Helen. "The Archeology of Gender in the Beat Movement." Lee 178–99.

Meyer, Dick. "The Truth of Truthiness." CBS News. CBS Interactive Inc., 12 Dec. 2006. www.cbsnews.com/news/the-truth-of-truthiness.

Middleton-Kaplan, Richard. "The New American Poetry, 1945–1960." Hemmer, *Encyclopedia* 225–33.

Miller, James A. "Amiri Baraka (LeRoi Jones)." Charters, *The Beats* 3–24.

Miller, Nancy K. *Subject to Change: Reading Feminist Writing*. New York: Columbia UP, 1988.

Mortenson, Erik. *Capturing the Beat Moment: Cultural Politics and the Poetics of Presence*. Carbondale: Southern Illinois UP, 2011.

Murphy, Patrick. "Gary Snyder." Hemmer, *Encyclopedia* 287–90.

Nicosia, Gerald. Introduction. *The Subterraneans*. By Jack Kerouac. New York: Grove, 1981. i–iv.

O'Neil, Paul. "The Only Rebellion Around." 1959. Charters, *Beat Down to Your Soul* 424–39.

Orr, Mary. *Intertextuality: Debates and Contexts*. Cambridge: Polity, 2008.

Peabody, Richard, ed. *A Different Beat: Writings by Women of the Beat Generation*. London: High Risk, 1997.

Perkins, Michael. "Bonnie Bremser." Charters, *The Beats* 33–35.

Quinn, Roseanne Giannini. "'The Willingness to Speak' Diane di Prima and Italian American Feminist Body Politics." *MELUS* 28.3 (2003): 175–93.

Rosen, Ruth. *The World Split Open: How the Women's Movement Changed America*. New York: Penguin, 2000.

Russo, Linda. "To Deal with Parts and Particulars: Joanne Kyger's Early Epic Poetics." Johnson and Grace, *Girls* 178–204.

Savran, David. *Taking It Like a Man: White Masculinity, Masochism, and Contemporary American Culture*. Princeton: Princeton UP, 1990.

Schelling, Andrew. "Joanne Kyger's Portable Poetics." *Jacket* 11 (April 2000). jacketmagazine.com/11/kyger-schelling.html.

Schlievert, Chelsea D. "Self-Narratives and Editorial Marks: Inventing Hettie Jones." *Women's Studies* 40 (2011): 1092–115.

Shattuck, Kathryn. "Kerouac's 'Road' Scroll Is Going to Auction." *New York Times* 22 Mar. 2001, E1+.

Siegel, Kristi. "Intersections: Women's Travel and Theory." *Gender, Genre & Identity in Women's Travel Writing.* Ed. Siegel. New York: Peter Lang, 2011. 1–11.

Skerl, Jennie, ed. *Reconstructing the Beats.* Introd. by Skerl. New York: Palgrave, 2004.

Skinner, Jonathan. "Generosity and Discipline: [Joanne Kyger's] Travel Poems." *Jacket* 11 (April 2000). jacketmagazine.com/11/kyger-skinner.html.

Smith, Sidonie. "Identity's Body." *Autobiography and Postmodernism* Ed. Kathleen Ashley, Leigh Gilmore, and Gerald Peters. Amherst: U of Massachusetts P, 1994. 266–92.

———. *A Poetics of Women's Autobiography: Marginality and the Fictions of Self-Representation.* Bloomington: Indiana UP, 1987.

Smith, Sidonie, and Julia Watson. Introduction. *Getting a Life: Everyday Uses of Autobiography.* Minneapolis: U of Minnesota P, 1996. 1–24.

———, eds. *Women, Autobiography, Theory.* Madison: U of Wisconsin P, 1998.

Strehle, Susan, and Mary Paniccia Carden. "Introduction: Reading Romance, Reading History." *Doubled Plots: Romance and History.* Ed. Strehle and Carden. Jackson: U of Mississippi P, 2003. xi–xxxiii.

Thomson, Gillian. "Gender Performance in the Literature of the Female Beats." *CLCWeb: Comparative Literature and Culture* 13.1 (2011). docs.lib.purdue.edu /cgi/viewcontent.cgi?article=1710&context=clcweb.

Thompson, Deborah. "Keeping up with the Joneses: The Naming of Racial Identities in the Autobiographical Writings of LeRoi Jones/Amiri Baraka, Hettie Jones, and Lisa Jones." *College Literature* 29.1 (2002): 83–101.

Tietchen, Todd F. *The Cubalogues: Beat Writers in Revolutionary Cuba.* Gainesville: UP of Florida, 2010.

Tri, Chon. *Zazen Practice.* Zen Guide. zenguide.com/practice/zazen.cfm.

Trigilio, Tony. Introduction. *Elise Cowen: Poems and Fragments.* Ed. Trigilio. Boise, ID: Ahsahta, 2014. xiii–xxviii.

———. "A New View of ruth weiss: An Introduction." *The E-Poets Network: The Book of Voices* (2003). voices.e-poets.net/weissr/intro.shtml.

"Truthiness." *Dictionary.com.* www.dictionary.com/browse/truthiness.

Tytell, John. *Naked Angels: The Lives and Literature of the Beat Generation.* New York: McGraw-Hill, 1976.

Van Den Abbeele, Georges. *Travel as Metaphor: From Montaigne to Rousseau.* Minneapolis: U of Minnesota P, 1992.

van Elteren, Mel. "The Subculture of the Beats: A Sociological Revisit." *Journal of American Culture* 22.3 (1999): 71–99.

Vega, Janine Pommy. *Tracking the Serpent: Journeys to Four Continents.* San Francisco: City Lights, 1997.

Waldman, Anne. "Fast Speaking Woman." Interview by Ronna C. Johnson and Nancy M. Grace. Grace and Johnson, *Breaking* 255–77.

———. Foreword. Knight, *Women of the Beat Generation* ix–xii.

———. Foreword. Kyger, *Strange Big Moon* vii–x.

Watten, Barrett. "What I See in *How I Became Hettie Jones*." Johnson and Grace, *Girls* 96–118.

weiss, ruth. "ALTAR-PIECE." *ruth weiss: a fool's journey* 42–46.

———. *CAN'T STOP THE BEAT: THE LIFE AND WORDS OF A BEAT POET.* Studio City, CA: Divine Arts, 2011.

———. *DESERT JOURNAL.* 1977. New Orleans: Trembling Pillow, 2012.

———. "FOR CAROL BERGÉ (1928–2006)." *Heartbeat No. 20: ruth weiss* 140–41.

———. *FOR THESE WOMEN OF THE BEAT.* San Francisco: 3300 Press, 1997.

———. *Heartbeat No. 20: ruth weiss. Einen Schritt weiter im Westen ist die See.* Wenzendorf, Germany: Stadtlichter Presse, 2012.

———. Interview by Nancy M. Grace. "Single Out." Grace and Johnson, *Breaking* 55–80.

———. "LIGHT." *Heartbeat No. 20.* 16–53.

———. *ruth weiss: a fool's journey/die reise des narren.* Vienna: edition exil, 2012.

———. "SOMETHING CURRENT." *Heartbeat No. 20.* 128–39.

———. "TURNABOUT." *Heartbeat No. 20.* 142–47.

Whitlock, Gillian. *Soft Weapons: Autobiography in Transit.* Chicago: U of Chicago P, 2007.

INDEX

Adam, Helen, 83, 92, 94
Adams, Timothy Dow, 32, 48, 49; *Telling Lies in Modern American Autobiography*, 35
Allen, Donald, 53, 122, 123
Allen, Graham, 25, 197nn15–16
Anderson, M. Christine, 201n1
Anderson, Sherwood, 35, 49
Angel Hair (magazine and press), 3–4
anxiety: in Bremser's works, 59, 67, 69–70, 72; in Jones's works, 181; in Kyger's works, 118, 121, 124
Art Students' League, 44
Auerhahn Press, 205n15

Bakhtin, Mikhail, 24
Ballet Theatre, 44
Baraka, Amiri. *See* Jones, LeRoi
Beat chick caricature, 2, 8, 17, 21–22, 23, 29, 35, 42, 46, 57, 59, 73, 78, 101, 146, 149, 190, 195n2
Beat identity, 7–9, 11–13, 26, 33, 92, 119, 121, 145, 150, 152, 190, 195n2. *See also* masculinity
Beatitude (periodical), 3
Beat Scene (periodical), 3
Bergé, Carol, 3, 97–98
Berkson, Bill, 210n6
Black Arts movement, 170–71, 177
Blackburn, Paul, 122
Blackburn, Sara, 166
Black Mountain poets, 6–7, 52
Black Mountain Review, 7

Black Nationalism, 170, 176
Bloom, Lynn, 206n7
Blue Beat (periodical), 3
Bowles, Jane, 209n3; *Two Serious Ladies*, 163
Boyle, Kay, 181
Breines, Wini, 196n7
Bremser, Bonnie (Brenda Frazer), 8, 59–81; *For Love of Ray*, 60, 63; intertextuality in works of, 23, 30; publishing of works, 3; travel tropes in works of, 189; *Troia: Beat Chronicles*, 78–81; *Troia: Mexican Memoirs*, 8–9, 59, 60–76, 201n1
Bremser, Ray, 59, 63–77, 79–80, 203n16, 210n6
BRINK, THE (film), 4
Bunkers, Suzanne, 112, 117
Burroughs, Joan Vollmer, 22, 143, 144, 157–58, 159
Burroughs, William S.: and Beat movement, 15, 34; and Bowles, 209n3; and Johnson, 143, 157–58; and Jones, 210n6; *Junky*, 196n10; *Naked Lunch*, 196n10, 199n6; *Queer*, 196n10
Butler, Judith, 43, 112; *Giving an Account of Oneself*, 27, 105

Caen, Herb, 198n3, 204n3
Carden, Mary Paniccia, 151, 196n9, 205n3
Carr, Cessa, 18
Carr, Lucien, 18, 21, 144
Cassady, Carolyn, 141, 155, 158, 159
Cassady, Neal, 89, 141, 155, 202n8
Charters, Ann, 44, 60, 63, 68, 201n1

222 / INDEX

Chase, Hal, 143
Cherry, Don, 210n6
civil rights movement, 173–74, 177
Clayton, Jay, 197n12, 197n15
Colbert, Stephen, 33, 199n4
Coleman, Ornette, 210n6
Congress of Racial Equality (CORE), 177
consociation, 5–7, 9, 10, 82–104, 168; and
Beat-claiming poetry, 91–103; and poet-
ics of identity, 85–91
contextuality, 11, 161–86; in *Drive* (Jones),
183–86; in *How I Became Hettie Jones*
(Jones), 161–83
Coontz, Stephanie, 196n7
Corso, Gregory, 6, 15, 165, 193n4, 210n6
Couser, G. Thomas, 198n2
Cowen, Elise: death of, 20–21; and Gins-
berg, 20, 196n8; and Johnson, 20–21, 141,
144–46, 152–53, 155–56, 158, 159, 208n8;
publishing of works, 5; and weiss, 96
Coyote's Journal, 3
Creeley, Robert, 52–53
cross-textuality, 10, 136–60, 161, 166, 167,
171
Croton Press, 60
Culler, Jonathan, 25
Culley, Margo, 112; *A Day at a Time*, 114

Dalai Lama, 121
Dalkey Archive Press, 60, 63
Damon, Maria, 34
Dardess, George, 194n6
defiant femininity: and iconoclasm, 18–23;
in di Prima's works, 34, 42, 49, 54, 56–57;
and intertextuality, 19–21, 31; in Johnson's works, 140, 148, 153, 160; in Kyger's
works, 124, 135; and road metaphors,
187–88, 191
defiant masculinity, 16, 19, 34
de Man, Paul, 25
Dickinson, Emily, 93
di Prima, Diane, 8, 32–58; and Beat identity,
6; *Dinners and Nightmares*, 4, 33, 199n9;
Earth Song, 4; *Haiku*, 4; identity as
writer, 1, 46, 49, 50–53, 55–56, 193n2; and
Jones, 165; "Keep the Beat," 5; *LA Odyssey*, 4; *Loba: Parts 1–16*, 4, 33; *Memoirs
of a Beatnik*, 8, 23, 30, 32–34, 35–46, 190;
The New Handbook of Heaven, 4; *New
Mexico Poem*, 4; *The Poetry Deal*, 199n7;
*Recollections of My Life as a Woman: The

New York Years, 2–3, 8, 20, 22, 32, 33–34,
46–57, 190, 199n7, 199n9; *Revolutionary
Letters*, 4, 33; *This Kind of Bird Flies
Backward*, 4, 44, 46, 51; travel tropes in
works of, 190; *War Poems*, 4
displacement, 9–10, 45, 64, 68, 105–35, 137,
148, 168, 189
diversification, 8–9, 59–81; and indiscriminate exchanges, 75–78; and sex text
exchanges, 71–75; and textual exchanges,
65–71
Dorn, Ed, 6, 210n6
Dorn, Helene, 166, 179, 181
Down Here (periodical), 3
Duncan, Robert, 105
Dunkel, Galatea, 95

Eakin, Paul John, 27, 29, 188; *Touching the
World: Reference in Autobiography*,
198n18
Egles, James, *Beats and Friends*, 194n3
Ehrenreich, Barbara, 16
Evergreen Review (periodical), 3, 120, 121

Falk, Jane, 106–7, 121, 125, 196n10, 207n13
female identity and self-concept: in Bremser's works, 79; in di Prima's works, 42,
54; and intertextuality, 10–11, 21, 26, 28,
29; in Johnson's works, 151, 153, 156, 158;
in Jones's works, 169, 182; in Kyger's
works, 115, 135; and road metaphors,
188, 189
femininity: in Bremser's works, 78; in di
Prima's works, 42–43, 54, 57; and intertextuality, 21, 26, 28–29; in Johnson's
works, 147, 149; in Jones's works, 161,
169, 179; in weiss's works, 101, 106. *See
also* defiant femininity
Ferlinghetti, Lawrence, 6, 83, 101, 116,
205n15; in *Oxford Companion to American Literature*, 193n4
First Zen Institute of America, 106, 205n5
Floating Bear (periodical), 3, 4, 33, 51, 180,
194n3
Foley, Jack, 201n15
Frank, Mary, 22
Frazer, Brenda. *See* Bremser, Bonnie
French, Warren, 204n4
Friedan, Betty, 19
Friedman, Amy, 3, 119, 193n2, 205n2,
206n12, 207n1

Recent Books in the Series
Cultural Frames, Framing Culture